teach® yourself

tracing your
family history

D1472362

teach
yourself

®

**tracing your
family history**
stella colwell

For over 60 years, more than
50 million people have learnt over
750 subjects the **teach yourself**
way, with impressive results.

be where you want to be
with **teach yourself**

For UK order enquiries: please contact Bookpoint Ltd, 130 Milton Park, Abingdon, Oxon, OX14 4SB. Telephone: +44 (0) 1235 827720. Fax: +44 (0) 1235 400454. Lines are open 09.00–17.00, Monday to Saturday, with a 24-hour message answering service. Details about our titles and how to order are available at www.teachyourself.co.uk

For USA order enquiries: please contact McGraw-Hill Customer Services, PO Box 545, Blacklick, OH 43004-0545, USA. Telephone: 1-800-722-4726. Fax: 1-614-755-5645.

For Canada order enquiries: please contact McGraw-Hill Ryerson Ltd, 300 Water St, Whitby, Ontario L1N 9B6, Canada. Telephone: 905 430 5000. Fax: 905 430 5020.

Long renowned as the authoritative source for self-guided learning – with more than 50 million copies sold worldwide – the **teach yourself** series includes over 500 titles in the fields of languages, crafts, hobbies, business, computing and education.

British Library Cataloguing in Publication Data: a catalogue record for this title is available from the British Library.

Library of Congress Catalog Card Number: on file.

First published in UK 1997 by Hodder Education, 338 Euston Road, London, NW1 3BH.

First published in US 1997 by The McGraw-Hill Companies, Inc.

This edition published 2007.

The **teach yourself** name is a registered trade mark of Hodder Headline.

Copyright © 1997, 2003, 2007 Stella Colwell

Typeset by Transet Limited, Coventry, England.
Printed in Great Britain for Hodder Education, a division of Hodder Headline, an Hachette Livre UK Company, 338 Euston Road, London, NW1 3BH, by Cox & Wyman Ltd, Reading, Berkshire.

The publisher has used its best endeavours to ensure that the URLs for external websites referred to in this book are correct and active at the time of going to press. However, the publisher and the author have no responsibility for the websites and can make no guarantee that a site will remain live or that the content will remain relevant, decent or appropriate.

Hodder Headline's policy is to use papers that are natural, renewable and recyclable products and made from wood grown in sustainable forests. The logging and manufacturing processes are expected to conform to the environmental regulations of the country of origin.

Impression number   10 9 8 7 6 5 4 3 2 1
Year   2010 2009 2008 2007

contents

acknowledgements		xii
preface		xiii
01	**getting started**	**1**
	how to begin	2
02	**getting help**	**4**
	first step	5
	second step	5
	third step	5
	getting in touch and setting up a visit	8
	questions to ask	8
	what to be wary of	9
	family souvenirs	10
	dealing with different types of relative	10
	seeing it from your relatives' point of view	11
	write or record?	12
	tape-recorded interviews	12
	copyright	13
	writing to relatives	14
	those moved away and the dead	15
	what to do if you have no known living relatives	16
	advertising in the press	17
	if you have no idea where your family came from	17
03	**sorting out the facts**	**20**
	fourth step	21
	some simple guidelines	22

	what to include	23
	fifth step	27
	collections of pedigrees	29
	other manuscript collections of pedigrees	30
	published family trees and family histories	33
	some words of warning	34
04	**starting your research: births, marriages and deaths**	**36**
	sixth step	37
	the indexes	38
	how to buy a certificate	40
	searching the local indexes	41
	looking for a birth	43
	adoption	46
	abandoned children	49
	stillbirths	49
	looking for a marriage	50
	divorce	53
	looking for a death	56
	coroners' inquests	60
	coming up against a brick wall	60
05	**births, marriages and deaths in the Channel Islands, Isle of Man, Scotland and Ireland**	**64**
	the Channel Islands	65
	Isle of Man	67
	Scotland	67
	Ireland	73
06	**births, marriages and deaths at sea and abroad**	**78**
	Britons at sea and on land	79
	service families	81
	men at war	82
	Scottish travellers	83
	Irish migrants	84

	Northern Irish records since 1922	85
	other places where you can find	
	British service personnel and their	
	families overseas	86
	the British in India and Asia	90
	United States of America	91
	Americans abroad	98
	American casualties of war	98
07	**searching the census**	**101**
	how the census was organized	102
	indexes, digital images and transcriptions	104
	what the censuses reveal	108
	Scotland	115
	Ireland	116
	earlier censuses in the United Kingdom	117
	census surveys overseas	118
	United States of America	119
	indexes, digital images and transcriptions	120
	what the censuses contain	121
	other American census surveys	128
	general advice on tackling the census	129
08	**other ways of finding your**	
	ancestors' whereabouts	**132**
	registers of voters	133
	directories of names	135
	what you can learn from directories	139
	maps	140
	tithe maps and apportionments	141
	Valuation Office records	145
	Old Poor Law settlement papers	150
	additional name lists	151
09	**finding your way to the records**	**152**
	seventh step	153
	drawing up a checklist	154
	finding historical documents	155

some practical points 157
handling old documents 158
problems reading old handwriting 159
meanings of words 162
understanding Latin documents 163
working with numbers 163
the dating of documents 164
interpreting your findings 165
filing and storage systems 165

10 searching parish registers in
England and Wales 168
where to find parish registers 171
indexes and transcriptions 172
the contents of parish registers 175
looking for a marriage? 179
family burials 186

11 the nonconformists 190
nonconformists' registers 192
Religious Society of Friends 197
Roman Catholics 201

12 parish registers in the rest of the
British Isles, Ireland and the USA 203
the Channel Islands 204
Isle of Man 204
Scotland 205
Ireland 212
United States of America 218

13 wills and other probate records in
England and Wales 221
where wills were taken to be proved
before 1858 222
wills proved since 1858 224
what wills tell you 227
contested wills 232
grants of letters of administration 233

what grants of letters of administration
    contain   235
probate inventories   236
probate accounts   236
tutors, curators and guardians   237
Death Duty registers   238
government stockholders   242

14 probate records elsewhere in the
    British Isles, Ireland and the USA   243
the Channel Islands   244
Isle of Man   245
Scotland   246
services (retours) of heirs and sasines   250
Ireland   253
The Registry of Deeds   257
Britons in India   258
United States of America   259
American estates in the
    United Kingdom and Ireland   263

15 across the divide: pursuing your
    migrant ancestors   266
ships' passenger lists and border crossings   268
some printed and electronic resources   274
special groups of emigrants   274
following an emigrant's paper trail   282
naturalization   285

16 writing it all up   291
when and where do you begin?   292
who is it for?   292
from present to past or fast forward?   293
the essentials   293
adding pictures   294
editing your script   295
how are you going to publish?   295

x contents

ensuring permanent preservation
and publicity 298
taking it further **300**
addresses and websites 300
bibliography 313
index **323**

dedication

First and second editions
For Shirley Hughes and the Manton family
(Les, Sue, Jen and Kate)

Third edition
And for Janice, Pat, Richard and Ruth,
and in loving memory of Cherry

acknowledgements

For this greatly revised and updated third edition I'd like to thank Else Churchill, Richard Colwell and Roger Kershaw for their much appreciated practical help and support, Richard Baxandall for replacing my hips, and Ian Hatcher for knocking me out and bringing me round. Jill Anderson, Deeann Kirton and Claire Race helped me to walk again, Elizabeth Donaldson and John Powell made me laugh and the rest of the staff of The Nuffield Hospital Ipswich gave me excellent care and food. My late cousin, Margaret Ure, helped me in more ways than she could know. I am extremely grateful to Elaine Clarke and the Stowmarket Occupational Therapy Team, and the Hadleigh Home Care Team, who all helped to make this book possible when I got home. Andy and Wendy Norman looked after Cherry to the very end, Steve Coker provided much needed technical assistance, Janice Bloomfield, Pat Brown, Bernard and Lucy Casburn, Patricia Kirkland, Dick MacGregor, Sue Manton, Bill Merrick, Christine and Stuart Miller, Frances Mount, Alan and Ruth Riddleston, Kate and Mark Tatham, and Vanessa Thompson-Royds all rallied round, helped me out of various pickles and inconveniences, and kept me in touch with the outside world, so thanks very much to them too.

Lastly, I'd like to thank Victoria Roddam, Katie Archer, and Jenny Organ of Hodder Education for their patience and understanding in seeing the project through.

Stella Colwell, May 2007

preface

In the three years since the last edition of this book, our approach to family history has been dramatically transformed. More and more databases and indexed digital images of major genealogical sources are now being made available online. You can search and view them whenever and wherever you want to pursue your ancestry.

Using the internet, you can share your discoveries with other people throughout the world. You can reach out to extended family members worldwide, some of whom may be quite distantly related to you and unknown before. You can post your results and seek help via the various online message- and notice-boards. You can join or set up a surname interest group. You can send and receive e-mailed answers to any queries in an instant.

As well as expanding your horizons globally, you can even submit a sample of your DNA and match it with the recorded genetic make-up of your remoter ancestors, whose relationship to you would otherwise remain undetected or beyond the realm of written records. If you want to do this, then visit a website such as **www.oxfordancestors.com**, **www.dnaancestryproject.com** or **www.familytreedna.com** for more information on what is involved.

You may already have visited one or two websites and be unsure about how best to set about tracing your own roots. There are millions of websites to tempt you – genealogy is the second most popular topic for internet users.

However, the internet doesn't offer quick fix genealogy. Treat online indexes and databases merely as time-saving research tools to help tease out the information you are looking for.

Avoid turning your research into a scattergun exercise. It is easy to get diverted into clicking on one website after another, until you lose sight of your original objective, so be self-disciplined.

You can end up spending a lot of money unnecessarily too. The content of some websites is accessible only by subscription, or you may have to pay to view indexed digital images of original documents, perhaps using a timed charged service. Look out for any free trial periods; make a list of exactly what you want to find out from each website, so that you fill such time wisely. Cast around to see if similar information is freely available elsewhere or where it is less costly. A search engine will help you to locate alternative websites.

Websites and online databases have no existence outside the computer. They are the creations of the people who designed them. They will tell you only what they want you to know, which may not always be the whole story. Before you begin, read the home page to find out what the website has to offer, and how it will and will not assist you with your own research. Have a look and see when the website was last updated. If this was not recently, then is the information still current? Many websites are short-lived, and you will find some recommended sites have disappeared or changed their addresses by the time you attempt to visit them, though usually there will be a direct link to any new site.

No indexes are perfect, so don't trust them entirely. If you think a person or family should be included, and isn't, don't give up, but use your imagination and try all the likely surname variants you can think of, or any other online indexes to the same source. The writing may have been difficult to decipher or names misinterpreted. Alternatively, you could go the long way round and examine the actual documents themselves, as many microform copies are now widely available. Because the information is arranged alphabetically, indexes ignore the way in which a document was written, so you lose the original context of individual names and the events they describe.

Databases can be annoying because information is hidden until retrieved in response to an exact or closely matching search command. The original record might contain more than was included in the given database fields, or the omitted parts lie outside its scope. Some online databases may be work-in-progress rather than complete, so always study the introductory text first.

Family history portal or gateway sites are signposts, directing you to websites listed by subject, place, personal-name, type of record or repository. The webmasters have found, sorted and listed all the appropriate sites for you. Portals and gateways involve a massive amount of work to keep all the links up to date and to add new ones. Examples of two invaluable genealogical portals are **www.familyrecords.gov.uk**, which can take you to the websites of the National Archives at Kew, the Family Records Centre, the National Library of Wales, the National Archives of Scotland, the Public Record Office of Northern Ireland, the General Register Offices for England and Wales, and for Scotland, the Asia, Pacific and Africa Collections in The British Library, the websites of Access to Archives and of the Scottish Archive Network, and to those of the Imperial War Museum and the Commonwealth War Graves Commission; the second, **www.cyndislist.com**, is hosted by Cyndi Howells, and is particularly strong on research sources in the United States of America and Canada, though she has links to genealogical websites of other countries worldwide. You can search for these using the Main Index on her home page, a Topical Index, an Alphabetical Index and a No Frills Index. You can also see at a glance when each section was last updated.

Alternatively, if you do not already have a specific website address, or want to know what is available online about a certain subject, person or place, employ a powerful search engine such as **www.google.com** or a web directory like **www.yahoo.com**, although this is not as comprehensive as a search engine. If you use several search engines and web directories, you will get different responses to your chosen keyword or phrase. Try **www.ixquick.com**, which is a metasearch engine. This will drill down many of the most popular search engines simultaneously, to save you having to trawl them individually. I find a search engine helpful in keeping track of fresh online census databases and indexes to birth, marriage and death registrations.

Many websites are enhanced by pictures, which take much longer to load up and also occupy a lot of space. When there are digital images of documents, you can print these out to study at leisure or even copy them into an online folder to build up a family scrapbook. Most websites will have a zoom-in facility to magnify images, transcriptions or text to help you understand them.

Many new family historians come unstuck simply because they expect the internet to come up with all the answers. Not everything is on the internet, nor is everything there honest, correct and authentic. A computer is brainless, so has no intuition, and cannot evaluate or analyse what is stored in its memory, nor is every potential source of information there. It is an encyclopaedia for you to dip into to select what you need. How you use this and apply your critical skills is up to you.

New websites are appearing daily, so by the time you read this book, some of the ones I mention may already be obsolete and fresh ones will have been uploaded to expand your range of inquiry even further. New records, databases and finding aids are surfacing all the time to make family research easier, but use these sensibly. If you want to read up about what's new, study the family history press, and subscribe to a newsletter such as **www.onlinegenealogy.com** or Dick Eastman's weekly updates at **http://blog.eogn.com**.

Read *Genealogy Online for Dummies*, by J.A. Thomas, M.L. and A.L. Helm and N. Barratt, *Getting Started in Genealogy Online*, by W. Dollarhide, and *The Genealogist's Internet*, by P. Christian, for more information about methodology.

You will gradually develop skills in identifying, locating and understanding some of the many available resources for tracing your ancestry. You will also learn to use the internet, copies, indexes and original documents effectively and efficiently as you hunt for the earlier generations of your family. You can never say that your family history is complete, for there will always be loose ends to tie up and another generation to look for. That is part of the attraction and why so many of us choose this as a hobby or profession.

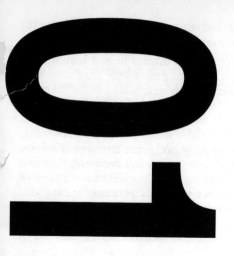

01

getting started

In this chapter you will learn:
- how to do your own research
- who this book will help
- what the prime sources are for people with British roots.

There is no substitute for finding out your family's history for yourself. You will definitely be in for surprises.

Adopt a step by step approach and always have a search plan. Identify those sources most likely to provide the answer to each of your queries, and discover their whereabouts, and if there are any finding aids. Satisfy yourself that you know their original purpose and scope. Do they cover the period and area in which you are interested? Will you be able to read the old handwriting, translate it from another language, decipher any abbreviations, learn the meanings of any archaic words and convert unfamiliar dating schemes? You will need to assess the relevance and value of each of your sources. Resist a ready acceptance of a statement or assertion simply because it seems to provide the solution to your problem. Tenacity, accuracy and a logical line of thought are important facets for research, as well as a certain amount of physical strength!

Work methodically and tidily. At all costs avoid stockpiling heaps of paper and scraps of unattributed notes with the intention of sorting them out on a rainy day. Family history research is fun, filing is not, so do this as you go along. Develop good habits at the outset, by adopting a simple filing system and sticking to it.

How to begin

This book is designed for people with British roots, including emigrants to the North American Continent, but it could apply to descendants of emigrants to other countries too. Its purpose is to help you teach yourself, step by step, where to look for key facts linking the various generations in your family and tracking down its members in time and place. It will explain why four pivotal sources were created (birth, marriage and death registrations, census returns of households, church and chapel registers of baptism, marriage and burial, and wills of individuals), as well as their genealogical content and limitations, because none was ever intended with the future family historian in mind. It will direct you to other material which might help where these records are deficient or unclear. There is a new chapter on how to trace emigrants too. The book ends with a list of useful addresses and websites I have referred to in the text and a select bibliography.

It is never too soon to start, and the best place to begin is with living relatives, not forgetting yourself, for who is better qualified than you to write an authoritative account of your life and times?

02

getting help

In this chapter you will learn:
- how to set down what you already know
- how to enlist the help of relatives
- what to do if you have no living relatives.

Your family's history starts with you, the golden rule being to work back from the known to the unknown, looking for names, family relationships, dates, places and occupations. None is much use without the other; a name without a date or place attached to it is next to useless, and likewise a name which is not connected in some way to that of another individual or family group will tell you nothing.

First step

Draw up a sketch family tree of your known relatives. Write down their names, dates and places of birth, marriage and death, where they have lived, and their occupations, indicating their relationship to each other. Your family tree may not extend very far vertically, but it may stretch out a long way horizontally. Be sure to include everyone of the same generation on the same line, whether brothers and sisters or cousins, because they are all related to you equally, and share the same ancestor. Now you can see the gaps.

Second step

Decide which side of the family you want to pursue. The paternal line is usually preferred by family historians because of the continuity of surname, but there is nothing to prevent you from tackling your mother's ancestry. It is, however, best to search one branch of your family at a time. If you get stuck with one line, you can turn to another, because each generation you push back doubles the pool of surnames to choose from: those of your parents (two), your grandparents (four), great-grandparents (eight), great-great-grandparents (16) and so on. Sometimes intermarriages occurred within a family or you will find that unrelated people of the same surname wed each other, so the actual number of surnames may not always be this great.

Third step

Identify the names and precise connection to you of living relatives recorded on your family tree, and their present addresses, so that you can contact them to see if they can add anything extra to the story. It is obviously wisest to approach older kinsfolk first, but do not ignore younger family members

(CA) DAVID COLWELL of Eland Hall, Ponteland, Northumberland, 1841; Prestwick, parish of Dinnington, Northumberland, 1851, farmer (retired by 1851), born c. 1781, at Elsdon, Northumberland, died 18 Jan 1852, at Prestwick
= MARY of Eland Hall, died 12 May 1838, at Eland Hall

1 son

(CA) MICHAEL COLWELL of Eland Hall, 1840, North Trewick, Belsay, parish of Bolam, Northumberland, 1851, Clickimin, Ponteland, 1861, farmer, born c. 1812 at Elsdon, aged 39 in 1851, died 26 Sept 1869, at Simonside, near South Shields, Co. Durham
= ANN daughter of JAMES HOWNAM, husbandman, born c. 1814, at Gosforth, Northumberland, married 12 Jan 1840, at Ponteland, by licence, died 6 May 1886, at High Simonside, Co. Durham

(C) WILLIAM COLWELL of Clickimin, Ponteland, 1861, Pilgrim Street, Newcastle-on-Tyne, Northumberland, 1877, Fellgate Farm, Jarrow, Northumberland, 1880, Laburnum Terrace, East Boldon, Co. Durham, 1912, clerk in an office, 1877, farmer, 1880, born 20 Nov 1841, at Eland Hall, died 1 Aug 1912, at South Shields Workhouse Infirmary, Harton, South Shields
= ELIZABETH daughter of MATTHEW GIBSON, waterman, born c. 1850, at South Shields, married 25 June 1877, at All Saints, Newcastle-on-Tyne, after Banns, aged 31 in 1881

(C) JAMES COLWELL of Simonside, farmer, born 19 March 1846, at Whalton North Middle Quarter, Northumberland, died 6 June 1919, at Simonside
= JANE daughter of WILLIAM WALKER, farmer, married 5 Mch 1878, at All Saints, Newcastle-on-Tyne, after Banns

1 son

(GC) WILLIAM COLWELL of East Boldon, Glasgow, Lanarkshire, and Middlesbrough, Yorkshire, hosier, born 21 Aug 1880, at Fellgate Farm, Jarrow
= MARGARET ELIZABETH daughter of JOHN URE, bottlemaker, married 1903, at Boldon, by licence

(GC) RICHARD WALKER COLWELL of Simonside, Staindrop, Co. Durham, Crookhill Farm, Stocksfield, Northumberland, farmer, and Sunderland, Co. Durham, grocer, born 26 Jan 1880, at Simonside Farm, near South Shields
= MARY daughter of WILLIAM HOLT, miner, married 1925, at Heighington, Co. Durham

(GGC) WILLIAM JAMES COLWELL of Glasgow, and Grasmere, Westmorland, merchant seaman, county milk analyst, and sub-postmaster, born 1903, at Sunderland
= ELSIE IRENE HARTLEY daughter of THOMAS ALFRED THEXTON, librarian, and sub-postmaster, married 1935, at Grasmere

(GGGC) STELLA born 1944

(GGC) RICHARD WILLIAM COLWELL born 1929

1 son
2 daughters

1 son
4 daughters

1 son
3 sons

figure 1 the Colwell family tree. My cousin Richard Colwell is my second cousin once removed. He is the great-grandchild (GGC) of our common ancestors, Michael and Ann Colwell (CA), and I am their great-great-grandchild (GGGC)

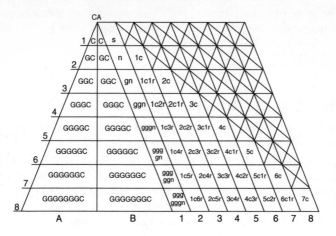

- Find the common ancestor of the two relatives.
- To work out a family relationship, identify the person of the earlier generation in column A. Note the number to the left.
- Then find the relative you want to link with the person in column B. Note the number to the left.

Look at the COLWELL pedigree on page 6; for example, RICHARD WILLIAM COLWELL is the great-grandson of MICHAEL COLWELL and ANN HOWNAM. The number next to this is 3.

STELLA COLWELL is the great-great-granddaughter of this couple, the common ancestors. The number next to this is 4.

- With your finger on the line at the higher diagonal number (4) move it across to find the box over the lower horizontal number (3). This shows that they are 2nd cousins once removed. RICHARD COLWELL is the 2nd cousin of STELLA'S father, one generation earlier.

In canon law they are related in the 4th degree, the maximum number of steps away from their common ancestor; in civil law it is the 7th degree, the total number of steps back and forwards separating them both.

Key:

CA	= common ancestor	s	= sibling (brother/sister)		
C	= child	n	= nephew or niece		
GC	= grandchild	gn	= great or grand nephew		
GGC	= great-grandchild		(or niece)		
		ggn	= great-great nephew (or niece) and so on		
GGGC	= great-great-grandchild and so on	1c	= 1st cousin		
		1c1r	= 1st cousin once removed and so on		

figure 2 how to work out family relationships

who may have cared for elderly parents or have memories of their grandparents. Find out if anyone in the family has already researched its history or would be interested in sharing the workload.

Getting in touch and setting up a visit

Spoken history has the advantage of immediacy and is a source that can be questioned or added to by others.

If you are regularly in touch with certain relatives, give reasonable advance warning (say three weeks) of what you are up to and an idea of the information you hope they can provide. A measured approach is preferable to springing a surprise call, which catches a person off-guard and unprepared.

If you begin with relatives you see often, you will feel more relaxed. Your relative's own home is probably the best place to meet, as he or she will be surrounded by family keepsakes within easy reach. Such a setting also ensures privacy, since some of what may be divulged may be intimate and sensitive. Try not to have anyone else around to inhibit the conversation or disturb its flow.

Compile a checklist of questions to steer you through the conversation and make sure you cover the essential points. You may not want to ask about everything on your list, certainly not in one sitting, so arrange to meet up again. This should prevent your informant becoming mentally and physically exhausted and perhaps even hostile to your efforts.

Questions to ask

Ask if anyone in the family has already done some research, and if so how that person can be contacted. This will avoid needless duplication and you might be able to exchange information.

A list of questions tracking a person's life story chronologically is the simplest method to adopt. If you have to break off the conversation, you will then both know at which point to pick up the threads of the story again.

If dates are imprecisely remembered, anecdotes recounted in sequence will fit more easily into the timeframe. A list gives the interview a structure, but need not be rigidly adhered to. Tailor your list to each individual and what you want in particular to elicit from them. Look in the next chapter for ideas on what information to aim for.

Your main objective is to draw out genealogical facts. Good listening skills and empathy are paramount. Don't be tempted to interrupt, make corrections or value judgements. Resist imposing your own life history unless called for, because you are trying to fill in gaps in your knowledge, not reiterate what you already know.

Refer to people's relatives in the way they were described during your conversation, as their father, grandfather, or brother, and not by their relationship to you, to prevent any later misinterpretation. The two grandfathers should be referred to as mother's father, or father's father, especially when it is unlikely that their forenames and surnames will be mentioned more than once.

What to be wary of

Personal descriptions can be misleading. For instance, 'aunts' and 'uncles' might have been family friends or connected by marriage rather than blood relatives. Occasionally you may need to track down these friends or their descendants to discover more about your family if there is no one left, or existing members are reticent.

Memories play tricks, as selective screening commences very soon after an experience. One person's editing process operates differently from another's, which can lead to several very interesting versions of the same incident. Memory is, after all, a mixture of fact and opinion, and reflects each person's unique standpoint. Family recollections may be re-interpreted over time, relate to occurrences which were insignificant in one person's life but had a far greater impact on someone else's. Events may be telescoped together or relayed out of order, whilst a person's role in them may be exaggerated by wishful thinking, or suppressed because of a feeling of guilt or embarrassment. Other stories may be based merely on hearsay, perhaps to protect the listener. Every time an anecdote is repeated it stands a chance of further embellishment or distortion.

Family souvenirs

Set aside some time to pore over family ephemera. Good examples are family photographs, old address books, franked letters, diaries, registration cards and passports, because they give valuable clues to what people looked like and where they were at set times, to their doings and observations, and to the relatives and friends with whom they stayed in touch. Artefacts such as medals, toys and jewellery as well as old rent and ration books, certificates and newspaper cuttings have all been saved for a special reason. A family Bible is a special treasure. It was often given as a wedding present, the first entry recording the recipients' marriage, followed by the names and birthdays of their children. Inscribed details about any infant deaths and the births of offspring before the introduction of civil registration may be the only surviving record of their existence. However, some family births and deaths were written up many years after they occurred, perhaps incorrectly, especially if a baby's arrival was uncomfortably close to or preceded the date of the parents' marriage. Always look at the Bible's publication date to check it was before the earliest recorded entry. Birthplaces may be omitted, leaving you with a chronicle of family events whose whereabouts are unknown.

Ask if you can list the things you have been shown and make copies of any documents and old photographs. Note the names, addresses and relationship to you of their various owners. It is worthwhile carrying copies of unidentified photographs with you on your travels because other family members may recognize who the people were or have similar copies of their own. Don't forget to photograph the relatives you have interviewed, to build up a lasting visual archive. Always return anything you have borrowed. If you want to make digital copies and e-mail them to family members, be sure to obtain the owners' prior permission, as you cannot control where else they might be forwarded. Digital copies also take up a lot of computer memory.

Dealing with different types of relative

One person's fascination may be viewed by another as an obsession, so do not outstay your welcome. Concentration flags after about an hour, too. The interview should not be rushed, but treat it as an opportunity for quiet reminiscence, not an interrogation. Reliving the past leaves people vulnerable and their feelings exposed, so respect their trust and confidence, and once the chat is over, do not hurry away but make sure any revelations have not caused emotional distress. Having your sole attention for even a short time may be enjoyable, allowing memories to flood back in which no one else has recently or ever expressed much interest, and he or she may have eagerly looked forward to your company. A gift, such as a box of good chocolates or biscuits or a home-made cake is also welcome and makes the person feel that you have thought of them. Before you leave, ask for the names, relationships and addresses of anyone else in the family in the district you might approach (especially married daughters, because their surnames may be different), as you may be able to combine a second agreed visit with a pre-arranged call on them.

You are almost certain to come across relatives who do not want to talk to you, or may clam up when you are sure they hold crucial information. This reluctance has to be respected however much you long to quiz them. Some memories might be too painful to resurrect, or there might be an embargo on discussion of some topics, so you will need to exercise sensitivity and tact. Other family members may be only too happy to reveal everything they know and will become valued allies, but be discreet about their revelations, as what they divulge might have been kept secret elsewhere in the family or cast them in an unfavourable light. At all costs, avoid stoking up a family feud or resurrecting buried resentments.

Seeing it from your relatives' point of view

Your questions are unlikely to be answered fully or unequivocally on a single visit. Be prepared to interview your relatives at least twice, but not so often that it becomes an ordeal. It is important that they do not feel exploited and their efforts on your behalf go unappreciated. Your relatives will probably like being kept in touch with your progress, but avoid bombarding them with minutiae. Christmas is a good time to send an updated family tree which is easy to understand and pass round, and any recent additions to the family can then be included on it. It may even generate yet more anecdotes.

The second interview gives you the chance to deliver a short, simple and clear progress report, accompanied by an explanatory family tree. Use this opportunity to fill in gaps and to sort out any conflicting assertions or misunderstandings. Your relative may value having a short list of these points to mull over beforehand. A suggested interval of a fortnight or so is usually sufficient after you have sent the list. Your informant will know what to expect this time. An excursion to your relative's childhood haunts, if it can be arranged, may trigger more memories and give them something to savour. Hopefully, your first meeting will have provided you with some ideas of places to visit.

Write or record?

You will need to decide how to record permanently your family chats. If you plan to keep a written account, an A4 pad with a narrow feint and margin for notes is recommended, for easy filing. Each new sheet of paper should be numbered, and headed by the name and relationship to you of the relative, plus the date and place of the interview. Do not try to commit what was said to paper verbatim as you will slow down the proceedings and distract the speaker. Jot down all the dates, places, names, relationships and other given key facts, with headings for memorable anecdotes which can then be written up later. Make sure you have plenty of writing implements with you and do not mark any documents or items shown to you. Pencils will not leak or run dry, but be sure they are sharpened beforehand to avoid interrupting the flow of conversation.

Make sure you have your relative's permission to use a laptop computer, if this is your chosen recording medium. Laptops are brilliant for information storage, but they are noisy and distracting, so be careful if you opt to record your conversations in this way. If you are focusing on the keyboard and screen as you write it all up, you cannot at the same time be giving your undivided attention to what is being said. It is more considerate to run the laptop on batteries, rather than use your interviewee's electricity supply.

Tape-recorded interviews

If you elect to tape-record, you can build up an oral archive, preserving any individual nuances of pronunciation, local dialect words and phrases. Be wary when using this equipment though, because the contributor may feel inhibited by it if he or she fears what purposes the tape-recording may be put to.

Copyright

The copyright of the tape content belongs to the speaker. If you wish to use it for later publication or to lodge a copy in a local oral history collection you must ask for the copyright to be assigned to you. Always secure the written consent of your interviewee in advance. A pro-forma which can be signed by each recorded relative is best, and this provides a safeguard in the event of your informant's death.

If you decide to use a tape-recorder, it is a good idea to opt for a portable cassette-player with two sockets for external microphones, one each for the speaker and the interviewer. A battery-operated type is more versatile than a plug-in recorder, as you can do the interviewing anywhere without requiring an adaptor, but always take spare batteries. The best types of microphone are the tie-clip or lapel type, worn about 20 centimetres away from the mouth, the lead being tucked under the person's arm. This allows the speaker to concentrate on the interview without affecting the quality of recording by any movement of the head. The most stable and reliable medium is a good quality ferric tape, running for 30 minutes each side (C60).

The room selected for tape-recording should be free of any extraneous background sounds. If possible, all phones should be temporarily immobilized. A microphone is very sensitive and will pick up every noise: a bad recording will forever remain a bad and irritating reminder of the occasion.

Try to place the tape-recorder out of the speaker's line of vision, and sit facing each other, at a slight angle. If you have to share the microphone, sit close together, and if the microphone is free-standing, place it at a different level to the recorder, on a soft, absorbent surface. The tape should run for at least five seconds before you begin recording. Start by announcing your own name, the date, place and name of the interviewee, and have your questions ready, preferably written down to stop you 'freezing'. This will relax you and assist you in achieving the correct sound level. It is helpful to discuss and agree your list of questions beforehand, so your interviewee knows what is coming and has mentally prepared his or her responses. Do not have more than 20 of these, and don't insist on asking all of them! Try not to rustle the pages on which your questions and answers are written.

Allow the person to respond at his or her own pace, and do not be tempted to break a particular train of thought. Silence can often be meaningful. A nod of the head as encouragement, and open questions which require more than a 'yes' or 'no' will produce a more fluent exchange, but expect the first few minutes to be slightly stilted until the speaker feels at ease. Let the interview run its course, and be ready for it to go off at a tangent occasionally. When this happens, pursue any promising avenue of information, or gently steer it back to what you want to know. This is where your structured list of questions will come in handy.

It is tiring listening attentively and picking up on unscripted topics, so practise with a friend first, until you feel comfortable in charge of the tape-recorder, and know what to do should anything mechanical go wrong. Ask to be interviewed yourself, and get to know how it feels. Training in oral history and interviewing skills under expert tuition will help too. Details about local courses and oral history society activities should be available in your local library.

Each recording is unique and irreplaceable. Once it is completed snap off the safety tab at the top of the cassette (there is one for each side of the tape) to prevent accidental erasure or over-recording. Label it with the date of the interview, the name of the speaker and his or her date of birth, plus your own name, and to whom the copyright belongs. Allocate a sequential number to each tape for listing and easy retrieval when it is stored away. A copy should be made and kept apart from the original (clearly marked as 'Master'). File your tapes upright in their boxes, in a shady, cool, dry and dust-free place away from a television set or any other electrical equipment which might interfere with their magnetic fields.

Next, listen to the recording and write a summary of the taped conversation. A complete transcript is not necessary, just a short precis of the salient points as you listen to the replay, and then arrange your summary under headings.

Writing to relatives

If your relatives live too far away for a visit, or you are contacting people that your relatives have told you about and you have never met, you may have to rely on e-mail exchanges or letters. With e-mails you can be certain of your intended recipient, but they may forward your message on without your knowledge, so be very careful what you say! You can of course send an e-mail as a confidential communication, but even then there is no guarantee your request will be honoured. Remember, though, that some people have an aversion to committing to writing anything intimate about themselves or their family.

Your written communication should be succinct. State your place in the family and list only the most important questions you want answered. If the list is kept short, you can always ask more later: if it is too long, then you may receive no answer at all. A list is easy to follow and gives your enquiries a framework. Always retain a copy, since the reply may simply refer to your questions by number. You may have to wait patiently for some time for an answer. Your request might even be mislaid. A second, friendly, letter, with your address on the outside of the envelope will offer another chance for a reply, and should the person have moved away the letter can then be returned to you. Remember that you are asking a favour and a reply is not obligatory. Always enclose a stamped self-addressed envelope or three International Reply Coupons.

Those moved away and the dead

If a relative was last known at a specific address, the new occupiers may have forwarding details or know where he or she went. Neighbours may have stayed in touch and can supply you with details. If you know only the name of the town they moved to, try the phone book, the online phone directory at **www.bt.com/index.jsp** (United Kingdom) or **www.infobel.com/teldir** (worldwide) or a recent online electoral register. The latest edited edition of the UK electoral register is available at **www.tracesmart.co.uk**. You could also **www.findmypast.com/LivingRelatives.jsp** for a person, address or business search.

If you are trying to locate a particular missing living relative in England and Wales, consider approaching Traceline, at **www.gro.gov.uk/gro/content/research/traceline**. This service is run by the Office for National Statistics, in Southport, and for a fee a search will be undertaken for you of the National Health Service Central Register. Both of you must be aged 18 or over, and you will need to specify your relationship to the named individual, and his or her date of birth or age, and any extra details such as the names of the person's parents, any previous names or the last known address. You will be notified if the person is still alive and for an extra fee you can send a letter which will be forwarded to the missing relative. No information as to their whereabouts is ever disclosed to the enquirer under the Data Protection Act 1998; it is left to the missing person to respond. If you are seeking a current or former partner, you will only be advised if he or she is still living, or has died, and should this be the situation, you will be supplied with enough information to enable you to obtain a copy of the death certificate. Traceline cannot assist with cases involving adoption, as there is a special Adoption Contact Register to deal with requests by adopted persons and their birth relatives. There is more information about adoption in Chapter 4.

Another option is to register yourself and the name of the relative with whom you want to renew contact at **www.genesreunited.com**. This is free, but you will have to pay to respond to any incoming e-mails.

You may discover that a relative you would have liked to have interviewed has died. Nursing home staff, neighbours and friends in the same street may be able to disclose more about the person than surviving relatives, as people often choose to unburden themselves elsewhere about subjects which might be too sensitive for family consumption. An appointment with the nursing home staff member or next-door neighbours can pay dividends, but always state in advance the purpose of your visit. Ask for the names and addresses of the person's solicitor and funeral director. The solicitor may have handled the deceased person's estate and let you have the names and addresses of the next of kin. He or she may also know what became of any family papers, but this approach requires tact, so explain the reason why you are making contact. The funeral director may be able to furnish similar information and can certainly reveal where the person was buried or cremated. A chat with the local priest or a churchwarden, a study of a local newspaper obituary or death notice, or the parish newsletter may tell you who were the chief mourners and friends with whom you can communicate.

What to do if you have no known living relatives

If you remember where your parents came from, a search of the phone book of that area may turn up the numbers and addresses of present-day subscribers bearing your surname.

Sometimes a visit to the street or district where your parents or grandparents once lived can elicit precious nuggets of information from their former friends, neighbours and their descendants about other family members who have since died or left the area. The headstone inscriptions in the local churchyard or cemetery may fill in gaps too. The cemetery owner may be willing to search the burial registers for details of family plot numbers to help you find particular graves. You can find out cemetery company contact numbers and addresses from the phone book or local district council office. Look also in *The Family and Local History Handbook*, edited and compiled by R. Blatchford, for a list of local cemeteries. Try the National Burial Index, on CD-ROM, for extracts from church, chapel and cemetery registers up to 2000, and the indexed transcriptions at **www.familyhistoryonline.org.uk**.

Advertising in the press

A short letter to the editor of the relevant local newspaper, briefly setting out what you know about your family's history, and requesting information from readers, can be worthwhile too. A similar letter to a local magazine, published less often, but subscribed to by people living further afield with family roots in the same area, is also worth considering. Consult *Willing's Press Guide*, in your local reference library, for an alphabetical listing of all national and provincial newspapers and magazines published in Great Britain, Ireland and overseas, together with their editorial addresses and publication dates.

Write to the local family history society to see if a member might already be researching your family. You can find details about many such societies at **www.ffhs.org.uk** and about family history societies worldwide in *The Family and Local History Handbook*.

If you have no idea where your family came from

Let a metasearch engine, search engine or a web directory retrieve the names of specific people, and online entries of your family surname. Try **www.cyndislist.com** and click on the section labelled 'Finding People' to discover what might be there. This includes access to online phone directories, e-mail addresses, mailing lists, queries and message boards, websites for lost and missing relatives, surname sites, online family associations and family newsletters. Try the huge database of names and specific records at **www.ancestry.com** too.

Use **www.genesreunited.com** to see if anyone has registered your surname. To learn about people on e-mailing lists in the United Kingdom and Ireland, visit **www.genuki.org.uk/indexes/ MailingLists.html** and for worldwide listings try **http://lists.rootsweb.com**. This is arranged by surname, A–Z, has a section devoted to the United States of America, an International section, where you select a country, and a section organized by subject. If you choose to register your own e-mail address, remember to regularly read incoming mail, and be prepared to receive some junk.

You may want to post a message on a website such as **http://boards.ancestry.com** or **http://boards.rootsweb.com** or scroll down the list of queries and message board website links at **www.cyndislist.com** to see if anyone is looking for you. The messages are listed alphabetically by surname, by locality and by topic so are easy to search. They reach a global audience, and you can contribute information without having to subscribe yourself to a mailing list. Advertise the questions you want answered, and then inspect the messages for any responses.

A letter to the national family history press may yield results too, as such magazines have a wide readership. In the United Kingdom, *Family Tree Magazine*, *Practical Family History* and *Family History Monthly*, in Ireland *Irish Roots*, and in North America, *Family Chronicle*, *Family Tree Magazine*, *Everton's Family History Magazine*, *Heritage Quest* and *Ancestry Magazine* are worth contacting to advertise your hunt for missing relatives.

Another ploy is to trawl through the current phone books of the whole country to discover the distribution of your surname and its variants, and where it is most concentrated. However, this does not always mean that the surname has been in the locality for a long time, as it could merely be an indication of a large family or of a common surname. Conversely, the scarcity or non-occurrence of your family name may not rule out its presence in an area, because phone books exclude ex-directory subscribers. Families move about and don't always stay close to their original roots, but the migration may have been relatively recent.

Inspect the surname distribution maps at **www.thegenealogist.co.uk/ namemap/help.php** which covers the period between 1851 and 2002, drawing on the civil registration indexes of England and Wales. The maps at **www.spatial-literacy.org/UCLnames/ surnames.aspx** show the distribution of more than 25,500 surnames in England, Wales and Scotland at the time of the 1881 census, and those with more than 100 occurrences in the 1998 electoral register. Colour codes indicate the postal areas where the fewest and most references to your surname were found. However, only the regional boundaries are outlined, not their names, so click on 'Geographical Location' for details. You can compare the results at each of these two dates to see how your surname has moved around and any changes in its main centres of density. The accompanying tables tell you those areas where your surname was most numerous in 1881 and 1998, and you can discover where it was most prevalent in Ireland, the United States of America, Australia, New Zealand, Africa and Asia. A second, extended, list of 255,000 family names will soon be available, many of which only appear a handful of times. A personal name distribution list is planned too.

The above survey, which was conducted by University College London, revealed that many surnames still have strong regional ties. Some surnames are intrinsically associated with particular areas, for instance, those beginning with 'Tre-' emanate from Celtic Cornwall, those ending with '-thwaite' from Norse Cumbria and Lancashire, so in themselves contain clues to where your family name should still be present and originated, however far back in time.

03

**sorting out
the facts**

In this chapter you will learn:
- how to draw up a family tree
- how to choose the most
  suitable pedigree layout
- how to find out if anyone
  else has researched your
  ancestry.

Fourth step

When you have amassed all the information you can from your living family members, you will need to sort it out. Devote a separate sheet of paper or card to each person. Arrange your loose sheets of paper in a ring binder or place your cards in a sturdy box for easy filing and retrieval. Put the details about yourself at the top of the file or at the front of the card box, followed by those relating to your father and mother, brothers and sisters (oldest first), their spouses and their children in family groups, then your grandparents, and their other children (oldest first), spouses and children, and so on, going back a generation at a time, keeping the two families separate.

You could invest in a set of family group sheets, which can be purchased from the Church of Jesus Christ of Latter-day Saints. Visit the website at **www.familysearch.org** to find out what they look like and how to order them. The forms incorporate details about one set of parents and their children, which can be cross-referenced to other family group sheets.

You can now begin to sift through the sheets or cards to draw up a pictorial summary of your ancestral line. Only include proven facts.

The sooner you start to transfer your information into a family tree, the easier it will be to see precisely what stage you have reached in your research. You can then add newly discovered facts as you go along. The pedigree chart should clearly and tidily show every generation link, and should be capable of being understood by anyone without any need for further explanation.

You may prefer to use one of the many available genealogical software packages to feed the details directly into a pre-set database, and then save it. Read up and ask friends who have used these for advice and recommendations on what to buy. There are regular reviews of the most recent packages in the family history press and in computer magazines. Examples are *Internet Genealogy, Your Family Tree, Computers in Genealogy, Ancestors,* **www.onlinegenealogy.com** and **www.ancestornews.com**. Usually there will be a choice of pedigree layout: this could be the traditional drop-line chart which starts with your name at the bottom (see Figure 1 on p. 6) or a horizontal birth-brief, which sets out your ancestry sideways from left to right. Family Tree Maker is one such package that a lot of family historians find especially helpful and easy to use. Following a set of simple clear instructions, you can insert the names of your forebears, their dates of birth, baptism, marriage and/or death and burial where indicated in the available fields shown on the screen. Inbuilt alerts warn you if any information looks suspicious, such as dates or filiations, and you can correct, amend, delete and add extra information at any time. Use GenSmart in association with Family Tree Maker. This program analyses your loaded files too, and suggests research avenues, together with a list of sources and lists.

Although being rather inflexible in the data such a package allows you to include, these products do save you time, and look professional. You can download, save and print as many copies as you like.

A web-based pedigree package is available at **www.pedigree soft.com**. This is useful because other members of your family can view it online and make corrections or additions. You can also upload an existing GEDCOM file containing your family tree into this database, and you can check its contents against all the entries in the various vital records and pedigree databases at **www.familysearch.org**.

Some simple guidelines

There are no hard rules for drafting your own pedigree chart, but you may find the following advice helpful. Plenty of time, sufficient work space, a large sheet of ruled paper (or several sheets of ruled A4 glued together), a sharpened pencil, rubber and ruler are all that are required.

- Start with yourself, towards the bottom of the page, and leave sufficient room to include your children and other descendants.
- Record everyone of the same generation on the same line, so that you can see their precise position in the family tree in relation to yourself.
- Place children of the same parents in birth order, the oldest on the left. Sometimes you may have to alter the order to slot in interfamily marriages, so indicate birth seniority by an appropriate number above each name.
- Write people's names in capital letters; record surnames only for males, and refer to females by their forenames.
- Write a wife's name to the right of her husband's. When he has married more than once place the name of the first wife to

the left of his name, and the second to the right. The same applies when it is the woman who has married twice.

- Use a vertical descent line from the marriage symbol (=) to connect parents to their children. Draw a horizontal line underneath this, and above the names of their children, and a short vertical line down from this horizontal line to each child.
- Indicate illegitimate children by a wavy vertical descent line from the names of the parents down to their names, with an X instead of = sign between the names of the parents.
- Record adopted children's names after the names of other children of a couple, but without a descent line, because there is no blood relationship.
- Where it is uncertain but likely that there is a parental or sibling link, use dotted lines.

What to include

Here is a checklist of items to include, although you will not manage all of them, and the further back you go in time the scantier the information will be:

1 full name
2 residence now, and previous ones, with dates if possible (earliest first), including county
3 occupation now and earlier occupations, with dates if possible (earliest first), any service rank or title, any awards and decorations, public appointments such as Justice of the Peace, degree and university
4 date of birth, and place, with the county (and date of adoption if appropriate)
5 date and place of baptism, with the county, and religious affiliation
6 where educated, starting with the first school, plus dates; date of any apprenticeship, and details of any wartime service
7 for females only: date and place of marriage, and the county; if divorced, the date of the decree absolute
8 ownership of land, and its whereabouts, including the county
9 if included in a census return, which years (earliest first), and at what age

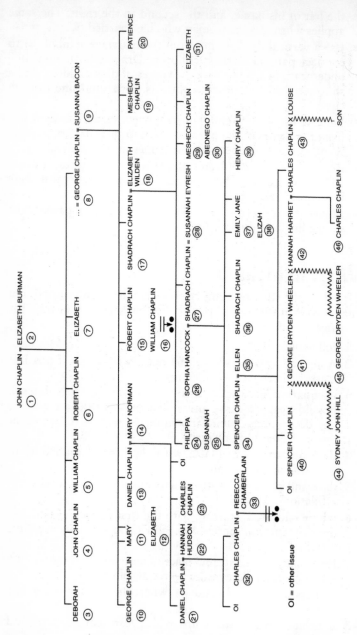

Figure 3 Chaplin pedigree (Charlie Chaplin's ancestry)

Key

① of Great Finborough, co. Suffolk, 1728, parish constable, 1744, 1746, overseer of the poor, 1768, 1773, churchwarden 1774, bur 12 Oct 1787, Great Finborough.

② marr 11 July 1728, Great Finborough afsd, after Banns.

③ bap 15 Dec 1728, Great Finborough, afsd.

④ bap 22 Nov 1730, Great Finborough, afsd.

⑤ bap 25 Dec 1732, Great Finborough, afsd.

⑥ bap 15 June 1734, Great Finborough, afsd.

⑦ bap 6 June 1737, Great Finborough, afsd.

⑧ of Great Finborough, afsd, farmer, 1771-1819, bap there 24 May 1741, parish constable, 1781, 1800, overseer of the poor, 1809, died 12, bur 19 May 1819 Great Finborough, aged 78, M.I., will dd 13 May, pr 30 Sept 1819.

⑨ marr 8 Sept 1771, Great Finborough afsd, after Banns, named executrix in husband's will, 1819, died 6, bur 10 April 1827, Great Finborough, aged 78 or 80, M.I.

⑩ bap 20 June 1773, Great Finborough, afsd.

⑪ bap 10 Sept 1775, Great Finborough, afsd, named in father's will, 1819.

⑫ bn 25 Apr, bap 17 May 1777, Great Finborough, afsd, received into the church 14 Sept 1783.

⑬ of Great Finborough, afsd, thatcher, 1802-50, there bn 8 Jly, bap 10 Aug 1779, and received into the church, 14 Sept 1783, aged c 60 in 1841, died 22, bur 28 Feb 1850, Great Finborough, aged 70, M.I.

⑭ of Ipswich, co. Suffolk, 1852, marr 9 Dec 1802, Great Finborough, afsd, after Banns, aged c 60 in 1841, died 7, bur 12 May 1852, Great Finborough, aged 71, M.I.

⑮ bn 15 Mch, bap 29 Aug 1781, Great Finborough afsd, received into the church 14 Sept 1783.

⑯ bn 2 Aug, bap 14 Sept 1783, Great Finborough, afsd, named in father's will as deceased, 1819.

⑰ of Great Finborough, afsd, 1809-19, Butter Market, Ipswich, afsd, 1851, shoemaker, 1814-22, retired farmer,1851, bap 21 May 1786, Great Finborough, named in father's will, 1819, aged 65 in 1851, dead by 1872.

⑱ (WILDING) of Buxhall, co. Suffolk, there marr 29 Aug 1809, after Banns, aged 67 in 1851.

⑲ of Hadleigh Road, Great Finborough, afsd, farmer, 1841, bap 3 Aug 1788, Great Finborough, overseer of the poor, 1828, 1840, 1847, aged c 50 in 1841, exectr of father's will, 1819, died 20, bur 25 Aug 1849, Great Finborough, aged 61, M.I.

⑳ bap 21 Jly 1793, Great Finborough, afsd, named in father's will, 1819.

㉑ of Village Green, Great Finborough, afsd, thatcher, 1841, bap 2 June 1803, Great Finborough, parish constable, 1851, 1855-61, aged c 35 in 1841.

㉒ Banns read at Great Finborough, afsd, 8, 15 Dec & 185-, aged 30 in 1841, died 8, bur 13 Dec 1878, Great Finborough, aged 69, M.I.

㉓ bap 22 Apr 1821, Great Finborough, afsd, parish constable, 1850, 1854, 1862-64, 1868, nominated but not chosen as overseer of the poor, 1869, parish clerk 1872, Rate Collector and Assistant Surveyor, 1875, Surveyor, 1876, aged c 20 in 1841.

㉔ bap 25 Dec 1809, Great Finborough,afsd.

㉕ bap 5 Jne 1812, Great Finborough, afsd.

㉖ bn c 1808, Tunstall, co. Stafford, marr 29 Apr 1834, St. Margaret, Ipswich, afsd, after Banns, aged 43 in 1851.

㉗ of Carr Street, Ipswich, afsd, 1851, and Old Cattle Market, Ipswich, 1881, master brewer, 1851, innkeeper, 1855, commercial traveller, 1872, boot-maker, 1881-87, bn 15 Jan, bap 8 Apr 1814, Great Finborough, afsd, aged 67 in 1881, died 2 Apr 1893, at Ipswich, aged 79, will dd 19 Feb 1887, Admon 12 May 1893.

㉘ dau of the late SAMUEL ROBIN-SON, labourer, deceased, marr 2nd, 25 Aug 1872, Crown Street Congregational Chapel of the Independents, Ipswich, died 3 Apr 1893, aged 65, Admon 5 May 1893.

㉙ bap 20 Apr 1817, Great Finborough, afsd.

㉚ of Butter Market, Ipswich, afsd, ironmonger, 1851, bap 6 Feb 1819, Great Finborough, afsd, aged 31 in 1851.

㉛ bap 12 May 1822, Great Finborough, afsd.

㉜ of Great Finborough, afsd, thatcher, 1873, bap 14 Jne 1846, Great Finborough.

㉝ Banns read at Great Finborough, afsd, 3, 10, 17 Dec 1871.

㉞ of St. Margaret, Ipswich, afsd, 1854, Orcus Street, Marylebone, co. Middx, 1881, Rillington Place, co. Middx, 1881, The Devonport Arms, Devonport Mews, Radnor Place, co. Middx, butcher, 1854-63, unemployed, 1881, public house manager, 1897, bn c 1835, Ipswich, aged 29 May 1897, aged 63, will dd 18 May 1897, Admon 2 Sept 1897.

㉟ dau of WILLIAM SMITH, dealer, marr 30 Oct 1854, St Margaret, Ipswich, afsd, by Licence, dead by 30 Mch 1851.

㊱ bn c 1839, Ipswich, afsd, aged 12 in 1851.

㊲ bn c 1843, Ipswich, afsd, aged 8 in 1851.

㊳ bn c 1845, Ipswich, afsd, aged 6 in 1851.

㊴ bn c 1849, Ipswich, afsd, aged 2 in 1851.

㊵ of Northcote Hotel, Battersea Rise, London, 1881, Queens Head, Lambeth, co. Surrey, 1891, manager to a publican, 1881, licensed victualler, 1891, bn c 1856, Ipswich, afsd, aged 25 in 1881.

㊶ (LEO DRYDEN), music hall singer.

㊷ (LILY HARLEY) of Southwark, 1881, Brandon Street,, Walworth, 1885, Oakden Street, Kennington Road, 1898, all co. Surrey, Golden Place, Chester Street, Lambeth, afsd, 1901, mantle machinist, 1881, dau of CHARLES HILL, bootmaker, marr 22 Jne 1885, St. John Walworth, after Banns.

㊸ of Northcote Hotel, Battersea Rise, afsd, 1881, Brandon Street afsd, 1885, Albert Street, Newington co. Surrey, 1891, Lambeth, afsd, 1901, barman, 1891, professional singer, 1885, music hall singer, 1891, comedian, 1901, bn 18 Mch 1863, Orcus Street, Marylebone, afsd, died 9 May 1901, St Thomas's Hospital, Lambeth.

㊹ bn 16/17 Mch 1885, Brandon Street, afsd.

㊺ (WHEELER DRYDEN), bn 31 Aug 1892.

㊻ (CHARLIE CHAPLIN) bn 12/15/16 Apr 1889.

10 whether named in someone else's will, giving its date, and the probate date if he or she was the executor

11 date and place of death, and the county; the given age might also be recorded here

12 date and place of burial, with the county, and if there is a gravestone inscription; the given age might be recorded here.

13 if a will was made, its date and when and where proved, or the date a grant of letters of administration was made and where

14 for people marrying into the family, the full name, address, occupation, rank, title and degree of the father are recorded immediately after the personal details about the man or woman concerned in 2–6, and whether that parent was deceased at the time of the marriage; then include the same information as in 7–13 above.

The above list could also form the basis of your line of questioning for family relatives.

All your given dates should record the day first, and write rather than number each month to avoid misinterpretation. Use 'Jan' for January and 'Jne' for June. Remember to link each place to its county, to avoid any ambiguity or uncertainty.

Your family tree will serve as your working document and summarize all you have been able to prove so far. However, as a reminder, you may want to include any doubtful information in square brackets or with a question-mark against it, so that you can check this up.

A birth-brief includes the names, births, baptisms, marriages, deaths and burials of parents, grandparents and great-great-grandparents, but rarely leaves any room for siblings. The space allowed for personal details shrinks as the number of names grows, but embedded in this kind of pedigree are the different families from which you are directly descended. This type of chart is employed at **www.familysearch.org**, where you can see only three generations of a family displayed on the screen at one time. This is deliberate, so that you concentrate on the given details about a limited number of people before clicking on to view more generations. You can order your own copy, or a vertical pedigree chart, at this website.

If you have lots of relatives to include, you may find it easier to have a master chart showing your own direct descent, cross-referenced to other numbered charts on which the descendants of individually numbered uncles and aunts and other collateral branches are set out. If you have to resort to this, remember to arrange each generation in the same way as on the master chart, so that you can fit them together and learn exactly where each person fits into your family's story. Above all, don't create extra work for yourself, and generate more paper than you have to, otherwise you may lose control. Keep it simple and keep it factual.

Sometimes you may come across a family tree written up in the form of an indented narrative. Examples of narrative pedigrees are to be found in published peerages and books tracing the antecedents and living members of the aristocracy and landed gentry. Such lineages can often be difficult to follow, whereas a pictorial chart can be quickly interpreted.

Once you are happy that your family tree is as complete as you can get it, send a copy to each of your informants in case they can add anything new, rectify any mistakes or omissions, or answer any queries which might have arisen. Once you have amended the relevant parts of the pedigree, you are ready to begin your research.

Fifth step

Having established what you know and don't know about your family's history, find out if anyone else has investigated or is investigating your ancestry. The annual *Genealogical Research Directory, National and International*, edited by K. A. Johnson and M. R. Sainty, lists family surnames, places and dates currently under examination, together with contributors' contact details. A consolidated version on CD-ROM covers all the entries between 1990 and 1999, and the 2000, 2003 and later editions are available both in book form and on CD-ROM. Be very careful if you find an entry which you think applies to your family, since not every contributor may be as generous as you in exchanging information, and never send any precious items to strangers which might not be returned. The *Directory* includes a section listing One-Name Study Groups, which specialize in extracting every mention of a particular surname and its variants from specific records and indexes to build up a picture of its regional distribution over time.

The Guild of One-Name Studies publishes a list of registered members' one-name surveys at its website (**www.one-name.org**). Whilst it is not the aim of name-collectors to establish blood relationships, nonetheless their results can indicate helpful geographic clusters, and may point to where you should be looking.

Look at the surname distribution maps for English and Welsh counties between 1851 and 2002 at **www.thegenealogist.co.uk/ namemap/help.php**. You can study individual county maps of Great Britain at **www.rootsmap.com**, which record the county and place of birth of everyone who was enumerated in the 1881 census returns and show late eighteenth- and early nineteenth-century surname distributions. The total number of surname references is specified for each country. Another set of county maps uses information prior to 1800, which was derived from the International Genealogical Index. This Index contains extracts of birth, baptism and marriage registrations from many parish and vital records. The date of the first reference to your surname in each parish is included as well, which may be a clue to its migration over more than two centuries. There are similar maps for Ireland, based on Griffith's Valuation between 1847 and 1864.

Consult *The Surnames of Scotland*, by G. F. Black, for information about their likely origins and distribution. Scottish and Irish clan names are listed at **www.scotlandsclans.com**. You can view maps marking out the domains of the major Scottish clans at **www.geocities.com/Athens/Parthenon/3145/scotmap.html**. If you visit **www.thecapitalscot.com/scotgenealogy/** you will find links to the websites of Scottish clans and family associations. For Ireland, visit **www.theclansofireland.ie/ register.html**. Clans of Ireland Ltd, in Lucan, maintains a list of associations of family surnames.

The British Isles Genealogical Register (BIG-R) is an index of family names, setting out the places, counties and periods currently being researched. This was produced in three microfiche editions (in 1994, 1997 and 2000), by the Federation of Family History Societies. The last edition is also available on CD-ROM. The numbered entries are linked to the names and contact details of contributors throughout the world, enabling you to get in touch.

The Federation of Family History Societies, is an umbrella body with a membership of more than 210 county, one-name, denominational and specialist societies as well as a number of overseas organizations. You can use its website, **www.ffhs.org.uk**, as a gateway to the websites of its member societies including the Guild of One-Name Studies. You can e-mail relevant local societies to see if anyone is registered as researching your family name and to post your own interest. There are similar Associations for Wales (**www.fhswales.info**) and Scotland (**www.safhs.org.uk**), and a Federation of Genealogical Societies for the United States (**www.fgs.org**), all of which have direct links to the websites of their member societies. There does not appear to be anything similar for Ireland, but you might try the Genealogy Society of Ireland (**www.familyhistory.ie**), and the Ulster Historical Foundation (**www.ancestryireland.com**). Umbrella organizations focusing on research into families with British roots include the International Society for British Genealogy and Family History (**www.isbgfh.org**) and the British Isles Family History Society (**www.rootsweb.com/~bifhsusa**), both of which are based in the United States. It might be worth contacting these as well.

Collections of pedigrees

The oldest family history society in the British Isles is the Society of Genealogists, in London. Its library is open to non-members for a time-based fee, and there is a limited pre-paid library search service available if you cannot visit in person. The Society's library contains thousands of copies of published family histories, deposited manuscript pedigrees and research notes and an extensive set of indexed members' birth-briefs, stretching back to 16 great-great-grandparents. None of this material has been independently authenticated, so you will need to evaluate it for yourself by double-checking the given information against the cited sources. The library catalogue is searchable at **www.sog.org.uk**, but the surnames in the birth-briefs are not included.

For information about researched family trees and family histories in the library of the Church of Jesus Christ of Latter-day Saints, in Salt Lake City, Utah, visit **www.familysearch.org**. Ancestral File is made up of millions of pedigree charts and family group sheets submitted by members of the Church so that certain temple ordinances could be performed. There are no accompanying source references or notes, so you will need to verify the given information on this website. The submitters' addresses may no longer be valid and in any case these people may not be willing to disclose anything more to you, because this was not the purpose of the compilations. Pedigree Resource File, accessible at the same website, consists of family group sheets too, but these do contain source citations.

Consult the online Family History Library catalogue, at the same website, for any references to books, microfilm or microfiche copies relating to your surname and family home. Note their call numbers, which you should quote if you want to hire them (for a small fee) to read in a family history centre of the church near you. You can find the whereabouts and contact details of family history centres throughout the world from the above website. Because family history centres are run by volunteers, their facilities and opening hours vary, so check before you visit.

Try **www.cyndislist.com,** **www.rootsweb.com** and **www.ancestry.com** for links to online pedigrees and family histories. You may prefer to use a powerful search engine to trace family trees or histories featuring your surname. Key in 'family tree' or 'family history' in the search box after your chosen surname and see how many numbered references are displayed on the screen. As before, if you make contact with any of the contributors do not give too much away, but treat it as a gradual exchange of information, once it is clear that you are interested in the same family. You may even find a relative in a different part of the world anxious to trace their British roots and with whom you can share your interest and ideas on how to solve research problems.

Other manuscript collections of pedigrees

A large collection of officially authenticated pedigrees is lodged in the College of Arms, in London (**www.college-of-arms.gov.uk**). From 1530 until 1689, about once in every generation, the heralds travelled into each English county to inspect family documents and other evidence produced by local gentry claiming a right to bear a coat of arms. One of the by-products of these Heraldic Visitations was the registration of thousands of family trees, some going back to the Middle Ages. You cannot examine the county volumes yourself, but for a fee a search will be undertaken for you. Unofficial copies of many of the pedigrees have been published in book-form and on CD-ROM. You can find out which these are from **www.uk-genealogy.org.uk** and **http://harleian.co.uk**. For a good description and some warnings about copies of Visitation pedigrees, read *Visitation Pedigrees and the Genealogist*, by G. D. Squibb. The majority of the more recent officially recorded pedigrees in the College are linked to applications for coats of arms, or bring previously registered family trees up to date. Such compilations can prove invaluable when you are trying to trace migrants or emigrants. Study *The Records and Collections of the College of Arms*, by A. R. Wagner, for a complete survey of the College's official and other holdings.

The Court of the Lord Lyon, in Edinburgh, preserves Scottish heraldic and genealogical archives, and the Genealogical Office, in the National Library of Ireland, in Dublin, holds similar Irish records. Like the College of Arms, the former is not open to the public, though members of the professional Association of Scottish Genealogists and Researchers in Archives can undertake research there for you. The Genealogical Office is open to personal callers and guidance can be given by staff of the Library's Genealogical Advisory Service. If you are not able to visit yourself, then a list of professional researchers is available. The Genealogical Office holds indexed research files relating to the family histories of Irish emigrants to America and elsewhere, and a notable set of sketch pedigrees drafted by Sir William Betham from his abstracts of Irish wills. Microfilm copies of the sketch pedigrees are in the Public Record Office of Northern Ireland, in Belfast, together with other indexed deposited genealogies.

Good catalogued collections of manuscript pedigrees and notes are in the British Library, in London, and in the Bodleian Library, in Oxford. You will need readers' tickets to examine them. Many of the pedigrees were assembled by antiquarians, heralds, herald painters or their assistants in the sixteenth and seventeenth centuries, from private family documents and inscriptions on monuments which no longer exist. Because most historical central government and legal records were not then accessible to the general public, you may be able to add flesh to the bare bones of such work. You can search the catalogues to some of the collections of pedigrees in the British Library at **www.bl.uk/catalogues/manuscripts**, but the catalogue to the Harleian Manuscripts, on which many of the Harleian Society publications of the Heraldic Visitations and additional unofficial pedigrees were based, has not yet been uploaded. Not all of the catalogues to manuscript material in the Bodleian Library are yet available at **www.bodley.ox.ac.uk/dept/scwmss/wmss/online/online.htm** either. Even though the pedigrees officially registered in the College of Arms or kept in the British Library and Bodleian Library may seem to concern only the higher reaches of society, because of our system of inheritance by primogeniture, and the high incidence of social mobility upwards and downwards, they do include references to family members who were relatively humble, or whose descendants went down the social scale.

The National Archives, at Kew (**www.nationalarchives.gov.uk**), the National Archives of Scotland, in Edinburgh (**www.nas.gov.uk**), the National Archives of Ireland, in Dublin (**www.nationalarchives.ie**),and the Public Record Office of Northern Ireland, in Belfast (**www.proni.gov.uk/records/ pedigree.htm**) contain thousands of pedigrees, many of which were produced as evidence for legal purposes in the central courts of law. Use the online catalogues of the National Archives at Kew and of the National Archives of Scotland to find document references to family trees listed under your surname.

Two excellent collections of manuscript Welsh pedigrees are in the National Library of Wales, in Aberystwyth (**www.llgc.org.uk**), and in the College of Arms. For more information, consult *Handlist of Manuscripts in the National Library of Wales*, produced by the National Library, and *A Catalogue of Manuscripts in the College of Arms: Vol. 1*, by L. Campbell, F. Steer and R. Yorke. A number of the pedigrees have been printed. You will need a reader's ticket to use the National Library of Wales.

Many of the Welsh pedigrees were written in the native language, and include fifteenth- and sixteenth-century recitals of ninth- and tenth-century genealogies which had been transmitted orally from generation to generation. Most of the manuscript copies end in the late seventeenth century. Welsh genealogies are remarkable for the many claimed descents from a handful of named 'patriarchs', and for the use of patronymics instead of hereditary surnames. Each individual was known by a genealogical string of personal names, which identified at least the father and grandfather, and thus changed every generation. Personal tags like someone's place of abode, farm or homestead name, occupation, trade, nickname or some other diminutive assume great importance in Welsh family history, because the pool of personal names was so small. Read *Welsh Surnames*, by T. J. Morgan and P. Morgan, to find out more.

County record offices and family history societies may also have copies of manuscript and printed pedigrees of local families. You can access the websites of most record offices via **www.genuki.org.uk/big** or **www.nationalarchives.gov.uk/archon**

and those of family history societies via **www.ffhs.org.uk**. The Family History Index of the Scottish Genealogy Society, in Edinburgh, is searchable online at **www.scotsgenealogy.com**, and includes references to both pedigrees and family histories in its collection.

The Library of Congress, in Washington, DC (**www.loc.gov**), has in its care thousands of manuscript pedigrees. These are indexed up to 1985 in *National Union Catalog of Manuscript Collections*, which from 1986 onwards can be accessed at **www.loc.gov.coll/nucmc/**. You should also trawl *Genealogies in the Library of Congress: A Bibliography*, edited by M. J. Kaminkow, and its three later *Supplements*, which record the Family Name Index entries of printed and manuscript pedigrees, together with their call numbers. *A Complement to Genealogies in the Library of Congress*, also compiled and edited by M.J. Kaminkow, covers other library holdings in the United States, including foreign and unpublished family trees. The National Society of Daughters of the American Revolution, in Washington, DC (**www.dar.org**), New York Genealogical and Biographical Society (**www.newyorkfamilyhistory.org**), New England Historic Genealogical Society, in Boston (**www.newenglandancestors.org**), and the Newberry Library, in Chicago (**www.newberry.org**), all boast notable collections of compiled pedigrees too. Visit their websites for advice on how you can access their catalogues and conditions for research.

Published family trees and family histories

Most printed pedigrees and their whereabouts in England are listed in S. A. Raymond's series of county genealogical bibliographies, which enshrine and bring up to date *The Genealogist's Guide*, by G. W. Marshall, which was first issued in 1903, and updated in 1953 by *A Genealogical Guide: An Index to British Pedigrees in Continuation of Marshall's Genealogical Guide*, by J. B. Whitmore and then by *The Genealogist's Guide: An Index to Printed British Pedigrees and Family Histories, 1950–1975*, by G. B. Barrow.

If your family's history has been written up and printed, then it too should be listed by Raymond and if published before 1980, by the *Catalogue of British Family Histories*, by T. R. Thomson. For printed Scottish pedigrees you will need to consult *Scottish*

Family History, Guide to Works of Reference on the Genealogy of Scottish Families, by M. Stuart and Sir James Balfour Paul, which was updated in *Scottish Family Histories*, by J. P. S. Ferguson. Published Irish pedigrees may be listed in *Bibliography of Irish Family History and Genealogy*, by B. de Breffny and *Bibliography of Irish Family History*, by E. MacLysaght. Copies of many of these publications are in the library of the Society of Genealogists, and can be hired from the Family History Library of the Church of Jesus Christ of Latter-day Saints to read in your local family history centre. Visit the National Library of Ireland's website for a catalogue to its collection of published family histories (**www.nli.ie/new_cat.htm**).

The American Genealogical–Biographical Index lists alphabetically all those genealogies and family histories which have been published in books, articles and in brief biographies up to 2005. Each entry sets out the person's name and state of birth, with an abbreviated biography, a book and page reference, and its year of publication. The index is available at **www.ancestralfindings.com/agbi.htm**. Most of the cited works are held in the Godfrey Memorial Library, in Middletown, Connecticut. You will need to subscribe to use the online index. Use the Library of Congress catalogue at **http://catalog.loc.gov** to find out what is available, as many of these books can be borrowed using the inter-library loan service.

Some words of warning

You will probably face an irritating void of several generations between what you know about your own ancestry and the broadcast researches that others have done. Your family may tantalizingly have stemmed from the same parish or district, so you may not require much more work to establish if there was any link. On the other hand, this may be purely coincidental if the surname was a common one or the family prolific.

Don't accept online, printed and manuscript pedigrees and family histories at face value as being authentic and accurate, especially if references to sources are lacking, because you need to know why each assertion was made. Always read any accompanying introductory notes to find out the compiler's intentions and scope of research. If given dates are sparse or look dubious, this should make you suspicious, particularly if someone's lifespan seems extraordinarily short or long. An unexplained migration to somewhere else may indicate that a set of facts about one family has been conveniently tacked onto those of an unrelated one of the same surname. This may be the result of wishful thinking or inexperience, rather than a deliberate misrepresentation.

High standards of evaluation of genealogical evidence have never been universally adopted, but that is not to decry the many scholarly, carefully researched pedigrees that are available.

04

starting your research: births, marriages and deaths

In this chapter you will learn:
- what is available online
- how to find and apply for copies of specific registrations
- how to solve some common research problems.

Look at your updated family tree. Have you been able to add anything more? Will you need to check some of the given sources, or can you rely on others' findings?

Sixth step

This is the point at which you start to spend money. Decide who and what you want to search for first. Do you want to bridge any gaps or to push back another generation?

What is the earliest date on your family tree? Most probably it will fall in the mid- or late nineteenth century. What does the date relate to? If it was a birth, do you know the names of the person's parents, including the mother's surname before marriage? What was that person's precise position in the family? If the date relates to a marriage, from where was the information taken? What type/denomination of wedding ceremony was it? Do you know the full names, ages and paternity of the couple? If the date was of a death, do you know the individual's purported age, and where he or she died? If the event occurred in the Channel Islands, Isle of Man, Scotland, Ireland or elsewhere, turn to Chapters 5 and 6.

Stay in control of your expenditure by drawing up a checklist of searches designed to prove only your direct ancestry. If you are feeling generous, you might want to include other branches of the family later on. You may need to do this anyway if you cannot locate your own forebears. The important thing is not to become distracted into spending time and money unnecessarily.

The first of the four basic sources covered by this book is the civil registration of births, marriages and deaths. In England and Wales, this began on 1 July 1837, under the control of the Registrar General, in London. The country was divided up into superintendent registration districts, based on the civil Poor Law Union boundaries created in 1834. These were sub-divided into smaller units called registration districts, each consisting of about seven civil parishes. The district registrars, appointed by the superintendents, recorded in special books the births and deaths in their area. Clergymen of the Established Church of England filled in two sets of marriage registers. Until 1898, the superintendent district registrars presided over all the weddings in dissenters' chapels, after which other legally authorized persons could do so. However, the Quakers and Jews maintained their own registrations of marriages. The superintendent district registrars also performed civil weddings in their offices. Civil marriages since 1970 have been allowed in exceptional circumstances by Registrar General's licence in other places such as hospitals, and where people are housebound or detained, and from April 1995 specially licensed hotels, country clubs and other premises outside the district of residence of either party have been deemed to be legal venues for weddings too.

Once every three months, the superintendents send to the Registrar General certified copies of the district registrars' returns of births and deaths which were registered in the quarter of the year up to the end of March, June, September and December. Copies of marriage registers are similarly furnished quarterly to the Registrar General by the clergy, the superintendent registrars, chapels and officers of the Quakers and Jews. When the original birth and death register books are full they are passed by the district registrar to the superintendent registrar for safekeeping, and from these, local district indexes are compiled. One of the duplicate church or chapel marriage registers is also deposited with the superintendent registrar when full, but if a parish is thinly populated, it might be many years before this happens.

The indexes

There are separate centralized indexes to births, marriages and deaths, which until 1984 cover registrations in each quarter of the year, and thereafter the indexes are annual. The entries run alphabetically by surname, then by forename, giving the registration district, volume and page number of each registration. From 1984 the registration district number was added, and from 1993, the month and year of registration.

You can search the Registrar General's indexes online. There are a number of options:

- **www.freebmd.org.uk** is a database which you can currently search for the registrations of specific births, marriages and deaths up to 1929. An excellent feature of the database is that if you are unsure of the name of someone's spouse, you can instigate a search for the names of people of the opposite sex whose marriages were registered in the same part of the year, district, volume and page as your ancestor's. However, there is no guarantee that they were married to each other. You can only discover this when you purchase a copy of the actual registration. This database is not yet complete, so check the website for a progress report on the year-by-year coverage so far for each event.

- **www.bmdindex.co.uk** is a pay-as-you-go or subscription website at which you can search digital images of the index pages between 1837 and 1983, and then a database up to 2004, using SmartSearch. This facility lets you find the birth registrations of all the children of a particular couple, details about both marriage partners and link people's birth and death registrations.
- **www.thegenealogist.co.uk** is identical to the above website, but you can also search for variant surnames, by their sound, and for nicknames.
- **http://ancestry.co.uk** You will need to subscribe or purchase pay per view vouchers to inspect the digital images of the index pages of births, marriages and deaths from 1 July 1837 until 31 December 1983, but the database of transcribed indexes of registrations from 1984 until 2004 is free. If you visit the National Archives, at Kew, or the Family Records Centre, in London, you can search these online indexes free of charge.
- **www.findmypast.com/HomeServlet** This too offers a subscription service for searching the birth, marriage and death indexes after 1837. However, you can also examine all the indexes to overseas returns made to the Registrar General in London up to 1994, of Britons, British Armed Service personnel and their families, and of British servicemen who were casualties in the South African and both World Wars, and to divorces and matrimonial causes between 1858 and 1903. The names of servicewomen are included in the death indexes for the First and Second World Wars.
- **www.familyrelatives.com** is similar to **www.findmypast.com/HomeServlet**, and you pay by credit or debit card to gain access to the digital images and transcriptions of the index pages, though some are free.
- **www.tracesmart.co.uk** offers pre-paid searches of the database containing indexed birth, marriage and death registrations between 1984 and 2004 only.

Microfilm or microfiche copies of many of the indexes to birth, marriage and death registrations in England and Wales and to the overseas returns up to 1992 are held in local libraries. An alphabetical place-name list of libraries is available at **www.familia.org.uk**. Sets of microfiche copies up to 1992 are held in the National Archives, at Kew, up to 1998 and on CD-ROM from 1984 to 2000 in the National Library of Wales, and you can study them in many family history centres of the Church of Jesus Christ of Latter-day Saints as well.

The original index books, running up to recent registrations, are in the Family Records Centre, in London, where you can examine them in the General Register Office search area.

How to buy a certificate

When you have obtained the correct index reference, you will need to buy a copy of the full registration details. All the above websites have a direct link to the General Register Office order form at **www.gro.gov.uk/gro/content/certificates**, or you can e-mail your request to **certificate.services@ons.gsi.gov.uk**, phone or fax the details, quoting the full index entry. You can also apply and pay for a certified copy of the registration by visiting the Family Records Centre or by sending full index details to the General Register Office, in Southport.

If the birth occurred within the last 50 years, you will need to supply the names of both of the child's parents including the mother's maiden name.

You can make requests for reference checks if you are undecided which of several index entries is likely to be relevant. Provide only those facts of which you are certain. In the event of a wrong reference, you will be charged for each one that is checked on the same application until the appropriate one is found.

If you haven't searched the indexes, you can apply online for a copy of any birth, marriage or death certificate issued between 1 January 1900 and the last 18 months, but you must specify the date and place of the event and maiden surname as applicable. If you don't have the exact date, then apply to the General Register Office by post, phone or fax for a three-year pre-paid search.

You will have to contact the appropriate district office for copies of registrations within the last 18 months (see opposite).

Searching the local indexes

A number of counties are now uploading their local registration district office indexes. If you visit **www.ukbmdsearch.org.uk**, you can either make a global search of all the available indexes in the database or select a specific county to view transcriptions of the index entries. This is recommended if you fail to find what you want from the General Register Office indexes, since these are known to be erroneous and are subject to omissions.

If you know when and where your antecedent was born or died, and the indexes are not online, it may be easier and cheaper to make an appointment to have the superintendent registrar's indexes checked. There is a set fee. For district office addresses, look under 'Registrations of births, deaths and marriages' in the phone book, or in the latest edition of *The Family and Local History Handbook*, or visit **www.gro.gov.uk/gro/content** and insert the place-name or postcode in the relevant search box to find out which offices served that area. If you click on the name of the district registration office you will be taken directly to its website and to any online indexes and order forms. You can find out at **www.fhsc.org.uk/genuki/reg/districts/index.html** which registrars' offices hold registers for districts which became defunct between 1837 and 31 March 1974. There is a complete alphabetical list of towns, villages and hamlets belonging to each district.

The Registrar General's index references cannot be used to order copies of certificates from superintendent registration district offices, and vice versa.

There are no superintendent registrars' consolidated indexes to local marriages. The duplicate church and chapel registers can be more easily (and freely) studied if they have been deposited in a county record office. You can find addresses and phone numbers in *Record Offices, How to Find Them*, by J. Gibson and P. Peskett and at **www.genuki.org.uk/big**. If the marriage registers are still in the church or chapel then you are likely to incur a search fee. Consult the current edition of *Crockford's Clerical Directory* or *Church of England Yearbook* for addresses of Anglican clergy, and similar yearly handbooks and directories should be available in your local library listing the names and addresses of ministers of other denominations. Find out the likely cost first, if you plan, and are allowed, to undertake this task yourself.

Tips

- When browsing birth, marriage and death indexes, be careful to look under all likely surnames. The first letter may vary, for instance Aughton might be an alternative spelling for Haughton; there may be latitude with vowels, for example as in Bermingham, Birmingham and Burmingham; and with consonants, such as Burmingham, Burringham and Burningham, and phonetic or dialect spellings like Tuddenham, Tudman, Studman, Birkett and Birkhead. Use the SmartSearch facility at **www.thegenealogist.co.uk** for phonetic spellings.

- Be wary of misread surnames beginning with 'L' instead of 'S', or 'T' in place of 'F'. Names may have been misspelled by the clerks compiling the central indexes.

- Because of the Welsh patronymic naming system, and the relatively few surnames and forenames in circulation, you may find it difficult sorting out who was who in the indexes, even if you know the district where an event occurred. In Wales, children of the same father might be registered under different surnames. In some cases hyphenated surnames were used, providing a clue to the mother's surname before marriage.

- Starting in the September quarter of 1911, the mother's given maiden name is recorded in the birth indexes, making it easier to identify the correct registrations of people with common names and to pick up the birth registrations of brothers and sisters.

- Inspect the index books or microform copies consecutively, as it is easy to miss one out. Note down every likely entry you come across. This will spare you having to repeat a search if you do not find exactly what you are looking for first time round.

- Sometimes two registration entries might be mistakenly combined to make one, or even omitted altogether. If you know when and where a birth or death occurred, it is worth approaching the local registrar's office.

- The online Registrar General's indexes are exact copies of the original indexes, so any errors and omissions have remained uncorrected.

- There is no alternative to purchasing a birth or death certificate if you want all the registration details.

- Make sure you order a 'full' birth certificate, because a 'short' one will omit parents' names and their personal details, and so is of little genealogical value other than confirming the child's registered name, sex, date and place of birth and the district where it was registered.

Looking for a birth

Until 1874, the district registrars were charged with collecting information about all the births within their jurisdiction. Thereafter responsibility for registration rested with the parents. If anecdotal evidence is to be believed, many births seem to have gone unregistered or were registered or indexed in such a way as to defeat us. In the early years of civil registration some parents elected either to register their children's births or to have them baptized, but not both, in the misguided belief that they had a choice. If you cannot locate a birth registration, investigate the baptism registers serving the place where your family lived.

By law, births should be registered within 42 days, with an extension up to six months, accompanied by a financial penalty. Always search at least the two quarterly indexes after a birth took place, as not everyone registered their children's births promptly.

Illegitimacy

The late registration of a child's birth to parents who had subsequently married each other might record a false birth date to conceal his or her illegitimacy. A child born out of wedlock was usually registered under its mother's surname, though before 1875 there was nothing to prevent an informant naming or inventing a putative father for an illegitimate baby. Later, only if the father agreed and was either present to register the birth, or his written or sworn acknowledgement of paternity was produced to the registrar, could his name be inserted as part of the entry. After the Legitimacy Act of 1926, if this child's parents subsequently married the child became legitimate and his or her birth was frequently registered a second time, under the married name. Sometimes children born to couples in an illicit relationship might have concocted the father's name to protect a man who was already married to someone else, or both parents passed themselves off as married to each other when they were nothing of the kind.

Some reasons why you may not find a birth registration

Your existing information about a birth year may be wrong, so trawl the indexes for a year on either side of the expected registration, then two years and so on. Even if you are unlucky in finding your ancestor, you may still be able to track down the birth registrations of his or her siblings, whose own birth certificates will put you back on the trail.

Don't ignore 'Male' and 'Female' birth registrations when searching the indexes. These appear at the end of each surname list. The chosen names were added to the registration entry later but are not recorded in the index.

Parents might alter their children's names at baptism. The officiating minister was obliged to inform the Registrar General, and although the registration itself was then emended, the index was not.

First names might subsequently be dropped or reversed, names shortened into nicknames, new or further names assumed, so always ask your relatives about this.

Occasionally, informal childhood names might stick with someone throughout life and the true registered name be lost.

Births were registered in the district where they took place. This might not be local to the parents' usual address, so faced with several indexed registrations of the same surname, forename and quarter of the year, you may inadvertently rule out the right district. If you do have this problem, list all the entries in order of probability and then request a reference check, to stop at the first entry which tallies, for example, with the known parents' names, date of birth or birthplace. You will be refunded any balance of the pre-paid search fee for the remaining unchecked references. Sometimes you can eliminate at least a few of the registrations by searching the International Genealogical Index. This includes births, baptisms and marriages of dead people extracted from vital records worldwide, and you can access it at **www.familysearch.org**, on microfiche and on CD-ROM. The British Isles Vital Records Index, on CD-ROM, is a similar database. Both indexes will give the date and place of birth or baptism, the infant's name and those of his or her parents.

The birth certificate

A full birth certificate sets out

- the date and place of birth,
- the registered forenames of the baby,
- the child's surname,
- its gender,

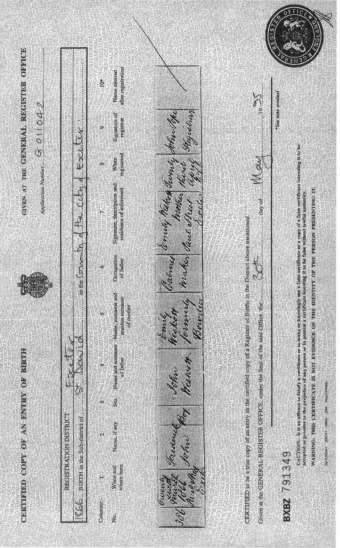

figure 4 Frederick John Westcott's birth certificate, in 1866. He later assumed the name of Fred Karno, and was a famous showman and impresario, running a troupe of comedians called 'Fred Karno's Army'. Charlie Chapman and Stan Laurel were among his recruits

© Crown copyright material is reproduced with the permission of the Controller of HMSO and Queen's Printer for Scotland

- the names of both parents, including the mother's former and/or maiden name,
- the father's current occupation,
- the name, address and relationship to the child of the informant, whether he or she signed or marked the register, and the date of registration.

Since 1 April 1969, the parents' birthplaces and usual address have been recorded too. There is extra space left on the certificate for any names given to the infant after registration.

When the informant was one of the parents, his or her usual address might be different from that of the birth. If the child was illegitimate, the informant might be another relative, whose name, address and relationship to the child will be specified.

Adoption

Adoptions before 1927 were often carried out privately between families, by parish officers, the Board of Guardians of the local Poor Law Union, or channelled through charities. There are no indexes open to the public. Most parish records are now in county record offices. *Poor Law Union Records*, by J. Gibson, C. Rogers and C. Webb, contains references to the known whereabouts of material relating to Union adoptions and boardings-out (fostering). Approach charitable bodies direct, using *Whitaker's Almanack*, the *Charities Digest* or the phone book as your guide. Up until the 1970s, adoption could still be arranged by an adoption society, local authority, or by a private agreement using the services of a doctor, solicitor, friend or mother. Some children were adopted by their grandparents or other relatives, or by step-parents, so ask around the family for more information.

Indexes to adoptions by court order in England and Wales since 1 January 1927 are accessible to the public only at the Family Records Centre in London, but you can request an index search of the Adopted Children Register at **www.gro.gov.uk/gro/content/adoptions/**, by phone or by sending your application to the Adoptions Section the General Register Office, in Southport, or by completing an application form for a copy of the entry in the Family Records Centre. If you are over 18, supply the full names of your adoptive parents as well as your full adoptive name, date of birth, year of adoption if you know it, and the name of the court making the adoption order, if this is known. Some overseas adoptions are included, if the child was born in England or Wales.

The adoption indexes cannot be used as a cross-reference to the indexes of birth registrations, because they are arranged by adoptive names.

To 31 March 1959, a full adoption certificate will disclose

- the child's date of birth,
- adoptive names,
- sex,
- the names and address of the adopting parents,
- the adoptive father's occupation,
- the date of the adoption order and the identity of the court making it, plus
- the date of entry in the Adopted Children Register.

From 1950 to 31 March 1959, the child's country of birth was recorded too, but later certificates give the English or Welsh registration or sub-registration district or the country of birth if elsewhere.

A short adoption certificate contains the person's adoptive forename and surname, sex, date of birth, and the birth registration or sub-registration district (and before 1 April 1959, the country of birth), if embedded in the adoption order. No reference is made to the adoption itself.

If you have been adopted, once you reach the age of 18, you can apply for a copy of your birth registration. You can do this in one of two ways. If you were adopted before 12 November 1975, you are obliged under the Adoption Act 1976 to see an approved adoption counsellor before you receive enough facts to enable you to obtain a copy of your birth certificate. This is because the adoption took place on the clear understanding that the child would never be able to find out its original registered name and those of his or her birth parents. The aim of the counselling is to help you understand the possible consequences of trying to establish contact with your true parents. You can ask for an interview with an adoption counsellor in the Family Records Centre, or if it is more convenient, via your local Social Services Department, or in certain circumstances, with the agency handling your adoption. The Registrar General will notify the counsellor of your original name, that of your birth mother and possibly that of your birth father, and the details of the adoption order, which is then passed on to you. If you live abroad, the General Register Office can let you have a list of approved overseas adoption organizations.

However, if you were adopted on or after 12 November 1975, a change in legislation has meant that you do not have to see a counsellor unless you choose to, and you can apply direct to the Registrar General for your birth details. You will receive a covering letter to show how and where to apply to the relevant court making the adoption order.

Once you have the name of the organization arranging your adoption get in touch to see if your adoption file still exists. You may be granted access to part of its contents. Adoption agencies used to preserve their records for only 25 years, but this has now been extended to between 75 and 100 years. Court records were not kept indefinitely, however. Your adoption adviser should be able to help you to locate the present whereabouts of any files. The National Organization for Counselling Adoptees and their Parents (NORCAP), in Wheatley (**www.norcap.org.uk**), can lend support too.

You might want to add your name and address to the Adoption Contact Register, which was created in 1991. Part 1 is for adopted persons, and Part 2 contains names and addresses supplied by the birth parents or other relatives of adopted people who would like to renew contact. You must be aged at least 18, know your full birth name, date of birth and parentage. If you don't have this information, your adoptive parents might, or you can apply to the General Register Office for a copy of your original birth registration. The birth relatives must likewise be aged 18 or more, and are required to show proof of their precise relationship to the adopted person. Adopted people wanting to make contact with adopted siblings can register themselves in both Parts 1 and 2. If a match is found, the Registrar General will send the adopted person the registered details of the relatives to enable them to get in touch, and the relatives will be advised that this has been done, although the adopted person's address will not be disclosed. Application forms are available from the Adoptions Section, and there is a fee for registration and for letter-forwarding. It is not recommended that you turn up on the doorstep or phone your relative, because you do not know their present circumstances, so act cautiously. It usually takes about two to three weeks to process applications. Don't forget that if you change your mind, or move to another address, to let the Adoptions Section know. NORCAP maintains a similar Adoption Contact Register.

Since 30 December 2005, adopted people over the age of 18 have been able to approach an approved intermediary agency about gaining access to their birth records, as part of the process of making contact with a birth relative. A birth relative wishing to renew a link with an adopted person can likewise use an intermediary agency, such as NORCAP. The agency applies to the General Register Office for the name of the organization involved in the adoption, and if this is not available, then the name of the court making the adoption order. It can also request information from the Adopted Children Register, and then, subject to the views of the adopted person, decide whether to proceed further. You can now record a 'specific' or 'no contact' registration with named individuals. It is otherwise assumed that you want to contact all of the registered family members or their chosen intermediaries. An intermediary is often registered to support the birth relative. If either party has made a 'no contact' request, each will be notified if a match occurs, but if both request no contact, neither will be informed of any match.

Abandoned children

The registrations of names given to foundlings are indexed under 'Unknown', following the listing of registered births of children whose surnames begin with 'Z'. Contact the Corrections and Re-registration Section of the General Register Office for details of entries in the Abandoned Children's Register.

Stillbirths

Stillbirths were registered within 42 days and no later than three months at the hospital or district register office. Certified copies of registrations of stillbirths from 1 July 1927 can be issued only to the parents, with the Registrar General's permission, or if they are both dead, to the siblings of a stillborn child. There are no indexes available to the public, so you will need to write to or phone the General Register Office for an application form. You will need to provide proof of your relationship to the child, and of the deaths of your parents, if appropriate.

Looking for a marriage

A full birth certificate should tell you the names of both parents, and the mother's former name. You can then start looking for their marriage. The earliest date on your family tree may be that of a marriage anyway. If you know exactly where it took place, remember that it might be easier and cheaper to inspect the original church or chapel registers, and thus see their signatures. Microfilm and microfiche copies of many registers are available for hire in family history centres. Visit the Family History Library catalogue at **www.familysearch.org** for a full list of parishes and date coverage.

The centralized marriage indexes after 1 July 1837 contain two entries for every marriage, with identical registration district, volume and page references for both the groom and bride. From the March quarter of 1912, each person's name is cross-referenced to the surname of the other partner.

Try using the database at **www.freebmd.org.uk** for marriages before 1919, though this is as yet far from complete, and **www.thegenealogist.co.uk** for marriages after 1984, if you don't know the partner's name. Otherwise, for marriages before 1984, begin searching in the same quarter of the year as the eldest known child's birth and work backwards, though you may have to take in several years afterwards as well! If you are unsure who was the eldest child this may involve a long period. If the wedding was earlier than 1912, look for the person with the more unusual surname or forename first as there will be fewer entries to cross-check.

Tips

- Sometimes you may not find the bride's name in the index. This might be because her maiden name was recorded on her child's birth certificate, but she went under her former married name when she wed the child's father, or vice versa. Request a General Register Office check of an indexed entry that otherwise looks correct in case there has been a clerical error, especially if the other known facts agree, or apply for a copy of the certificate anyway to see what it says.

- If there is no index entry at all, and you have searched back over more than 20 years, and a few years forward too, try the indexes to Scottish, Irish or overseas marriages, particularly if the husband was in the armed forces.

- Occasionally the parents did not marry each other, but cohabited in a common law union, perhaps because one of them was already married to someone else, which might be explained by an unexpected marriage registration of one of the parties.

The marriage certificate

Having found the relevant entry, apply for a copy of the certificate. This will tell you

- the date and where the wedding ceremony took place,
- the religious denomination if in a church or chapel, and whether the wedding was after banns, by licence or by registrar's certificate,
- the full names of the groom and bride,
- their ages,
- their current marital status,
- their rank, profession or occupation,
- their places of residence,
- their fathers' names and occupations, plus
- the names of at least two witnesses who were signatories, and that of the officiating minister or registrar.

The asserted ages can be misleading, or a party be described as of 'full age' or as a 'minor'. Until raised to 16 in 1929, 12 was the minimum age at which a girl could marry, and 14 for a boy. Up to 1969, parental consent was necessary until a minor attained 21, since when it has been 18. An under-age couple marrying against their parents' wishes might lie to make them seem full adults; conversely where there was a significant age difference, one partner might add on or deduct some years.

If one of the marriage partners was widowed, you should find the bride's birth surname from her father's given name on the marriage certificate. Multiple marriages were by no means uncommon, as women often died in childbirth or relatively young, so your family may contain step- and half-brothers and sisters as well as issue of the full blood.

In 1907 it became legal for a man to marry his deceased wife's sister, and from 1960 the sister of his divorced wife. Since 1968 a step-parent has been able to marry a step-child aged 18 or over, provided that person has not been treated as a child of the prospective partner's family while under age.

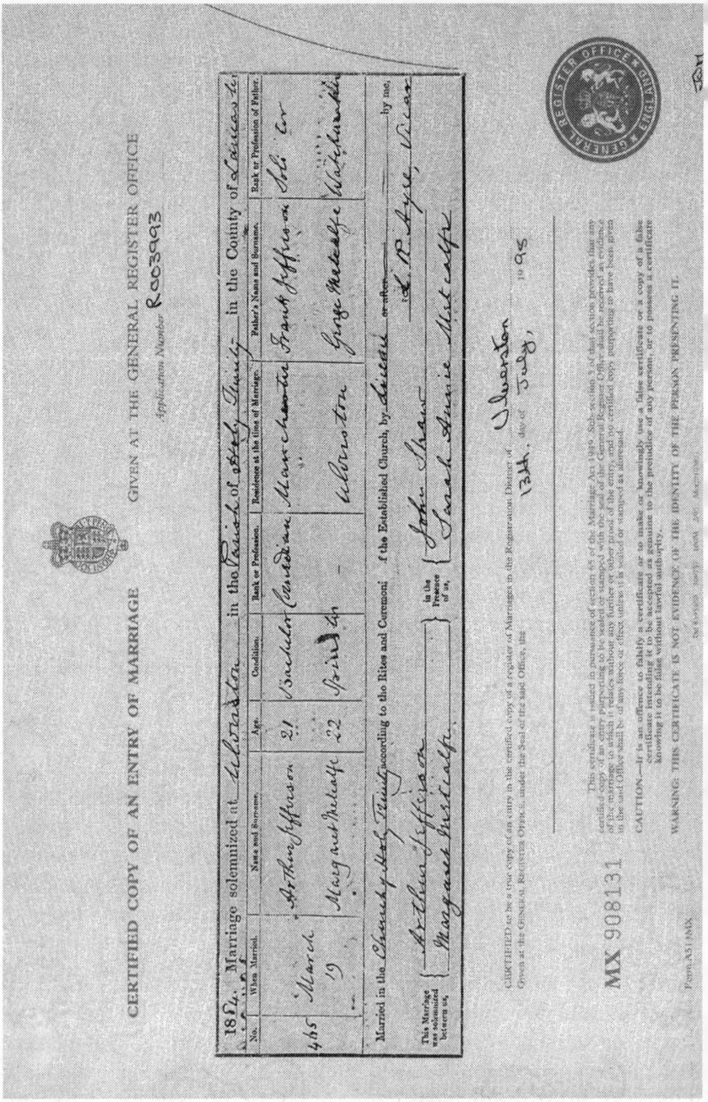

figure 5 Arthur Jefferson and Margaret Metcalfe's marriage certificate, in 1884. The couple were the parents of Arthur Stanley Jefferson, later known as Stan Laurel. Arthur gave his father's name here as Frank Jefferson, but when he married for a second time in 1912, it was Christopher Jefferson. Arthur's exact parentage, date and place of birth are so far unknown

© Crown copyright material is reproduced with the permission of the Controller of HMSO and Queen's Printer for Scotland

Given occupations were frequently exaggerated to suggest a higher social or employment status, whilst the precise nature of others now seems obscure. You may need to consult the *Oxford English Dictionary*, or *A Dictionary of Old Trades, Titles and Occupations*, by C. Waters, for explanations.

The given addresses were often temporary lodgings, to comply with the legal residential requirement of three weeks for the reading of church banns, or 15 days for a licence, in order to marry in the chosen church.

Be wary of the father's given name, since this might have been invented to conceal illegitimacy, or have been given in good faith when the person had been brought up by his or her grandparents or as part of someone else's family. If the father had died some time before the wedding, his forename might have been forgotten or never known by his offspring, so a guess might have been made from his initials. A certificate does not invariably disclose the previous death of a father. If he had disappeared out of his child's life and was thought to be no longer living, he might be described as deceased. Where the father's surname is different from that of the child, this may indicate adoption or fostering just as much as natural parentage. The absence of a father's name altogether may suggest illegitimacy, but this is not guaranteed.

Don't ignore the names of witnesses. If your searches grind to a halt, investigate their recent family backgrounds, as witnesses were frequently relatives of the couple.

Divorce

Divorced people are described as such upon remarriage. After 11 January 1858 and until 1922, all petitions for divorce dissolving a marriage by decree absolute were heard in the Court for Divorce and Matrimonial Causes, in London. After 1873 this became part of the Probate, Family and Admiralty Division of the High Court of Justice, and since 1970 has been in the Family Division. From 1922 until 1971, a number of Assize towns were empowered to hear undefended divorce petitions, whereupon county courts have granted uncontested divorces.

Indexed copies of all the decrees are held in the Principal Registry of the Family Division, in London, as well as of those filed in the regional district registries set up in 1927 to receive the local divorce records. You can search indexes to both successful and unsuccessful petitions filed in London between 1858 and 1903 at **www.findmypast.com/HomeServlet**, then pay to view the digital image of the full index entry. Microfilmed copies of the indexes up to 1958 are in the Family Records Centre, and in the National Archives. Embedded in the indexes as well are applications for legitimation of children, judicial separation, protection of a wife's earnings and property, and for the restitution of conjugal rights of co-habitation. The indexes are arranged in blocks of years, then initial-alphabetically by surname. The surname of any alleged co-respondent is cited too, plus an abbreviation representing the type of petition. Each cause was assigned a unique number and filed under the year the petition was lodged, which might be a few years before any divorce. Between November 1946 and 1949, however, the indexes relate to divorce receipt book entries rather than to petitions.

All the numbered petitions between 1858 and 1927, and other relevant papers, can be inspected in the National Archives. The files may include sworn affidavits, the responses of defendants and alleged co-respondents, amended petitions, copies of marriage certificates, children's birth certificates, and a brief summary of the evidence produced to the court. There is rarely an indication of the final outcome, nor was a copy always attached of the decree nisi or decree absolute which was issued to the petitioner. From 1928 to 1937, however, the paperwork relating only to those cases heard in London (about 80 per cent of all the petitions) has been preserved in the National Archives, and from 1938 to 2002, merely a heavily weeded selection of London matrimonial causes deemed to be of especial interest, which are subject to a 30-year closure rule. The document references to these are searchable by name at **www.nationalarchives.gov.uk/catalogue**.

Because the file numbering was inconsistent and often overlapped after 1866, you may need to look at the files for several years until you find the one that corresponds with the given index reference up to 1937. The later indexes contain references to petitions which no longer exist.

For locally heard causes, only the decrees have been saved, so you will need to apply to the Decree Absolute Search Section of the Principal Registry of the Family Division, for an index search and a copy of the decree. There is a charge for every ten-year period or part of a ten-year period examined, which includes the decree copy. You can also contact this address for a copy of any

London decree, quoting the National Archives index reference number and year, as this may cost you less. However, the Registry indexes are arranged by year of decree rather than of the petition. Conversely, if you obtain a copy of the decree first, it may be easier to locate the file containing any pre-1938 petition in the National Archives. If the divorce was granted in a county court within the last five years, approach it direct, as the research fee will be smaller. You can find the addresses and contact details of the county courts at **www.hmcourts-service.gov.uk/HMCSCourtFinder**.

Until 1923, a wife could sue for divorce only if she could prove her husband's adultery and life-threatening cruelty towards her. This meant that divorce was often denied her, so she might have to settle for a judicial separation which did not free either party to remarry. Under the law, and until the Married Women's Property Acts of the 1880s, a deserting husband could resurface at any time to claim his wife's property, earnings or inheritance, and she might be forced to petition the court for a protection order over them. This was expensive, as was the divorce procedure itself, so was viewed as the last resort and the province of the wealthier classes. Financial assistance was available under the Poor Persons Rules 1914, and the Poor Persons Procedure 1926, the latter reflecting the post-War increase in divorce applications.

Before 1858, marriages ended in a variety of ways other than death. Divorce permitting remarriage could only be granted by a private act of parliament or if the union had been declared null and void by a church court. The legal effect of this was as if the marriage had never happened. A church court annulment caused a marriage to become voidable. It still remained valid and the children legitimate, but the marriage could later be declared null and void by a church court. A divorce '*a mensa et thoro*' granted by a church court merely led to a lifetime suspension of a marriage. As with an annulment, neither party was released to remarry.

Local church court material is now usually either in the diocesan record office or county record office. However, some provincial marital disputes were pursued in the Consistory Court of London, because they were seen to be dealt with more quickly and professionally. The records of the London Consistory Court are held by London Metropolitan Archives. Appeals against church court decisions were presented first to the Court of Arches and finally, up to 1833, to the High Court of Delegates and thereafter to the Judicial Committee of the Privy Council. Look at *Index of Cases in the Records of the Court of Arches in Lambeth Palace Library, 1660-1913*, by J. Houston, for the names of appellants. The indexed records of the High Court of Delegates and its successor are in the National Archives. You can search for document references at **www.nationalarchives.gov.uk/ catalogue**.

Private separation deeds were signed mutual agreements to maintain the status quo, the husband promising to pay the wife alimony and the wife indemnifying him against future liability for any debts which might be claimed or pursued against her. They were not enforceable in a court of law. Desertion, wife-selling, and bigamy were other resorts. The children of bigamous unions were legally illegitimate, but not every bigamist got caught!

Looking for a death

Until 1953, deaths were supposed to be registered within eight, now reduced to five, days. This is undertaken by a witness, someone who was in attendance during the last illness, the occupier of the premises where the person died, or by the individual causing disposal of the body, such as a coroner. Since 1874 a doctor's medical certificate has been mandatory, stating the time and cause of demise and length of the last illness, and after 1 January 1927, any secondary causes. Starting in 1902 two doctors' signatures have been necessary to authorize a cremation. The doctor's medical certificate is presented by the informant to the district registrar, and the resulting death certificate is the undertaker's authority to arrange for the disposal of the body.

Try the online database at **www.freebmd.org.uk** for deaths registered up to 1919, although this is not yet complete. The quarterly indexes from September 1837 until 1983, and the yearly indexes thereafter, contain the surname, forenames, registration district, volume and page number of the entry for each dead person and between the first quarter of 1866 and the March quarter of 1969, the indexes include given ages as well. After this, the indexes record the date of birth, instead of age, if known. Indexes to the deaths of unknown people appear after those whose surnames began with 'Z'.

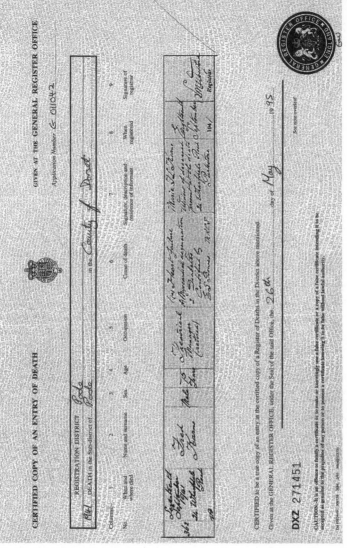

Figure 6 Fred Karno's death certificate, 1941. When he died, Fred left assets of less than £50. He was declared a bankrupt in 1828, when his fun palace 'Karsino' on Tagg's Island on the River Thames, and the rest of his theatrical tackle were sold off to pay his debts

© Crown copyright material is reproduced with the permission of the Controller of HMSO and Queen's Printer for Scotland

Family historians tend to overlook death certificates as a genealogical source, yet they reveal:

- a person's date and place of death,
- his or her full name,
- his or her sex,
- the given age,
- his or her rank, profession or occupation,
- the cause of decease and duration of the last illness,
- the signature, relationship to the defunct and the address of the named informant, and
- where and when the death was registered.

The death certificate of a married woman or a widow will give her husband's name and occupation as well.

Since 1 April 1969, the deceased's date and place of birth and usual address have been recorded, and the maiden name of any married woman. This information will enable you to look for the deceased woman's marriage, her late husband's death, and her birth certificate.

A death certificate marks a date beyond which you are unlikely to discover anything more about the deceased, unless from a will or administration grant, an obituary notice or gravestone inscription. If demise occurred close to a census year, you can search the returns for the given addresses for details about other occupants as well as about the named person and the informant.

Tips

- The date (and up to 1891 the place) of death from 1858 onwards can be gleaned from the annual published National Probate Indexes of wills and administration grants of people leaving property in England and Wales. You can search these in the public search room of the Principal Probate Registry in London, and in most of the 12 local district and 18 sub-district probate registries. Consult **www.hmcourts-service.gov.uk/ HMCSCourtFinder** for their addresses and contact details, or *The Family and Local History Handbook*. Microfiche copies of the indexes are widely available too, though the end dates vary. *Probate Jurisdictions: Where to Look for Wills*, edited by J. Gibson and E. Churchill, lists the cut-off dates of holdings. It may be quicker to search these before tackling the three-monthly General Register Office indexes, and having found the date of death you can then locate the indexed registration and order a death certificate. However, not everyone made a will, nor were letters of administration always applied for when someone died intestate.

- A person's identity at death might be different from that at the time his or her birth was registered. Formal name changes are not obligatory. People sometimes disappear, and start life afresh under a new identity.

- The identity of a relative dying outside his or her usual area may be difficult to recognize from the indexes, especially before 1866, particularly if the name was a common one.

- Given ages at death may be wildly inaccurate, as they might have been guessed by the informant. People often had no idea of their true age, or lied about them. When applying for a certificate of a death registered before 1866, specify the minimum age you would expect the deceased to have been, to avoid buying that of an infant, as ages were not included in the indexes.

- The cause of death may indicate an inherited condition, genetic disorder, family proneness to certain illnesses or an occupational disease.

- Churchyard, cemetery and cremation registers should reveal at least the person's date of death and age. Gravestone inscriptions frequently not only set out the same information, but often refer to the deaths of other family members interred in the same plot.

The second edition of the National Burial Index, produced by the Federation of Family History Societies in 2004, on CD-ROM, contains extracts of 13.2 million entries in the burial registers of well over 8,000 churches, chapels and cemeteries throughout England and Wales, including those in the first edition, which was published in 2001. The given dates and places of interment, some running up to 2000, enable you to go straight to the General Register Office indexes to find the appropriate death registration. You can discover which places and periods are covered by the National Burial Index from the database itself and at **www.ffhs.org.uk/General/Projects/NBI.htm**. A third edition is in progress.

Coroners' inquests

When registration was by coroner's order, this was noted on the death certificate. Look for a local newspaper report of the inquest. Coroners are obliged to retain their records for 15 years, after which they can exercise their discretion about their disposal (usually to the county record office) or destruction. Generally, coroners' records remain closed to the public for 75 years, and not all are transferred to county record offices; the coroner's prior written consent is required before you can inspect them. Many coroners' reports before 1875 survive, and *Coroners' Records in England and Wales*, edited by J. Gibson and C. Rogers, gives a county by county listing of most known local holdings. Try the catalogue at **www.a2a.org.uk** for references to some of these. Post-mortem examination reports are also kept by coroners, but again there should be a local press item. If the coroner's inquest ruled that a person had died as a result of foul play and the assailant could be identified, his report served as an indictment. The bundles of Assize indictments for each county session, up until the Assizes were abolished in 1971, are in the National Archives. Document references to surviving bundles can be found in the online catalogue.

Coming up against a brick wall

If the centralized indexes to births, marriages and deaths have yielded nothing, you may wonder what to try next. If you have some idea of the year and district, then the following sources may help, assuming you have already trawled the International Genealogical Index (at **www.familysearch.org**), and British Isles Vital Records Index (on CD-ROM), for extracts of births, baptisms and marriages of people who are no longer living, and have explored the local registration indexes:

- Church or chapel baptism registers may contain entries of children whose births were not registered. However, in the nineteenth century fewer parents took their offspring for baptism.
- From 1862, statutory admission and discharge registers began to be kept by the head teachers of schools receiving government funding. Many of these commence only in 1880, when education became compulsory nationwide for children between the ages of five and ten, though local districts could

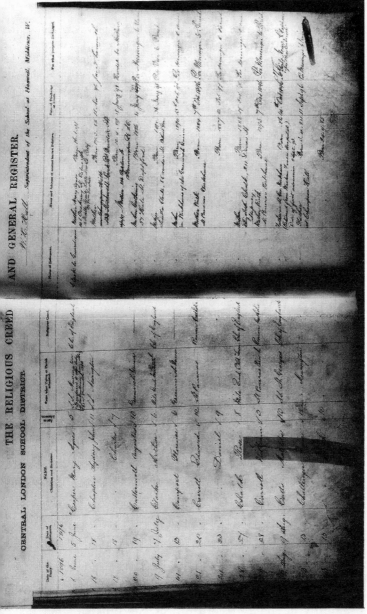

Figure 7 Religious Creed and General Register of Hanwell School, London,
recording the admission on 18 June 1896 of Sydney John Chaplin and his half-
brother, Charles Chaplin. The birth date of Charles was given as 12 or 14 April
1889, an event that seems to have gone unregistered (reproduced by permission of
City of London, London Metropolitan Archives)

make it so in board schools after 1870. The registers may still be stored in the school, or may now be in the local county record office. The entries generally record every new pupil's name, his or her date of birth, father's name, place of residence and occupation, the date of admission, and his or her progress through each stage from infant to senior class, or until the date of departure, giving the reason for leaving and the place removed to if changing schools. The books are often indexed making it possible to trace the school attendance of several generations of a family. Where there is no other written evidence of a person's birth, baptism or parentage, school registers are invaluable.

- School attendance registers were compiled by local education authorities after 1875. These disclose similar information, as well as the placement of youngsters in schools throughout the county.

- The 'particulars registered … concerning the deaths and births of children' submitted to the local education authority by the district registrars record the date and place of each event, the child's name and sex, his or her father's name, and the description and abode of the informant. Like the school attendance registers, the extant returns are most likely to be found in county record offices.

- Often unknown and untouched by family historians are the compulsory smallpox vaccination registers, which date from a series of enactments after 1853, and run up to 1948. Parents were put on three months' notice by the district registrar to take their baby for vaccination by the public vaccinator or by the medical practitioner where they lived. A vaccination certificate was then issued. The registers are arranged by English and Welsh registration sub-district and record the date and place of birth, the child's name and sex, the father's name (or that of the mother if illegitimate), his or her occupation, and the date when the district registrar notified the birth to the local vaccination officer. The registers also set down the date of the medical certificate confirming a successful vaccination, instances where all attempts at vaccination had failed or where a named child had already had smallpox, or the date of death if it happened before vaccination could take place. *Poor Law Union Records* indicates the whereabouts of surviving registers, which are mostly in county record offices. Since parents may have registered a birth away from their usual place of residence, vaccination could prove difficult to enforce, and similarly newcomers with children whose births had been registered in another district might not have bothered. Six-monthly parish lists, identifying children who were known to be lacking vaccination certificates were presented by the district registrar to the Poor Law Union Board of Guardians, and to the governing parish vestry meeting or council so that its officers could make further enquiries. The dates and location of these are mentioned in the above guide too.

- Monthly returns of registered deaths of infants under a year old were presented by the district registrars to the vaccination officers. The returns furnished the date and place of death, the child's name and age, and his or her father's name and occupation. The father's home address was supplied if the death occurred elsewhere, such as in a hospital. The deaths were cross-referenced to the weekly returns of births if both events occurred in the same district. However, the precise dates or places of birth, and parents' names are excluded from the birth returns.

A major drawback of the above records is that if a birth went unregistered then the child slipped through the vaccination net, but they can help if you have overlooked entries or names have been omitted from the centralized indexes.

- Local press announcements of births, marriages and deaths provide another source of information. You will need to know the approximate date of the event to make use of these, since such newspapers were generally published weekly, and few have been extensively indexed. You can find out which newspapers served your area from *Willing's Press Guide*.
- UK hospital records of births and deaths are not open to the public, but searches may be made of them for you. Visit **www.nationalarchives.gov.uk/hospitalrecords/search.asp** for details of their dates and whereabouts.

05

births, marriages and deaths in the Channel Islands, Isle of Man, Scotland and Ireland

In this chapter you will learn:
- what is available online
- how to apply for copies of registrations
- how the registrations compare.

The Channel Islands

The statutory registrations of births and deaths in Guernsey, Jehou and Herm date from 1840, and of marriages since 1919, although there are some earlier voluntary registrations after 1840. The indexed records are held in the Greffe, in St Peter Port, and you can search these yourself on payment of a fee, but phone first to find out about opening hours and charges. Copies of the indexes and civil registers of births to 1981, indexes to marriages and to deaths to 1966, civil registers of marriages to 1901 and to deaths up to 1981 are available on microfilm in the Priaulx Library, in St Peter Port. You can inspect microfilm copies of the birth indexes and registers, 1840–1966, death indexes and registers, 1840–1963, marriage indexes, 1841–1966, and registers, 1841–1901, in family history centres, where you may have to hire them in. The civil registration indexes from 1842 to 1969 are also available on microfilm in the Society of Genealogists. The weddings before 1919 and deaths earlier than 1963 are indexed under each of the ten parishes, married women dying before 1949 being listed under their maiden names.

Registers of births and deaths in Alderney from 1850, and of marriages since 1886 are preserved in the Registry for Births, Deaths, Companies, Land and Marriages, in St Anne, although there are gaps. The registrations in Alderney after 1925 are housed in the Greffe, in St Peter Port. There is a gap between 1940 and 1945, during the period of the German Occupation, and some other records no longer survive before 1945 because they were left behind at the time of the evacuation and were probably burnt. Mrs E. Mignot, of St Martins, has transcribed all the island's entries, and you are advised to write directly to her for any searches. The Priaulx Library holds microfilm copies of birth registrations up to August 1885, and of death registrations between 1850 and 1855 and from 1907 to 1925.

If you have ancestors who came from Sark, the civil registration of births and deaths only started there in 1915 and of marriages in 1925. You can search for entries in the duplicate registers in the Greffe, in St Peter Port. The original records are kept in the Greffe, in Sark.

Civil registration of births, deaths and marriages began in Jersey in August 1842. The records are in the custody of the Superintendent Registrar, in St Helier. There are limited public search facilities, so phone first, if you plan to visit. A five-year pre-paid search can be undertaken by staff, if you can provide the date of the relevant event, and the name of the person you are after. Copies of the indexes to 1900 are available in the Lord Coutanche Library, in St Helier (**www.société-jersiaise.org**). You can search the catalogue online. All the indexes to births and deaths since 1842, compiled by members of the Channel Islands Family History Society, are kept on the open shelves in Jersey Archive, also in St Helier (**www.jerseyheritagetrust.com**). You will need a reader's ticket to gain admission. Research assistance is available in both venues.

The certificates are similar in content to those of England and Wales, though marriage certificates include the couple's birthplaces.

Some indexed births, marriages and deaths between 1831 and 1958 in the Channel Islands are included in the Registrar General's Miscellaneous Non-statutory Foreign Returns, which are available on microfilm in the Family Records Centre, the National Archives, and for hire in family history centres. These are to be made digitally available at **www.thegenealogist.co.uk**. The International Genealogical Index is also worth consulting.

Adoption

If you were born in Guernsey and then adopted, non-identifying information from the Adopted Persons File can be released to you before you apply for your original birth certificate, but you are required to undergo counselling first so that you understand the possible consequences if you want to make contact with your birth relatives. An application form can be obtained from the Greffe, and a fee is payable. Your counsellor will forward the completed form to the Children Board, for transmission back to the Greffe, who will then write to you and request a further fee for a copy of your birth registration. The Greffe has a Contact Register of names of adopted people and of birth relatives, and if there is a match the Children Board will act as an intermediary to put you in touch.

If you were born in Jersey, a similar Adopted Persons File is held by the Superintendent Registrar. In this instance, approach him first, and he will refer you to the Children's Service, in St Helier. You will need to supply your name (including your maiden name if appropriate), date of birth, and the names of your adoptive parents. Alternatively, you could deal direct with the Children's

Service itself. However, there are no earlier legal adoption records than 1947, and between then and 1959, when the Children's Service was set up, adoptions were mainly arranged by health visitors and doctors, so the information surrounding your adoption may be limited to the name and address of your birth mother at the time of your placement. The Children's Service counsellor will apply for your original birth certificate, and this can be done even if your adoption took place elsewhere in the United Kingdom. The Superintendent Registrar has a Contact Register too, and the Children's Service will let you know if there is a match, and act as your intermediary.

Isle of Man

Registers of births and deaths occurring in the Isle of Man after 1878, of marriages from 1884, and an Adopted Children Register starting in 1928, are in the care of the Civil Registry Office, in Douglas. Voluntary civil registration of births and dissenters' marriages had, however, been possible since 1821 and 1849 respectively. An appointment is not necessary, but recommended, to search the indexes, and there is no fee. Microfiche copies of the civil registration indexes are held in the Manx National Heritage Library and Archives, in Douglas. At a family history centre you can hire in copies of the registrations of births from 1821 to 1964, of marriages from 1849 and of deaths from 1878 until the same year. You can also order in microfilm copies of the full registrations up to 1911.

There is a charge if you want to purchase a certificate from the Civil Registry. You can apply for copies of the registrations at **www.gov.im/registries/general/civilregistry/welcome.xml**, and staff are able to conduct index searches on your behalf, based on a fixed charge for each three-year period covered.

Scotland

Civil registration of births, marriages and deaths in Scotland commenced on 1 January 1855, and indexed self-service digitized images and microform copies of the registers running up to a year ago are available in the General Register Office, in Edinburgh. You will need a pass to use the records. It is advisable to book ahead of your planned visit, as otherwise seats are offered on a first come first served basis.

You do not need to go to Edinburgh, however. The indexes to registered births to 1906, marriages to 1931, and to deaths up to 1956, can be inspected at **www.scotlandspeople.gov.uk** with an extra year being added annually. The service is operated on a page-credit basis. Digital images of the registrations can be viewed at this website too, and you can order an official extract (certificate) or abbreviated (short) certificate online. Postal applications can also be made. Alternatively you can order transcriptions of registered births, marriages and deaths from 1855 to 1990 using the charged service operated by **www.originsnetwork.com**.

There are computerized links to the centralized indexes in some local Scottish registration offices, which may also have facilities for you to consult microfilm copies of the statutory registers for their area. A list of all the Scottish parishes, registration districts and their dates and addresses can be found at **www.scotlandspeople.gov.uk** and in *The Family and Local History Handbook*. You can also search the yearly Scottish indexes between 1855 and 1956 on microfilm in family history centres, plus filmed copies of registrations between 1855 and 1875, for 1881, and for 1891. Visit **www.familia.org.uk** for details of local library holdings of birth, marriage and death indexes on microform and on computer.

The indexes list males and females separately, by surname, forename, parish or registration district, county, and entry number. From 1966, the district or parish registration number is cited too. The mother's maiden name is written alongside her child's name in the birth indexes after 1929. Be careful to look under surnames with the prefix Mc- and Mac- or do a wild card search, such as M*. There is also a soundex search facility at the website. Married women's deaths may be registered twice or more under their married and maiden names.

Indexed digital images of the Register of Connected Entries from 1855 onwards are available at **www.scotlandspeople.gov.uk**, too. The affected registrations are indicated by 'RLE' in the margin, and a reference number.

Scottish birth registrations

Scottish birth, marriage and death certificates are far more informative than their English and Welsh counterparts. The birth registrations add

- the child's exact time of birth,
- the ages and birthplaces of both parents (1855 only),
- their usual address,

- their date and place of marriage (1855, then 1861 onwards),
- the number and sex of any older siblings but not their names, and whether living or dead (1855 only).

Thus you can discover where the parents came from and their approximate birth years, where they were married and how many earlier offspring you should be looking for. As these events took place before civil registration began, you can pursue them in the indexes to the Old Parochial Registers, which are available at **www.scotlandspeople.gov.uk**, at **www.familysearch.org**, on CD-ROM, and on microfilm. A certificate from 1855 may also guide you to the whereabouts of the parents in the 1851 and 1861 census returns, and these too are searchable at **www.scotlandspeople.gov.uk**.

Adoptions and stillbirths

Before 1930, adoption in Soctland was arranged privately, as in England and Wales. An Adopted Children Register was then introduced. Information about birth parents can be released to adopted persons aged 16 and over. None of the entries relate to people born before October 1909. The indexes to adoptions in Scotland are embedded in the computerized birth indexes, but the resulting certificates will not divulge the names of the birth parents or the child's original registered name. In order to trace your birth entry, write to the Adoption Unit of the General Register Office, giving details about your adoptive name, and your date of birth. You will be sent a declaration form to complete and return. The following information might be released to you: your date and place of birth and original registered name, your mother's name and possibly her occupation, your father's name if it was recorded at the time of registration, and the name and relationship to you of the informant of your birth. You may be told about the adoption agency or civil court which ratified the adoption order. You will be advised of the present whereabouts of such documents. Although there is no public access to them for 100 years, you may be alllowed to consult them on production of your birth certificate and some other proof of your identity. You have a statutory right to counselling before you go any further. Birthlink, in Edinburgh (**www.birthlink.org.uk**), offers voluntary counselling and operates an Adoption Contact Register for adopted people, their birth parents, siblings and other birth relatives.

Disclosures about stillbirths in Scotland after 1939 are only issued by the Registrar General in exceptional circumstances.

Looking for a marriage in Scotland

From the outset, the Scottish marriage indexes show the married name of the wife in brackets next to her maiden name, but only from 1929 is there a cross-reference to her surname beside that of her husband. The marriage registers contain the following extra details to those appearing on English certificates:

- usual residences of the couple,
- the dates and places of birth of the couple (1855, then from 1972 onwards)
- any blood relationship between them (to 1860),
- whether this was a second, third or later union (1855 only),
- the number (but not the names) of living and deceased children by each previous marriage (1855 only),
- the forenames and maiden names of the couple's mothers, and if now dead, and
- if the marriage was regular or irregular.

The irregular, though legal, marriages are indexed in the usual way, and each registration up to 1965 records the date of any conviction, decree of declarator or sheriff's warrant issued by the local sheriff court.

Divorce

From 1922, the registers note if a person was divorced. Until 1560, annulments of marriages and divorces *a mensa et thoro* were dealt with by the Church and amounted only to a lifetime separation. Full divorce has been possible in Scotland since then, and until 1830 the commissary courts handled all matrimonial cases, including the legitimation of children. Since 1831, such cases have been heard by the Court of Session, sitting in Edinburgh, though some continued to be heard by the Edinburgh Commissary Court to 1835. The grounds for divorce were adultery or the lengthy desertion of one spouse by the other and, from 1938, cruelty. The records are held by the National Archives of Scotland, in Edinburgh. Look in *The Commissariot of Edinburgh – Consistorial Processes and Decreets, 1658–1800*, which contains a personal-name index, then at an index volume for the years between 1801 and 1835, which is arranged by the first initial letter of each surname, for cases in the Commissary Court, and at the indexed printed minute books of the Court of Session for the relevant years from 1831 onwards, to find the document references you require.

From 1855 until 30 April 1984, decrees of divorce inside and outside Scotland which were notified to the Registrar General were annotated as 'divorce RCE' (Register of Corrected Entries) against the marriage registration, though not in the index. However, a central register of divorces in Scotland has been kept since February 1984 (when the sheriff courts also began to hear cases). The register records the names of both spouses, the dates and places of their marriage and divorce, with details of any court order relating to the provision of financial assistance or the custody of any children. This information does not appear in the marriage entry itself, but the online marriage indexes in the General Register Office from 1 May 1984 disclose the other partner's name, the date of the marriage, the divorce year, the court, and serial number of the decree.

Looking for a death in Scotland

The 1855 index records in brackets the maiden name of any married woman, and from 1855 to 1858 the deceased's mother's surname, if known. After 1859, the indexes consist of two entries, under each of a married woman's surnames. Starting in 1974, the maiden name of the deceased's mother has been restored. The indexes to deaths in Scotland include ages from 1866, as in England and Wales.

The Scottish death registrations will also tell you

- the time of death,
- his or her usual address if it was not the place of death,
- his or her birthplace (1855 only),
- the date of birth (1966 onwards),
- how long the person had lived in the district (1855 only),
- the duration of the last illness (to 1964),
- the name of the medical attendant certifying death and when he last saw the deceased,
- the spouse's name (1855, then 1861 onwards); marital status only, 1856–60
- the names of any offspring (1855 only),
- the father's name and occupation,
- the mother's name and maiden name,
- whether the parents were dead,
- the place of burial, name of the undertaker, and when last seen alive by the doctor (to 1860).

Potentially these certificates span three generations of a family.

28938

1861–1965

Extract of an entry in a REGISTER of DEATHS

Registration of Births, Deaths and Marriages (Scotland) Act 1965

No.	1 Name and surname Rank or profession and whether single, married or widowed	2 When and where died	3 Sex	4 Age	5 Name, surname and rank or profession of father Name and maiden surname of mother	6 Cause of death, duration of disease and medical attendant by whom certified	7 Signature and qualification of informant and residence, if out of the house in which the death occurred	8 When and where registered and signature of registrar
636	Margaret Jefferson Married to Arthur Jefferson Theatrical Manager	190 8. December First 8 h. 30 m. a.m 17 Craigmillar Road Langside	F	50 Years	George Metcalfe Bootmaker (Retired) Sarah Metcalfe M.S. Brindly	General Debility as certified by Robert Macleod Watson L.R.C.P.&S.	Arthur Jefferson Widower (Present)	190 8. December 2 nd A: Mount Florida George Purcell Artist : Registrar 17

The above particulars are extracted from a Register of Deaths for the District of Cathcart

in the County of Renfrew

Figure 8 Margaret (Madge) Jefferson's Scottish death registration, 1908. She first met her husband, Arthur Jefferson, when he appeared on stage in her home town of Ulverston, in Lancashire, and bore him five children

© Crown copyright material is reproduced with the permission of the Controller of HMSO and Queen's Printer for Scotland

Ireland

Irish civil registration of births, Roman Catholic marriages, and deaths began on 1 January 1864, although marriages between non-Catholics had been centrally recorded since 1 April 1845.

Indexes and microfilm copies of the original registers transmitted to the Registrar General, in Dublin, by superintendent registrars for all Ireland up to 31 December 1921, and those in the Republic after 1 January 1922 up to two years ago, are held at the General Register Office, in Dublin (**www.groireland.ie**). If you want to search the indexes yourself, a fee will be charged for a particular search of up to five years, or for a day's general search for any longer period. You can request a pre-paid search of the indexes by staff by post or fax, but you will need to supply enough information to enable them to identify the correct entry so that you can obtain a photocopy or certified copy of the registration. Microfilm copies of the indexes between 1845 and 1958 may be hired in and searched in family history centres, along with copies of the birth registers until the March quarter of 1881, from 1900 to 1913, and between 1930 and the March quarter of 1955, the marriage registers from 1845 to 1870, and of the death registers from 1864 to 1870. Extracts of Irish births registered between 1864 and 1875, and non-Catholic marriages between 1845 and 1863 are included in the International Genealogical Index.

The indexes are arranged by quarter of each year between 1878 and 1903, and from 1928 until 1965, and otherwise by year. The indexes to birth registrations up to 1965, except for 1903–27, give the child's name, registration district, volume and page reference, whilst those between 1903 and 1927 and from 1966 onwards reveal the child's name, mother's maiden name, the date of birth, registration district, volume, page and entry number and the quarter of the year in which it was notified. Any late registrations were recorded at the back of the index for each year. If you are looking for a marriage, the indexes contain two entries, each of which will give you the person's name, and the surname of the other partner, the date of the marriage, the registration district, volume, page and entry numbers, and the quarter of the year of registration. Late marriage registrations were inserted alphabetically by place amongst the other registrations. The death indexes reveal the name, age, sex, marital condition, date of death, registration district, volume, page and entry numbers and the quarter of the year and, again, late entries were listed at the end of the relevant annual index.

By law, births in Ireland should be registered within 21 days, extended to three months with a financial penalty.

When the mother's maiden name is included in the indexes, you can pick up the birth registrations of siblings.

Unfortunately, non-registration of births, marriages and deaths seems to have been widespread, so you may not be successful.

Tips

- When searching the indexes, look under surnames with and without the prefix O'–, Mc–, and Mac–.
- Where the pool of surname ranges was relatively small, positive identification of one of several people registered with the same names in the same period can seem daunting, so it helps to know the district or townland of birth.

Searching the indexes in Northern Ireland

Online and microfilmed duplicate indexes and registers of births and of deaths for the whole of Ireland from 1 January 1864 up to 31 December 1921, and indexes to non-Catholic marriages from 1845 and to all marriages from 1864 to the end of 1921, are available in the General Register Office, in Belfast (**www.groni.gov.uk**). Thereafter, the indexes relate to births, marriages and deaths registered only in the six northern counties (Antrim, Armagh, Derry, Down, Fermanagh and Tyrone) up to two years ago, and these too are computerized. The more recent registrations remain in the district registrars' offices, as well as the marriage registers up to 31 December 1921. Copies of the indexes to centrally registered marriages in all of Ireland from 1845 to 1921 are also available in local district registrars' offices. You can find their addresses at the above website and in *The Family and Local History Handbook*. Use these indexes to find the relevant district and religious denomination and then apply to the appropriate registrar's office for a copy of the marriage registration.

Filmed copies of the indexes and registers from 1922 to 1959 can be hired for inspection in family history centres.

You can search the indexes in the General Register Office yourself, but it is best to book an appointment a few weeks ahead of your planned visit, as space is limited. There are two types of search: you can undertake an assisted search with a member of staff, or opt to make an index search yourself, for which there is a charge, and this includes four verifications of entries by staff. Alternatively, you can complete an online application form at the above website or make a postal request, giving as much information as possible about the person concerned. There is a charge for each five-year search or any part of it.

The contents of an Irish certificate

The details recorded in the Irish birth, marriage and death registers match those for England and Wales. Photocopies of registered entries may be purchased as an alternative to the certificates, which may be preferable if the original handwriting is difficult to decipher.

Tips

- Dates and places of death may also be gleaned from the post-1858 annual printed calendars of wills and administrations in the National Archives of Ireland, and for the six northern counties, in the Public Record Office of Northern Ireland.

- If there is no death certificate or you want to see if there is any extra family information on a gravestone inscription, visit **www.ireland.com/ancestor/browse/addresses/major.htm** for the addresses of county heritage centres throughout Ireland, many of which hold transcriptions of local headstones. You will not be able to examine these yourself, but searches can be undertaken on your behalf for a fee. The Genealogical Office also has copies of many of these transcriptions. Another useful source is *Gravestone Inscriptions*, edited by R. S. J. Clarke, which purports to include all those before 1865 and some as late as 1900. They are arranged alphabetically by graveyard and then by name, provide an Ordnance Survey grid reference and, where appropriate, are cross-referenced to entries in the *Journal of the Association for the Preservation of the Memorials of the Dead*. This was published annually between 1888 and 1934 and there is a consolidated index up to 1910, to surnames and place-names, and thereafter the volumes are integrally indexed.

- Cemetery registry books are rare, and are generally associated with modern municipal cemeteries, but it is always worth approaching the sexton or record-keeper, just in case.

Adoptions and stillbirths

An Adopted Children Register was started in Ireland on 10 July 1953, and you can examine the index in the General Register Office, in Dublin, or request a postal search for an entry and certified copy. The adoption certificate will show your adoptive name, your date and place of birth, the names of your adoptive parents, the name of the court and date of the court order or identify the adoption agency or health board concerned. If you are over the age of 18, you can then request a copy of your birth registration, by writing to the Irish Adoption Board, in Dublin (**www.adoptionboard.ie**). The Board has a file for each adoption since 1953, and some earlier ones which were carried out informally without the intervention of an adoption agency or health board. If you do not know which adoption agency or health board was involved, the Adoption Board Information and Tracing Unit can help. The Adoption Board can also assist adopted people, their birth parents and birth relatives to register their desire to renew contact, but you will need to approach the appropriate adoption agency or health board first. A list of their titles and addresses is at **www.adoptionboard.ie/info/contacts.php**. This website also provides addresses of support groups in Northern Ireland.

Adoptions by court order in Northern Ireland commenced on 1 January 1931, and an Adopted Children Register is held in the General Register Office, in Belfast. You can apply for a pre-paid search online at **www.groni.gov.uk** or by post. The certificate should tell you enough to be able to identify your birth parents, birthplace, date and method of adoption. Then, if you are 18, you can request your full birth details, by completing an application form, which can be obtained from the General Register Office. An interview is first required with a social worker who will help you to locate the name of the adoption agency or court. There is an Adoption Contact Register in Northern Ireland similar to that for England and Wales, and both the adopted person and birth relatives can ask to have their details placed on it.

Copies of registrations of stillbirths in Ireland since 1 January 1995 are only released to the parents, and similarly of those in Northern Ireland after 1 January 1961. You will need to apply in writing to the appropriate Registrar General.

Divorce

You will need to contact the High Court, in Dublin, or the relevant circuit court issuing a decree of divorce in Ireland for information about a grant in the Republic. You can discover the addresses of the circuit courts from **www.courts.ie**. Records of divorces in Northern Ireland are held by the Royal Courts of Justice, in Belfast.

06

births, marriages and deaths at sea and abroad

In this chapter you will learn:

- how to find Britons overseas in UK records
- how to find records about UK armed service personnel and their families
- how to trace American civil registrations and military service records.

Britons at sea and on land

Any births and deaths of Britons at sea or in the air were notified to the Registrars General for England and Wales, Scotland or Ireland, as well as many births, marriages and deaths of Britons overseas. No returns were made from the British Empire or Commonwealth before independence.

You can search the following indexes to registers held by the Registrar General of England and Wales at **www.findmypast.com/ HomeServlet** and at **www.familyrelatives.com**:

- Births and deaths at sea between 1 July 1837 and 1965 (Marine Returns). From 1875 these relate also to passengers on foreign-registered ships leaving and arriving in British ports as well as those registered in the United Kingdom. Unknown deceased are listed after surnames beginning with 'Z'.

- Births and deaths on British civil aircraft from 1947 to 1965 (Air Register Book). This includes people missing, presumed dead, between 1948 and 1980, whose names are listed at the end of the index.

- Consular Returns of births, marriages and deaths of British subjects abroad from July 1849 to 1965. Starting in 1906, each marriage entry is cross-referenced to the surname of the partner, and from 1901, the death indexes record ages.

- UK and British High Commission Returns of births to 1966, marriages and deaths up to 1965, from the date of independence of the Commonwealth country.

- Returns of births and deaths at sea and abroad, and marriages overseas, from 1966 to 1994. These include births and deaths on British-registered hovercraft from 1 November 1972, and deaths on off-shore installations since 30 November the same year.

Microfiche copies of the indexes are widely available up to 1992, in the National Archives, at Kew, in family history centres, and many record offices and reference libraries. The original index volumes run up to recent registrations and these are kept on the open shelves in the General Register Office search area of the Family Records Centre.

You will need to pay for a certified copy of a full registration, which can be applied for in the same way as English and Welsh certificates, although you should address your enquiry to the Overseas Section of the General Register Office or apply online at **www.gro.uk/gro/content/certificates**.

Microfilmed copies of the indexes, 1627–1960, and of the Registrar General's Miscellaneous Non-statutory Foreign Returns of births, baptisms, marriages, deaths and burials recorded between 1627 and 1965, are available in the Family Records Centre, the National Archives, and for hire in family history centres. Some of the returns relate to foreign nationals at sea, to people in the British Colonies, and to the British African and Asian Protectorates. The indexes are incomplete, so inspect the returns as well to be really sure you have not missed anything. However, most entries begin only in the early nineteenth century, and a number overlap or duplicate the General Register Office registrations, so are well worth seeking out. Indexed digital images of the registers are to be made available at **www.thegenealogist.co.uk**.

Reports sent to the Board of Trade of the deaths of merchant seamen from 1852 to 1960, of births to passengers between 1854 and 1960, and of any passengers' deaths on board ship between 1854 and 1964, can be examined in the National Archives, at Kew. There are separate volumes from 1875 to 1891 relating to births to English, Welsh and non-British subjects, for Scots and for Irish citizens, and to deaths from 1875 to 1888. Included are events reported to the Registrar General of England and Wales, for Scotland and of Ireland between 1910 and 1918, though some of the births and deaths were excluded from the official Marine Returns, principally when a ship was lost at sea. A single indexed Board of Trade register relates to marriages performed on voyages between 1854 and 1972, whose legality was uncertain. Most of the volumes are indexed, as well as being microfilmed for the years up to 1890. Indexed digital images of the returns of births and deaths of passengers at sea from 1884 to 1887, and 1854 to 1890 respectively, and of marriages from 1854–83, can be viewed at **www.findmypast. com/HomeServlet**. The earlier returns of births and deaths will soon appear online too.

For other returns of births, marriages and deaths of Britons abroad, try the online catalogue of the National Archives at **www.nationalarchives.gov.uk/catalogue**. You could also look up the country by country listing of references in *Tracing Your Ancestors in the National Archives*, by A. Bevan. *The British Overseas: a Guide to Records of Births, Baptisms, Marriages, Deaths and Burials available in the UK*, produced by the Guildhall Library, in London, is well worth consulting too. For information about filmed copies of indexes and registration records of countries throughout the world, which you might be able to hire in to search in your local family history centre, look at *International Vital Records Handbook*, by T. J. Kemp. This guide tells you about the start dates of birth, marriage, death and divorce records, arranged alphabetically by country, or American state (see later in this chapter). You can search indexes to the vital records of Mexico and of Scandinavia at **www.familysearch.org**.

If your relatives were born, married or died in one of the British Colonies, Commonwealth, Dominions or Territories it is more than likely that you will have to approach the registration authorities direct. However, the Australian Vital Records Index, on CD-ROM, covers registrations of births, marriages and deaths in New South Wales from 1788 to 1888, in Tasmania from 1803 to 1899, the State of Victoria from 1837 to 1888 and in Western Australia between 1841 and 1905. You can search this database as part of the Online Publications and Electronic Resources Archive in the Family Records Centre and in the National Archives.

More and more vital registration indexes are being loaded onto the internet, so for up-to-date information on how to access them, try **www.cyndislist.com** under 'Vital Records' or use a search engine and key in 'births, marriages and deaths' and the country, state, or province in which you are interested.

Service families

Digital images of the indexes to the General Register Office returns of births, baptisms, marriages and deaths of British armed personnel and their families can be seen at **www.findmypast.com/HomeServlet** and at **www.familyrelatives.com**. The entries from 1966 run up to 1994 as part of the union indexes to overseas births, marriages and deaths. Index volumes are on the open shelves in the General Register Office search area in the Family Records Centre, and microfiche copies are available up to 1992 in the National Archives, Kew, in family history centres, many local reference libraries and county record offices.

The indexes relate to:

- Regimental Registers of births and baptisms, 1761–1924, which include some in Britain and Ireland. You will need to write to the Overseas Section of the General Register Office, for a search of surviving regimental marriage registers. A list of these is in the Family Records Centre, next to the indexes to the regimental registers of births and deaths.

- Army chaplains' returns of births and marriages, 1796–1955, and of deaths, 1796–1950, of officers, soldiers and their families recorded at overseas stations. These contain references to Royal Air Force families from 1920 onwards.
- Military, civil and chaplains' registers of births, marriages and deaths in the Ionian Islands, 1818–64.
- Service Departments' Registers of births and marriages, 1956–65, and deaths, 1951–65, of Army and Royal Air Force personnel and their families, and of Royal Naval families from 1959.
- Annual union indexes to births, to marriages, and to deaths at sea and abroad from 1966.

Certified copies of the full registrations can be applied for in the usual way, although any online, e-mailed, phoned or postal applications should be addressed to the Overseas Section.

It is worth trying the Registrar General's Miscellaneous Non-statutory Foreign Returns, described above, for additional or overlapping entries.

Men at war

There are special General Register Office indexes to registers recording war casualties. Digital images of the indexes are searchable at the above two websites. Whilst the index volumes are held in the Family Records Centre, microfiche copies can be examined in the National Archives, family history centres, many local reference libraries and record offices. The indexes relate to:

- Natal and South African Field Forces, 1899–1902 (Boer War deaths).
- Army officers, 1914–21 (First World War), including officers in the Royal Flying Corps, and from 1 April 1918, the Royal Air Force.
- Army other ranks, 1914–21, including airmen and airwomen in the Royal Flying Corps, and from 1 April 1918, the Royal Air Force.
- Royal Navy, all ranks, 1914–21, including submariners, Royal Marines, and members of the Royal Naval Air Service up to 31 March 1918. Look in the General Register Office indexes to Marine Returns, described earlier, for this period as well.

- Indian Services, all ranks, 1914–21.
- Army officers, 3 September 1939 to 30 June 1948 (Second World War).
- Army other ranks, for the same period.
- Royal Navy officers, for the same period.
- Royal Navy ratings and petty officers, for the same period.
- Royal Air Force, all ranks, for the same period.
- Indian Services, all ranks, for the same period.

All of the above indexes also relate to service deaths after the war, which resulted from wounds.

Once you have located the correct entry you will need to order a certificate, again directing your application to the Overseas Section.

Deaths of servicemen and women in England and Wales during both wars, such as in hospitals or air crashes, were registered with the local district registrar, so consult the civil registration indexes for these.

Scottish travellers

Details about Scots born, marrying or dying at sea or abroad can be tracked via the following indexes to 'minor records' in the General Register Office, in Edinburgh:

- The Marine Register, which includes births and deaths on board British-registered merchant ships from 1855, where at least one of the parents or the deceased was usually resident in Scotland.*
- The Air Register, which extends to births and deaths on UK-registered civil aircraft from 1948 onwards. Digital images of the death indexes to 1956 are accessible at **www.scotlands people.gov.uk**.
- Separate indexes to the Foreign Returns of births of children of Scottish parentage, to marriages, and to deaths of Scots in foreign countries notified between 1860 and 1965, and to marriages taking place *lex loci* (according to local law) after 1947 when a British consular official was not present.*
- Consular Returns of births and deaths of people of Scottish birth or descent from 1914, and marriages from 1917.*
- High Commissioners' Returns of births and deaths of persons of Scottish descent or birth in Commonwealth countries from at least 1964. There are some returns of marriages too.

- Army Returns of births, marriages and deaths of Scots at overseas military stations, 1881–1959, marriages performed by army chaplains abroad since 1892, where one party was Scottish and at least one serving in the Armed Forces.*
- Service Departments Registers, which date from 1 April 1959 and relate to the births, marriages and deaths of Scots and their families serving overseas or employed by the Armed Forces.
- Army fatalities of Scots, 1899–1902 (Boer War). Digital images of the indexes are at www.scotlandspeople.gov.uk.
- War deaths of warrant officers, non-commissioned officers and men in the Army, 1914–18. Digital images of these indexes are similarly available.
- War deaths of Royal Navy petty officers and ratings, 1914–18. Digital images of the indexes are available at the above website.
- Incomplete returns of Scots killed in all three Armed Forces, 1939–45. Digital images of the indexes are accessible at the same website.

*Digital images of the indexes to births up to 1906, marriages to 1931, and deaths up to 1956 are available at www.scotlandspeople. gov.uk. You will need to purchase a copy of the full registration. You can do this online.

Irish migrants

The births, marriages and deaths of Irish people outside Ireland may be found in records held at the General Register Office, in Dublin. These cover

- Births of children at sea, with at least one parent who was Irish, and deaths of Irish-born people at sea, 1864–85 (indexes are available on request). From 1886 onwards, the entries are listed at the end of each yearly index to births and deaths in Ireland itself, and only concern subjects of the Republic after 1 January 1922.
- Births, marriages and deaths of Irish servicemen and their families in the British Army stationed abroad. Look for these at the back of the yearly Irish birth indexes from 1888 to 1930, and the marriage and death indexes between 1888 and 1931. Deaths of Irish soldiers serving during the South African War, 1899–1902, are included in the 1902 death

index. Further birth and death registers of Irish Armed personnel and their families overseas run from 1960 onwards.

- British Consular Registers of births abroad to Irish parents, and deaths of Irish-born people from 1864 to 1921.
- Registers of births, marriages and deaths of Irish subjects outside the State, following the Registration Act 1972.
- A register of Lourdes marriages from 1972 onwards.

The last three sets of registers are not indexed.

To apply for a copy of any of the above registrations, contact the General Register Office, in Roscommon, or a local registration office. However, you will need to apply to the relevant superintendent registrar's office for marriage certificates between 1845 and 1919, and deaths from 1864 to 1923.

Northern Irish records since 1922

The General Register Office in Belfast (**www.groni.gov.uk**) holds indexes to the following overseas registrations:

- The Marine Register, containing details of births at sea of children with at least one Irish parent, and deaths of Northern Irish-born people from 1 January 1922 onwards.
- Consular Returns of births and deaths abroad of people with Irish connections as above, from 1 January 1922 onwards, and of marriages since 1923. Marriages in foreign countries, according to local law and without a British consular official being present, starting in 1947.
- High Commissioners' Returns of births, marriages and deaths in Commonwealth countries since 1950.
- Service Department Registers of births of children to fathers who were born in Northern Ireland, and of marriages and deaths from 1927.
- War deaths of servicemen and servicewomen who were natives of Northern Ireland, 1939–48. Online indexes to these registrations are available in the General Register Office.

You can order certificates at **www.groni.gov.uk**.

Don't forget that births, marriages and deaths at sea and abroad of Scottish and Irish nationals may also be found in other deposited material in the National Archives, at Kew, particularly those of ships' passengers and crew, described earlier in this chapter, and in Armed Service records (see below).

Other places where you can find British service personnel and their families overseas

The names of First World War military personnel who died away from the theatres of war in France and Belgium between 1914 and 1921 may be located in the microfilmed copies of the Registrar General's Miscellaneous Non-statutory Foreign Returns, and similarly those of civilian victims in the Far East between 1941 and 1945. The former entries are not indexed, and were written in the vernacular.

You can also search the Debt of Honour Register of the Commonwealth War Graves Commission at **www.cwgc.org** for the dates and places of death and burial or commemoration of more than 1.7 million servicemen and women who were casualties during the First and Second World Wars, and of over 67,000 Commonwealth civilians who died as a result of enemy action in the Second World War. You can read a brief summary of the action in which a person died or was reported missing, presumed dead, and find out the age, parentage and parental residence, rank or rating, regiment and service number, battalion, unit, ship, station, squadron or Royal Marine Division of each man and woman. A couple of databases, 'Soldiers (Officers) Died in the Great War', are accessible online in the Family Records Centre, and in the National Archives, at **www.familyrelatives.com**, **www.findmypast.com/HomeServlet**, and on CD-ROM. These will tell you the person's dates and places of birth and death, and family home, plus the regiment, rank and regimental number. The National Roll of the Great War, 1914–18, and the Army Roll of Honour, for soldiers killed or dying between 1 September 1939 and 31 December 1946, are similarly available, with the exception of **www.familyrelatives.com**. The databases exclude all 'dishonourable deaths'.

The service and pension records of soldiers in the British Army who were discharged or who died in service before 1920, are in the National Archives. The pre-First World War papers should contain details of age at enlistment, birthplace, usual residence and occupation or trade, and a physical description, and from 1882, the name of the next of kin. You can search for document references to the microfilmed attestation and discharge papers of soldiers who became pensioners between 1760 and 1854 at **www.nationalarchives.gov.uk/catalogue**. The catalogue entries reveal each soldier's name, including any aliases, his place of birth, last regiment, age at discharge, length and dates of service or the year he left the army. Less than half of the First World War service records now survive, as 'burnt documents', but this collection is boosted by a series of service and disablement pension records. From these you can piece together information about each soldier's army service, medical record, conduct and medals, his age and birthplace, physical appearance, occupation or trade on joining up, and his date and place of discharge or death. Crucially, if you are lucky, the papers will include the names and addresses of his parents or grandparents and of his wife, the birth dates of any children, the names and ages of any siblings, and identify the next of kin. Digital images of all of the above First World War documents are gradually being made available at **www.ancestry.co.uk**.

The earliest, signed, regimental service returns made to the War Office by commissioned officers date from 1828, and these, like similar returns in 1847, recorded men who were already retired on full or half-pay. Service returns were sent in by officers on the active list in 1829 and between 1870 and 1872. The very first returns gave only the officer's age when first commissioned, his date and place of marriage, wife's name and those of any children and their dates and places of baptism, whereas from 1829 the returns invariably contained each officer's dates and places of birth and marriage and the dates and places of birth or baptism of his children. All the returns are available on microfilm, and can be hired in to examine in a family history centre near you. Later army officers' files in the National Archives concern men who died or left the army before 1 April 1922. The document references can be found listed at **www.nationalarchives.gov.uk/catalogue** by the surnames, initials, rank and period of service of officers in the First World War. Some careers began as far back as 1898 or continued to 1939. Although the original records were heavily pruned, you can still discover an officer's date and place of birth, his former profession or occupation, and marital status, his date and place of death whilst in service, and any correspondence about his war service, hospitalization, capture or loss.

The indexed registers of deaths of Royal Naval officers and ratings from 1854 to 1957, and of Royal Marines between 1854 and 1911, in the National Archives, at Kew, exclude those as a result of enemy action. For such deaths separate registers cover the years between 1854 and 1929 for Royal Naval personnel, and from 1914 up to 1929 for Royal Marines. The volumes are indexed after 1915 by surname range. You can discover the date and cause of death and place of burial, the date and place of birth, and the name, address and relationship to the deceased of the next of kin.

The names of Royal Naval ratings and Royal Marines who lost their lives between 1914 and 1918 are included in the War Graves Roll, which is also in the National Archives. This is arranged alphabetically by name. Entries on the Roll about officers who died between 1914 and 1920 are accessed via a series of personal-name index cards. The Roll records the last ship and rank, dates and places of birth and death and the names and addresses of the next of kin of each casualty.

Indexed continuous service engagement books of ratings in the Royal Navy between 1853 and 1872 are in the National Archives too. From the numbered entries you can learn each man's date and place of birth, accompanied by a physical description of his appearance on engagement, date on first entering the Navy, a summary of his naval career and the names of the ships on which he served and at what rates. The books include the names of men who joined much earlier in the century. You can glean similar information from the registers of seamen's services between 1873 and 1928 of entrants up to 1923. Indexed digital images of the entries are searchable at **www.nationalarchives.gov.uk/documentsonline**, and access is free in the Family Records Centre and in the National Archives, but you will have to pay a flat fee to view the images elsewhere. Each rating's former occupation or trade, date and place of death if this happened in service, or his date, place and reason for discharge are recorded. Royal Naval lieutenants' passing certificates, in the National Archives, run from 1691 until 1902, and from 1761 they will usually be accompanied by a certified copy of the candidate's baptism entry as proof of his minimum qualifying age of 20. Look in *Royal Naval Lieutenants: Passing Certificates 1691–1902*, by B. Pappalardo, for full document references. The signed returns of officers' services compiled at various dates between 1756 and 1931 include careers which continued to 1966, but only from the mid-nineteenth century do they reveal warrant or commissioned officers' birthplaces and dates of death, as well as the name of any wife.

You can study the indexed service records of men joining the Royal Marines before 1925 in the National Archives as well. Some services are recorded up to 1940, and include date and place of birth, a physical description, the former trade or occupation, and a career outline. Indexed records of service between 1793 and 1966 of entrants up to 1923, give the dates of birth of both warrant and commissioned officers. Consult *A Register of Royal Marine Deaths, 1914-1919*, and *A Register of Royal Marine Deaths, 1939-1945*, both by J. A. Good, for information about casualties.

Indexed digital images of the service records of the Royal Naval Division from 1914 to 1919 are available at **www.national archives.gov.uk/documentsonline**. These will tell you about each reserve's date of birth, home address, the occupation and the name and address of the next of kin.

If you are looking for the births, other personal details and careers of officers and men in the Royal Flying Corps (RFC) who died or left the service before the Royal Air Force (RAF) was established on 1 April 1918, try the Army 'burnt documents' and pension records outlined above. Royal Naval Air Service (RNAS) personnel up to the same date are included in the Royal Navy registers of seamen's services, also described earlier. If your relative transferred to the RAF from the RFC or RNAS or joined before 1923, his or her date and place of birth, place of residence, former occupation and career up to 1928 can be extracted from the indexed RAF service records in the National Archives. The dates of death were written in for airmen and airwomen who died on duty. For personal information about commissioned RAF officers, whose service ended before 1921, search the alphabetical records, on microfilm, in the National Archives, for their date and place of birth, former address, profession or occupation, and the address of their named next of kin.

There are various alphabetical or indexed registers of tickets issued to merchant seamen between 1836 and 1857, and again between 1918 and 1972, in the National Archives. The earlier registers divulge either age and birthplace or actual date of birth. The birth dates and places of merchant seamen who were discharged between 1918 and 1941 are set out on several sets of cards, which are available on microfiche. A surviving alphabetical collection of seamen's pouches, spanning the years between 1913 and 1972, will provide you with this information too. You can search for their document references by personal-name at **www.nationalarchives.gov.uk/catalogue**. If you want to find out the given years of birth of officers, examine the papers relating to men voluntarily submitting themselves to an examination of competency as masters and mates from 1845 until 1849. The mandatory examination certificates from 1854 up to 1921 for masters and mates engaged in the home trade (in territorial waters), and from 1846 until 1906 for masters and mates involved in the foreign trade, contain their actual birth dates and places. Similar colonial certificates between 1833 and 1934 specify only the year of birth and the birthplace, and possibly the date of death. Compulsory certificates of long service were issued to masters and mates after 1850 and you can trawl these for the same information. All of the certificates are indexed and are available on microfilm in the National Archives.

You can find out more about deceased or injured merchant seamen from applications made to Trinity House for financial help. Indexed digital copies of the summarized petitions between 1787 and 1854 are searchable at **www.originsnetwork.com** and in print. Embedded in the bound papers, which are in the library of the Society of Genealogists, are copies of marriage, birth, baptism, burial and death certificates.

The British in India and Asia

If your ancestors spent time living, working or were stationed in India, try the ecclesiastical returns of baptisms, marriages and burials of Britons (excluding Roman Catholics before 1836), and the civil registrations of births, marriages and deaths, in the Asia, Pacific and Africa Collections of the British Library (**www.bl.uk/collections/asiapacificafrica.html**). The indexed ecclesiastical registers relate to the three Presidencies of Madras from 1698, Bengal from 1713, and Bombay from 1709, and Roman Catholic church and mission registers from 1836 until 1854 in each Presidency. To help you locate in which Presidency your ancestor was based the website includes a map.

Birth registration was not compulsory, but was usual from the 1920s, and should then be complete as far as the date of independence in 1947, though some entries run up to 1968. The registrations include former parts of India (Burma, Pakistan and Bangladesh) prior to partition. There are separate indexes for each Presidency. You can discover the name, date and place of birth of each registered child, the names of his or her parents and a wealth of other information. The ecclesiastical registers also record the date and place of baptism and may add the names of godparents. The civil registrations of marriages include the ages of each bridal pair, details about the ceremony, the names of the couple's fathers and the witnesses. The church marriage registers supply similar information, plus the couple's addresses. The registers of burials record the person's date of death, age, occupation, date and place of interment. After about 1850, you can discover cause of death too. Look in *The British Overseas: A Guide to Records of Births, Baptisms, Marriages, Deaths and Burials available in the UK* for the whereabouts and dates of other sources about Britons in India.

The British Association for Cemeteries in South Asia's research notes and photographs relating to graves and epitaphs of Europeans in the sub-continent form part of the British Library's Asia, Pacific and Africa Collections. The Association's monograph booklets contain full inscriptions copied from gravestones in various cemeteries, and potted biographies and articles about the social lives of residents. A list of its publications is available at **www.bacsa.org.uk** as well as the catalogue to the Association's cemetery records.

You can search **www.a2a.org.uk** for document references to a lot of the material in the Asia, Pacific and Africa Collections.

For more information about how you can trace your ancestors in India visit the online exhibition and research guide at **www.movinghere.org.uk**. There is also a Families in British India Society (**www.fibis.org**) for people interested in the period before Independence.

United States of America

From the eighteenth century, some American colonial assemblies required town and county clerks to keep records of both births and deaths. However, recording was often haphazard, so a family Bible or other surviving evidence might be a better source. Microfilmed copies of many of the town and county volumes are available for hire in family history centres, or scan the North American Vital Records Index, which covers more than 4.5 million births, baptisms and marriages in America between 1700 and 1888, on CD-ROM, for brief extracts. Visit **www.genealogy. com/gbnk/keyword.html** for indexed digital images of birth, marriage and death announcements in over 1,300 newspapers between 1690 and 1977, and in historical documents after 1789.

In certain states, particularly those in the south, civil registration of birth, marriage and death only began in the USA as recently as the twentieth century, but the system was universally in place by 1917. The indexes and registers are mostly held in the relevant county courthouse, and duplicates are sent and preserved in the state vital records departments. Searches can be undertaken for you for a fee. You will need to provide as much information as you can, including your relationship to the person concerned. However, the privacy laws may prevent access to a copy of a registration more recent than 75 or 100 years ago. Ask for a photocopy or digital copy rather than a handwritten certificate, to avoid any misreading of what was often a horrible script, which may have made indexing difficult.

You can learn the start dates and whereabouts of vital records, and how to order copies, state by state, at **http://vitalrec. com/index.html**, which has overseas links too. The map can be used to identify the names of counties by state. Kemp's *International Vital Records Handbook* provides similar information, as well as filmed copies of indexes and registers, many of which you can hire in to study in your local family history centre.

A few of the state registration indexes are available online. There are links to these at **http://vitalrec.com** and at **www.cyndislist.com**. Some indexes are included in **www.ancestry.com**, though you may have to subscribe to use them. If you cannot find the name you want, try all possible variant spellings, and be wary of possible confusions between 'T' and 'F', 'P' and 'R', or 'L' and 'S'.

Although there is no overall standardization of content, a birth certificate will generally tell you

- the name,
- date and county of birth of the baby,
- his or her parentage and their birthplaces (state, territory or country),
- the mother's maiden name,
- both parents' ages, their address, occupations, and the number of any other living children.

After 1910, you are likely to find more family details, such as the child's seniority of birth.

Most states record late birth registrations, which were filed mainly after 1937 by applicants for Social Security benefits. Unfortunately, such registrations are usually kept in the county in which the person lived, which may not be where he or she was born. The applications had to be accompanied by supporting documentary evidence as to age, such as sworn affidavits, entries from the 1880 and 1900 census schedules, school records, a baptism certificate or family Bible, so they are worth tracking down for their ancillary information.

If you are looking for a marriage certificate, you should find:

- the date and place,
- the names of both parties,
- the names and birthplaces (again, the state, territory or country) of both sets of parents,
- possibly the ages and birth dates and birth county or country of the bridal couple, their places of residence, and occupations, current marital status, number of any previous marriages, and
- the names of the witnesses and officiating minister or clerk.

Look at the table in the next chapter for ways in which you can limit the scope of your search for a marriage by using the census schedules between 1850 and 1910.

The minimum age at marriage varies from state to state, and the consent of a parent or guardian is usually essential up to the age of 21 for males and until 18 for females. Signed affidavits to this effect are lodged in the town or county courthouse.

During the colonial period, most weddings took place after the reading of banns in church, or by filing couples' intentions to marry with the town or county clerk, which were then publicly posted. The groom entered a bond with or without a surety, guaranteeing the wedding at a specific place, and within a prescribed period, which was generally a few days. The date of the marriage was often endorsed on the bond. Marriage bonds were common in New England and in the southern states. Look for the existence of a marriage contract, which was designed to protect the inheritance of family property by the rightful heirs, especially the children of a widow if she were to remarry.

Marriage licences gradually replaced banns and the posting of intentions to marry. The applications and actual licences were also filed in the town or county courthouse, and they were usually indexed under the groom's name. The application papers should reveal the couple's names, ages, addresses, birth dates and places, and occupations, to which were often added the names, state, territory or country of birth of their parents. The licence will tell you the date and place of the marriage, when the licence was issued and the name of the person performing the ceremony. If the clergyman did not report the marriage to the town or county clerk, the marriage applications and licences can be extremely useful. Lots of these records have been filmed by the Church of Jesus Christ of Latter-day Saints, so consult the library catalogue at **www.familysearch.org** for information on what is available for hire in your local family history centre.

If you cannot locate a specific marriage, consult the indexed marriage records of the nearest large city for an irregular ceremony, when the above formalities were dispensed with or minors lied about their ages.

A death certificate can be especially rewarding.

The early death registrations will usually only tell you the

- date and place of demise,
- the person's name, and
- possibly that of his or her spouse.

As the nineteenth century progressed, the registrations became much more instructive, and listed:

- the cause of death,
- the person's age, and birthplace (county, or country),
- his or her occupation,
- spouse's name and maiden name, as well as
- his or her parents' names, and
- the name and relationship to the defunct of the informant.

After 1910, the deceased's date of birth, and the name of the funeral home, the name of the attending physician or medical examiner, the date and place of burial or cremation were recorded too, and from 1937, his or her Social Security number, so the registrations are genealogically invaluable.

Some states even set out the birthplaces (state, territory or country) of both parents. If the individual or either parent was a first-generation settler, such details will tell you the country of origin. You can search for the names of people registered for Social Security benefits and who have died since 1937, at **http://vitalrec.com**, **www.familysearch.org** and at **www.family relatives.com**, although most of the entries relate to deaths after 1962. The database will disclose the name of the deceased, the Social Security number, the state in which he or she lived when it was issued, the birth and death dates, last address, and the amount of death benefit, plus the address to which it was to be sent. However, death benefit was not always applied for, or there might have been a recording error, so you may not be lucky.

See the next chapter for advice on how the ten-yearly 1850–80 mortality schedules can reduce the years you have to search for a death.

Sometimes, you may learn more about a person's life from gravestone inscriptions. A tombstone may be your only source about birth and death dates which fell before civil registration began or which went unnotified, and often show the original spelling of an immigrant's name. Many urban church burial places were moved out to the suburbs as property values and populations soared and the pressure for space was at a premium. Non-sectarian public, municipal cemeteries and commercial Memorial Parks were established and national and state graveyards set aside for military veterans and their families. In rural areas, family burial plots were common at least until the nineteenth century. If you consult a local directory or map of the period, you should be able to identify where local people were taken for burial. Use **www.cyndislist.com** and **www.ancestral findings.com/cemetery.htm** to find any gravestone inscriptions which are searchable online.

Newspaper obituaries are another useful resource, and a number of these have been uploaded, so try the above websites for links to free websites. A state-by-state list of websites containing newspaper obituaries and gravestone inscriptions is available at **www.libraryspot.com/ask/askobit.htm**. You can also conduct a free surname search for newspaper obituaries, again state by state, at **www.Obitcentral.com/obitsearch/**. This includes details about the ongoing USGenWeb project, hosted by **www.rootsweb.com**, to transcribe and index newspaper obituaries. Indexed digital images of newspaper obituaries can also be accessed at **www.genealogybank.com/gbnk/keyboard.html**.

Probate packets and files, coroners' reports, and military pension applications also note deaths. The probate material is described in Chapter 14. Coroners' reports are deposited in the state, county or city coroner's office, and searches can be made for you.

Adoption records

Adoption can take place by agreement between the parties with or without any formal court proceedings resulting in a court order, or by a petition leading to the issue of a court order. Private agreements are not considered to be legally binding in most states today, so most adoptions are conducted through the courts.

If you are adopted, contact the relevant adoption agency or state court for non-identifying information. You may be able to examine the records yourself, although some papers may be withheld under the privacy laws. The court docket books or indexes will furnish your family name enabling you to identify the number and title of your case file. This information can also be released to your adoptive parents and birthparents. In some states you can obtain your original birth certificate on demand and the files can be similarly opened, and in other states only at the court's discretion. The adoption petitions divulge the name(s) and addresses of your biological parent(s) and adopting parents, and generally they include your name, abode, age or date of birth, with details about any property you might have owned at the time of the planned adoption. Occasionally you can discover your given religion, and place of birth, and the names of any siblings, plus the ages, religious denominations, marital status, date and place of marriage of the adopting parents and remarks about their fitness and suitability to adopt. The adoption decree will normally include the child's new name, and the original birth certificate is then altered accordingly.

Alien children adopted by American parents do not automatically become American citizens, but the residency requirement for applications for naturalization is reduced to two years in such cases.

If you are 18, you, your birth parents, siblings and other birth relatives can register, as can the adoptive parents of adoptees under the age of 18, with the State and National Reunion Registries (Mutual Consent Registries) to find a match with someone else in the family who might be looking for them. The best of these registries is possibly the International Soundex Reunion Registry, based in Carson City. Always advise each registry if you are already listed with another one.

Divorce

Divorce was uncommon in the United States until the twentieth century. Originally, the only grounds for divorce were adultery or prolonged desertion by one party of the other.

In colonial New England, where marriage was a civil contract, divorces were granted by local courts from early times. A notice might be posted in the town or county courthouse, and in the local newspaper, of a pending divorce application, especially if the defendant's whereabouts were unknown. The publications often ran for months, but as communications improved the period of publication shortened to about three or four weeks. In New York, New Jersey and Pennsylvania, however, divorce proceedings were dealt with by the governor and his council or by a petition to the assembly. In the south, few civil divorce laws came into being before the Revolution, but couples could separate by mutual consent, have this legally ratified, and formalize the payment of alimony. This did not free either partner to remarry, but in states such as South Carolina, where divorce was illegal, this was the only alternative, other than a ride to the Western frontier and anonymity. There were certain places where it was known to be easier to obtain a divorce, for instance in cities in Pennsylvania and New England, in Chicago after the Civil War, in Utah, and in Ontario, over the Canadian border.

The divorces granted in New England were recorded in the county or town courthouse, which is where any surviving documentation remains today. However, the colonial governing councils and assemblies had to submit copies of their private acts of divorce to the British government for approval. You can find records of such colonial divorces in the registers and papers of the Privy Council after 1607 and in the Treasury Plantation Books from 1678, both of which are in the National Archives, at Kew. Indexed printed summaries are included in *Acts of the Privy Council of England, Colonial Series, 1613–1783*.

There is no consistency among the states about the courts in which divorce petitions are now heard, but once you have located them, the court divorce case files are most informative. The files are not always indexed, but you can usually discover the date of the court hearing and of the judgment from the dockets and minute books and the local press. The case files reveal the names of each couple and the dates of their marriage and divorce, sometimes accompanied by their ages and birth dates, and invariably by details of their current addresses, an inventory of their property, the names and birth dates of their children, and the reasons for divorce. Copies of divorce decrees are now required to be filed in some state vital statistics offices. Visit **http://vitalrec.com/divorce.html** for their addresses and those of the county courts. Divorce certificates issued within the last 50 years are often protected by the privacy laws and the permission of a divorced party is needed before their release.

Americans abroad

You can glean details about births and marriages and reports of deaths until 1974 of American citizens overseas, in the Consular Despatches from 1789 until 1870, the Correspondence of the Department of State from 1870 until 1906, and then in yearly files, which are assigned a number code for each country. The records are in the National Archives at College Park. You can examine the indexes from 1828 to 1906 on microfilm, and thereafter name index cards for the respective number code. Alternatively, apply for an order form by post, at **www.archives.gov/contact/inquire-form.html** or by fax. No fee for a search and copy is required until you receive this.

Death notices concerning American citizens who died abroad were sent by the Department of State for publication in the press between 1835 and 1855, and these, like similar notices from 1857 until 1922, are arranged chronologically, but almost all the later volumes are indexed. The notices tell you the person's name, date and place of death, the consul or consulate reporting the death, and the number and date of his despatch.

If you are an American citizen, contact Passport Services, in Washington, DC (**www.travel.state.gov/passport/get/first/first_825.html**), for events since 1975. Otherwise you will need to approach the nearest consular office of the relevant country.

American casualties of war

You can search for information about American casualties and missing personnel in the Army and Army Air Force during the Second World War at **www.archives.gov/research/arc/ww2/army-casualties/index.html**, and in the Navy, Marine Corps and Coastguard at **www.archives.gov/research/arc/ww2/navy-casualties/index.html**. The databases are arranged by state and county. For casualties during the Korean War, 1950-57, and in Vietnam, 1956-98, search **www.archives.gov/research/korean-war/casualty-lists/index.html** and **www.archives.gov/research/vietnam-war/casualty-lists/index.html** respectively. A US Military Index can also be searched at **www.familysearch.org**. This database contains details about American servicemen and women who perished in Korea between 1951 and 1957, and in Vietnam between 1956 and 1975. Embedded in the index are the birth and death dates of each casualty, an indication of his or her marital status, religious affiliation, given home when first recorded (the town, city, county and state), country of death, rank, serial number and Service branch, and the date of the last tour of duty. Details about army casualties in the Korean War are available at **www.familyrelatives.com**. The casualty case files are held by in the Army Casualty and Memorial Affairs Center, in Alexandria.

If you want information from an overseas Second World War military cemetery, visit **www.ancestry.com** or contact the American Battle Monuments Commission, in Arlington (**www.abmc.gov**).

Other service records

Service papers of the military, dating from the Revolutionary War until 1912, are preserved in the National Archives Building in Washington, DC, whilst those from the First World War onwards are in the custody of the National Personnel Records Center, in St Louis, Missouri. The documents include details about service, pension applications and payments to veterans, their widows and other heirs. The pension papers in the National Archives Building relate to service between 1775 and 1916, but are well worth seeking out for the wealth and range of documents which they contain, such as marriage, birth and death certificates of the veterans and their immediate families, and pages from family Bibles. The bounty-land warrant application files concerning claims based on wartime service from 1775 until 3 March 1855, consist of similar information. The warrants were granted in lieu of pay. Many of the Revolutionary War and War of 1812 land applications have been combined with the above pension files. Selected records of Revolutionary War pensions, bounty-land application files and casualty lists are available at **www.heritagequestonline.com** and at **www.genealogybank.com**. For information about local records relating to the state militia, visit **www.archives.gov/research/ alic/reference/state-archives.html** for a list of addresses of state archives and historical societies.

You can search the draft Army Registration Cards of men aged between 18 and 45 in 1917 and 1918 on microfilm in the National Archives Building, and a database containing Army Enlistment records for the Second World War between 1938 and 1946 is searchable at **http://aad.archives.gov/aad**, **www.familyrelatives.com**, and at **www.ancestry.com**. All three of these sources are likely to disclose your subject's current address, age and birthplace and marital status. The registration cards also provided a physical description, the man's occupation and the name of his employer, the names of any dependent relatives, his father's birthplace and the name and address of the next of kin.

Surviving American Navy veterans' personnel files from 1906 onwards are also in the National Personnel Records Center, from which you can obtain an application form for a search and copy. To obtain a pension, men who were invalided out and applying for a pension were required to produce personal testimonies about themselves. The indexed pension applications, from 1861 to 1934, are in the National Archives Building. From these you should be able to discover the veteran's rank, last ship, details of his service, his age or date of birth, and current address. Dependants who were claimants had to prove their relationship to the veteran officer or sailor, so embedded in the application files are sworn affidavits, copies of their marriage licences and birth certifications. The files relating to disapproved pension applications for the same period can help you as well.

Unfortunately, few Confederate records survive and are usually to be tracked down in state archives, or local historical society libraries. The National Archives staff should be able to assist you in identifying their known whereabouts.

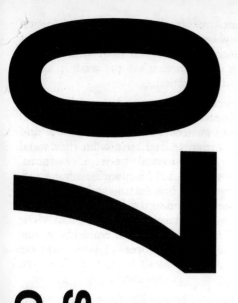

07

searching the census

In this chapter you will learn:
- how to access census returns online
- how to search the census schedules elsewhere
- how to solve some common problems when using the census schedules.

Having obtained a clutch of birth, marriage and death certificates, you should now be able to plug some of the holes in your family tree, or to take it back several more generations. However, you will reach a stage where what you want to know lies beyond the start of civil registration.

The next prime genealogical resource, the ten-yearly census returns, should tell you approximately when and where your ancestors were born. You can discover the household in which they slept overnight at a particular date, and what they were doing to earn their keep. If you haven't been successful in locating the registration of someone's birth, your best hope will be to find him or her in the parental home with any brothers and sisters and other family members. Indexed digital images and/or transcriptions of all the census returns between 1841 and 1901 are now available for Great Britain, so if you know the approximate year of birth, in theory, your task should be relatively straightforward.

The first census, or complete population count, was undertaken in Great Britain on Tuesday 10 March 1801, and in Ireland on Monday 28 May 1821. From 1841, a Sunday night was always chosen, when families and workers were thought most likely to be at their usual addresses. People's names were not systematically recorded until 1841 either, but because the parish clergy, overseers of the poor and schoolmasters were among the first census enumerators, some parochial lists of the names of heads of household exist for earlier years. You can find their dates and whereabouts from *Local Census Listings, 1522–1930: Holdings in the British Isles*, by J. Gibson and M. Medlycott.

How the census was organized

The civil registration districts created in 1837 were adopted as census districts, and divided into enumeration districts, each comprising about 200 households. This number was considered to be what an enumerator could cover in a day. The district registrars, under the supervision of the superintendent district registrars, were responsible for appointing and paying the local enumerators. The enumerators delivered a numbered schedule to every head of household for completion on census night, and then collected them all up again the following week, helping the householder to fill in the schedule if necessary. A household was defined as people sharing the same roof, boarding and eating together. The schedules requested personal details about each household member. This information was duly copied into special enumerators' books which were presented with the schedules for checking by the district and superintendent registrars and for eventual transmission to the Registrar General in London. The household schedules were then destroyed.

The census returns are made available to the public on the first working day in January once a full 100 years have elapsed, because the personal information contained in them was confidential. The returns for 1931 no longer survive and no census was taken in 1941. If you are interested in information about yourself or your family from the 1911 returns, written applications for a paid search on your behalf of a specific address can be made to the National Archives, for consideration under the Freedom of Information Act. It is planned to make available indexed digital images of most of the personal data in 2009 earlier than the full release in 2012, and this will be cheaper. Early access to information in the 1921 returns is prohibited and exempt under the Freedom of Information Act.

Microfilmed copies of the returns up to 1891 are held in the Family Records Centre, and a microfiche copy of the 1901 census returns can be consulted there and in the National Archives, whilst copies of the Welsh returns for each census year are available in the National Library of Wales, for Jersey in the Jersey Archive, in St Helier, and in the Lord Coutanche Library, for Guernsey, Alderney and Sark in the Priaulx Library, and indexes in the Lord Coutanche Library, and for the Isle of Man in the Manx National Heritage Library and Archives. For details of copies in local libraries, visit **www.familia.org.uk**.

Though never intended for use by genealogists, census returns are a key nineteenth-century source, because they open a window on the lives of people at ten-yearly intervals over a period of 60 years, and trace the whereabouts of three or four generations of a family. They bridge the divide between the centralized civil registrations of birth, marriage and death and the earlier local records of baptism, marriage and burial and tell you at which places and at what dates to start looking for these events. Unlike vital registrations, which link a single individual to his or her parents, spouse or informant, the census returns capture an entire family or household unit on a specific night. You can find out who were their nearest neighbours and build up a picture of the sort of community in which they found themselves.

The UK census was taken on the following nights:

- Sunday 6 June 1841
- Sunday 30 March 1851
- Sunday 7 April 1861
- Sunday 2 April 1871
- Sunday 3 April 1881
- Sunday 5 April 1891
- Sunday 31 March 1901.

Someone born early the following morning was not enumerated, nor anyone dying during census night. Night-workers were recorded at the addresses to which they returned on the morning after their last shift. Travellers by coach or train and on the move were listed in whichever hotel or house they rested the morning after their journey, or if they alighted, wherever they spent census night. As such strangers might arrive late and leave early their given details might be extremely vague, because they were not personally known to the head of household.

Indexes, digital images and transcriptions

Website links to the indexed digital images of the returns for the whole of England, Wales, the Channel Islands and the Isle of Man from 1841 to 1901 can be made via **www.nationalarchives. gov.uk/census** or you can go directly to **www.ancestry.co.uk** to view all of the returns or to **www.1901censusonline.com** to inspect the returns excluding 1881. The transcriptions and digital images are freely accessible in the Family Records Centre, and in the National Archives, but you will have to pay to examine them in most other places. Indexed digital images of the 1841, 1861, 1871 and 1891 returns can be viewed at **www.findmypast.comHomeServlet** too. Indexed transcriptions of the 1881 census returns are freely available at **www.familysearch.org**, on CD-ROM and on microfiche, whilst indexed transcriptions of all the other English and Welsh returns up to 1901 are at **www.thegenealogist.co.uk**. Many of these transcriptions are linked to digital images of the census pages. Other transcriptions for 1841 and 1861 are available at **www.originsnetwork.com**.

The online indexes to the 1901 census returns at **www.1901censusonline.com** offer you six choices:

- Person Search;
- Address Search (of particular houses, streets or roads. If these were not transcribed and indexed because they ran over from a previous page, they will not be included, nor in the digital image. Watch out for abbreviated addresses, which will defy your search command);
- Place Search (of specific towns, villages or hamlets);
- Institution Search (schools, army barracks, prisons, hospitals, asylums, workhouses and other institutions with more than 100 inmates);
- Vessel Search (for boats and ships); or
- Reference Number (this is useful if you already have a full National Archives film, folio and page reference, as you can go straight to the digital image).

You will probably want to try the Person Search first. You will have to enter the surname or forename in the search box, whereas the age and birthplace boxes are optional. For a double-barrelled name, you may need to search separately under each of the names. The first two letters of a surname must always be entered. Forename searches are especially useful when you do not know the married or maiden names of female relatives, but know when they were born. Since surnames and forenames were occasionally recorded in reverse, if you fail to find an entry, try this as an option too.

An Advanced Person Search is available to retrieve synonyms and abbreviated names, and you can do wild card searches using * to represent missing letters, or _ if a single letter is in doubt. Try not to be too specific about birthplaces, ages and addresses.

The results set out each person's name, given age, place of birth, the place and county where enumerated, and his or her occupation. A number of 'hits' may correspond to your search command. Select the one most closely matching the facts you already know. You now have two choices: to view the digital 'Image' of the whole original census page on which the person was recorded, or to inspect the 'Transcription' relating only to that household. If you decide to view the digital images or transcriptions, you will have to use a special voucher, which is time-based, or use your credit or debit card. Vouchers are sold in the Family Records Centre, the National Archives, in many local libraries, record offices and by family history societies. You can find details about sales outlets at the website.

Should a household run over to two census pages, you will need to pay to view them both if selecting the first option, whereas the transcription will include everyone in the household, but nothing else that appeared on the same census page.

> ## Tip
>
> Open your account only when you are ready to pay to view if you are using a voucher, because the clock starts ticking from the moment you log on. At the end of the session don't forget to 'Log out'.

The indexed digital images of the other census returns, at **www.ancestry.co.uk**, are searchable by surname, forename, and by year of birth, birthplace, residence and year of death. The 'Ranked Search' option will display the results using a starred system, with the entries most closely matching your search terms listed first, in descending order. The 'Exact Search' option will only display precise matches, so don't be too specific with your requests. You can have all of the returns searched and retrieved simultaneously, or take each census year in turn. Another helpful feature is that you can confine your search to the first name, adding other identifying tags, such as year of birth and birthplace, to pick up on spelling errors or unfamiliar ways of writing your surname. Wildcard * and missing letter ? searches are permitted as well. When you are ready, click on to see the transcription for each person, and the names of the rest of the family or household, and then decide whether you want to view the digital image, or the full household transcription. You can also move from one census page to another to find the neighbours. If you want to browse all the census pages for a particular place, click on the name of the county and select the civil parish. Because the transcriptions (and digital images of the census pages) cite the National Archives film, enumeration district, folio and page numbers you can use these to locate the same individuals on any unindexed copies you may have on CD-ROM or microform.

You can conduct both person and address searches at **www.findmypast.com/HomeServlet**.

You do not need to key in the first two letters of each surname or forename to hunt for the transcriptions of the 1881 returns at **www.familysearch.org** or on CD-ROM. If you prefer, you can search the indexed transcriptions of the 1881 returns on microfiche: there is a complete national personal-name index, which gives full National Archives film, folio and page references for each individual, another identical index is arranged county by county, a third as enumerated (the complete transcription), and the fourth runs alphabetically by county and birthplace. Copies of the indexes are held in the Family Records Centre, in many local libraries, record offices and family history centres. The local family history society will have a set at least for its own county, since its members were responsible for helping to compile the index.

The fully indexed census returns are a wonderful resource, because more than 165 million people's names lie just a click away. They include people at different stages in their lives, and you can see how households changed over time.

If you are using microfilm copies of the returns, there is a good collection of personal-name indexes in the Family Records Centre, listed by place for each of the census years from 1841–91. Many local libraries and record offices have compiled their own indexes too. Some personal-name indexes are in private hands, and you may need to pay a small fee to have them searched by writing to the address given in *Marriage and Census Indexes for Family Historians*, by J. Gibson and E. Hampson.

If there is no personal-name index for your place or locality, you will need to identify the film reference for the street or place itself. The returns for towns with populations over 40,000 have all been street-indexed and you can search the indexes in the Family Records Centre. Locally-held street indexes are listed county by county in *Marriage and Census Indexes for Family Historians*.

Sometimes you may not find your street mentioned in an index, so you may need to look at a contemporary map of the district to identify nearby streets, and then start again. Present-day locations can be identified at **http://uk.multimap.com/map/places.cgi**. For London, consult *Names of London Streets and Places and their Localities*, a copy of which is in the Family Records Centre. This lists the street names alphabetically, giving their locality and parish, enabling you to find the census reference to a larger neighbouring or nearby street in the street index, and thus the whereabouts of the one you want. Street directories of London and larger towns and cities, published around census years, will indicate which roads, streets and terraces intersected each other. A number of directories are now available on CD-ROM, and some are searchable as part of the Online Publications and Electronic Resources Archive in the Family Records Centre. You can study copies of nineteenth-century Ordnance Survey street plans of some larger towns and cities in the Family Records Centre, and your local studies collection and record office should have copies too.

Don't rely on the name of the registration district in the centralized birth, marriage and death indexes as being the exact place where someone lived because each one covered up to seven different parishes. In any case, the family's usual address might have been somewhere altogether different from that at the time of registration.

For unlisted townships, communities or settlements try the 'Hamlet Index', in the Family Records Centre, and the above website. For Welsh localities look in *Welsh Administrative and Territorial Units*, by M. Richards, too.

What the censuses reveal

Every enumerator's book was numbered and prefaced by a short description of the hamlets, townships, roads and streets it encompassed.

Each page of the 1841 returns is headed by the title of the relevant township, hamlet, village, town, city ward and parish to which the entries relate but the various columns recorded only limited personal details about people, household by household. You will find

- their names (first forename and initials for any others, and the surname. Sometimes these were reversed),
- their approximate ages (rounded down to the nearest five for people over the age of 15),
- their occupations, and
- merely the vaguest indication of birthplaces (whether in the same county where the person was enumerated 'Y', or not 'N', or not known 'NK', or in Scotland 'S', Ireland 'I' or in Foreign Parts 'F', if someone was a non-British subject).

Road, street and house names were rarely identified, so when picking your way down the strings of names be careful to note when one building ends and another starts. This will be signified by two diagonal lines drawn through the margin immediately to the left of a person's name. If a building was divided into apartments or was occupied by more than one household who did not eat together, then a single diagonal line will be shown. The name of the head of the household came first followed by those of the other people sharing the same household. The surnames of people which were the same as that of the person recorded immediately preceding them were indicated by 'do' (ditto). Because of the idiosyncratic spelling of some forenames it may be difficult to decide someone's gender, so look in the age columns, which are separate for males and females.

Neither family relationships nor marital status were inserted in the 1841 census returns, and it was not always the oldest member who headed the household. Don't assume that a man and woman of similar ages and bearing the same surname who were sharing a household were a married couple, as they might actually be a brother and sister or related by marriage to someone else in the family, whilst younger people of the same surname staying with them may turn out to be the offspring of neither.

Every household in an enumeration district in the 1851 and later census returns was individually numbered, and the names of roads, streets and houses or house numbers were written in. You can even discover how many rooms the household occupied in 1891 and 1901, if it was less than five, so you can learn about your ancestors' housing conditions.

From 1851, under a series of headed columns were recorded

- each person's name (first forename and initials for any other names, and the surname, or vice versa),
- his or her relationship to the head of household,
- marital status,
- given age,
- occupation, and
- the place and county of birth (for non-English or non-Welsh residents or foreigners this may merely be the country).

In 1851 too, the returns began to note who was blind, deaf and dumb, and from 1871 anyone who was suffering from certain mental disabilities.

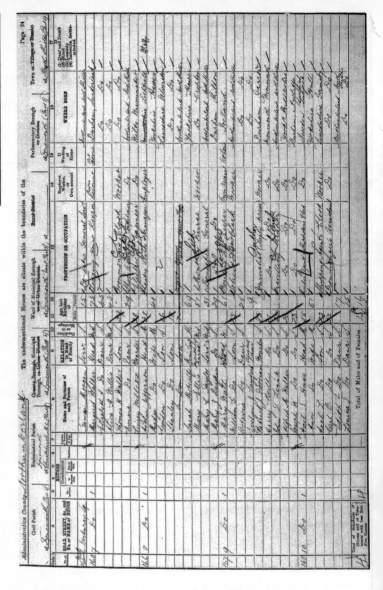

Figure 9 part of the 1901 census return for part of North Shields, Northumberland. Schedule number 166 relates to Arthur Jefferson's family at 8 Dockurray Square. A son was born to his wife Madge at 3.45 am on 1 April, whose details were crossed out because it happened the morning after census night. Arthur's mother-in-law, Sarah Metcalfe, was on hand to support (reproduced by permission of The National Archives)

Tips

- As generally only the first forename was set down, with initials for any others, if you cannot find the expected name of someone, but the age tallies, this may be the explanation.
- A youngster might take on the surname of a step-parent.
- A child born to his present wife, but by a former husband or some other partner, might be described as the head of household's son or daughter, under his surname. Conversely, the head of household's children might not all belong to his current wife. All the given relationships were to the head.
- Any change in a person's marital status between census years, or a differently named spouse, will point to a marriage, the death of a husband or wife and a remarriage. If you do not know the new partner's surname, try the cross-referenced marriage database at **www.freebmd.org.uk** for registration details, and the International Genealogical Index and British Isles Vital Records Index to see if you can locate the date and place of the wedding. You may have to resort to obtaining a copy of the birth certificate of one of the children of the fresh family in order to discover the mother's former name. The birth certificate of one of the older children will reveal the full name of the missing partner if you do not know this.
- Some of the people described as servants, boarders, lodgers, visitors and apprentices might be kinsfolk or related to the head or spouse by marriage. It is always worth writing down their details, and following up their immediate family histories because you may not have to search long before you find a connection.
- The given ages were allegedly as of the last birthday before the census. They did not invariably increase or decrease by ten years and the birthplaces may vary from census to census, because it was the head, not each household member, who filled in the schedule.
- Common occupations were often abbreviated by the enumerators. An agricultural labourer was described as an 'ag lab', a framework knitter as 'fwk', and a handloom weaver as 'hlw'. If you find an occupation and do not understand what it involved have a look in *The Oxford English Dictionary*, or *A Dictionary of Old Trades, Titles and Occupations. Instructions to the Clerks Employed in Classifying the Occupations and Ages of the People* grouped together similar types of employment for government statistical purposes. Copies are

available in the Family Records Centre. 'Living on their own means' usually denoted a person deriving an income from rents or investments, whereas an annuitant was described as such. Anyone receiving poor relief was listed as a pauper. A pensioner is likely to have been a former Serviceman, so you might want to pursue his army or naval career in the National Archives.

- Up to 1861, it was the most recent or usual job that was set down. This can be misleading if a person was out of work at the time. When several occupations were carried out, the census recorded the one which earned the most during that season. From 1871, however, retired or unemployed people were described as such. After 1891, the returns should indicate whether a person was an employer, employee, or neither (including the self-employed).

- Between 1851 and 1881, the returns noted farm acreages and how many labourers, men and boys were employed by each farmer. Business employees and apprentices were totted up during this period too. However, wives and children, who assisted in family enterprises but did not receive wages, were discounted before 1891. Children were frequently termed as scholars, regardless of how many hours' weekly formal teaching they were getting compared with the time they spent at work. It was only in 1891 that occupations began to be recorded for children aged ten and over, who by then were legally allowed to leave school to take up paid employment.

Some workers slept under the same roof as their employers, and were listed as lodgers or as occupiers of a separate household. Other employees lived nearby, generally no more than a day's return walk (about 14 or so miles in all), before the introduction of cheap wheeled transport made longer distance commuting possible.

In the 1841 and 1851 returns, people sleeping in places not designated as dwelling houses, for instance in barns, sheds, tents or the open air, were merely counted rather than named. Because the 1841 census was taken in summer there must therefore have been many seasonal harvest workers whose personal details do not feature at all. In 1861, such temporary residents appeared in a separate 'list of persons not in households' at the end of the main schedules for each place, and from 1871 in whichever named road or street they slept on census night.

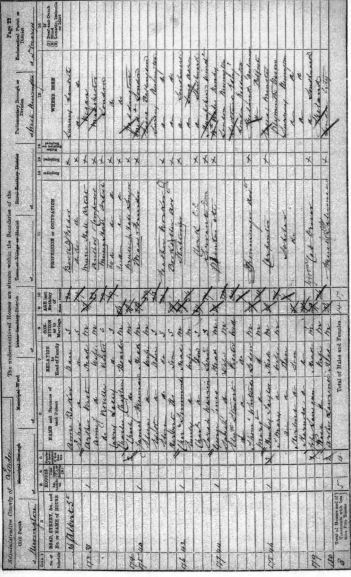

Figure 10 This page from the censor enumerator's book for Newington, Surrey, in 1891, shows two entries for Charlie Chaplin's father, Charles Chaplin, at 38 Albert Street (schedules number 173 and 174). He was recorded as boarding with Arthur West, but appears to have completed a schedule of his own for the two rooms he occupied there. Note the slight variation in the given information about his age, occupation and birthplace (reproduced by permission of The National Archives)

People in institutions, not in a dwelling

Special schedules were devoted to households exceeding 100 occupants. The returns were filed at the end of the relevant town, registration district or hundred (an administrative division of a county). The staff, their families and servants were listed first, and usually only the initials of inmates of gaols, houses of correction and lunatic asylums. The personal information was otherwise the same as for the main returns.

People at sea or on inland waterways

The commanding officers of Royal Naval and merchant vessels in harbour or putting into port on or within a prescribed period around census night handed in special schedules to the local customs officer. The indexed digital images are accessible at the listed census websites described earlier.

The first surviving Royal Navy ships' enumerations date from 1861, although there are a few, earlier, 1851 returns of British merchant shipping in port or at sea in the home trade. After 1861, they relate to British shipping in port and at sea throughout the world, but they are not fully comprehensive. The schedules listed all the crew and passengers by vessel, and furnished the name, rank, rating, profession or occupation of everyone on board, as well as his or her marital status, age and birthplace. There is a complete personal-name index on microfiche to the 1861 shipping returns.

These marine returns are worth searching for passengers on ships sailing to and from the Continent, trans-migrants changing ship for a larger ocean-going vessel, emigrants already on board in the port of departure on census night, and newly arrived immigrants. Trawl the local hotels and other establishments close to the harbour for details about intending or recently landed passengers, and for lodgers in and around the trans-Atlantic ports trying to earn enough to pay for their passage overseas.

The earliest known returns of fishing boats and trawlers putting in to port during April 1861 were filed with those of Royal Naval and merchant shipping. In 1891 and 1901 they included returns made by foreign fishing boats landing their catches at ports throughout the United Kingdom.

People on canals and inland navigable waterways were listed under the enumeration district or sub-district where they were moored on census night, using schedules similar to those for ships.

Scotland

Ten-yearly census enumerations were carried out in Scotland from 1801 onwards, on the same dates as above. Until 1851, the task was undertaken by local schoolteachers under the supervision of the county sheriff or his deputy. Each enumeration district was based on the parish, the larger ones being sub-divided. From 1861, the census was organized by the Registrar General for Scotland, using his district registrars and the local registration districts as the basis of the population count. You can find out to which registration district any parish belonged at **www.scotlandspeople.gov.uk**.

Indexes and copies

Indexed digital images of the census returns from 1841 until 1901, excluding 1881, are accessible at **www.scotlands people.gov.uk** but you will have to pay to view both the indexes and the images. Indexed transcriptions of the 1881 returns can be searched at this website too, and on CD-ROM. Indexed digital images and transcriptions of the 1841–71 and 1891 census returns are also available at **www.ancestry.co.uk**.

What the census returns will tell you

The contents of the census returns are identical to those for England, Wales, the Channel Islands and Isle of Man, except that in 1841 the birthplace column will indicate if a person was born in England 'E', Ireland 'I', or in Foreign Parts 'F'.

You may have to use wildcards and different spellings of people's names and place-names to get to the images you want. Married women, especially widows, were recorded either by their married or maiden names. Look out for misspelled and abbreviated addresses too.

Passengers and crews at sea

Indexed digital images of the returns of Royal Naval vessels after 1881, and of merchant shipping between 1861 and 1901 can be viewed at **www.scotlandspeople.gov.uk** as well. The content of the schedules is similar to that for vessels putting in to English and Welsh ports.

Ireland

The first full Irish census was undertaken on Monday 28 May 1821, and unlike for the rest of the United Kingdom the 1911 census returns are open to the public. Only a few returns between 1841 and 1891 survive, those between 1861 and 1891 being officially destroyed. The whereabouts of existing material, copies and indexes can be found in *Local Census Listings, 1522-1930: Holdings in the British Isles*, by J. Gibson and M. Medlycott, and in *Tracing Your Irish Ancestors*, by J. Grenham.

For census purposes, Ireland adopted the existing arrangement of counties, baronies, civil parishes, and townlands. In 1901 and 1911, however, the enumeration was based on counties, electoral divisions or wards and townlands, and by streets for towns and cities.

Microfilmed copies of the returns for 31 March 1901 and the original schedules for 2 April 1911 are held in the National Archives of Ireland; filmed copies of the 1901 returns are available for the six northern counties in the Public Record Office of Northern Ireland. You can also hire in microfilm copies of the 1901 returns to search in a family history centre.

Indexes and transcriptions

Indexed digital images of the 1911 census returns are to be made freely available via **www.nationalarchives.ie** and **www.collectionscanada.ca/ireland/index-e.html**, to be followed by those for 1901. Personal-name indexes to many of the returns from 1851 until 1911 are listed and accessible online via **www.census-online.com/links/Ireland**. The links are arranged alphabetically by county and then by place-name.

If you are using the microfilmed copies, the 1901 *Alphabetical Index to the Townlands and Towns, Parishes and Baronies of Ireland*, notes each electoral division name and number; there is a *Supplement* for 1911. Urban streets are each assigned numbers, and there are discrete street indexes for Belfast, Cork, Dublin, Dún Laoghaire (Kingstown) and Limerick in 1901. If you don't know in which street your family lived, try one of the contemporary city directories, which were generally arranged by name, address and occupation.

The National Archives of Ireland, and the Public Record Office of Northern Ireland, hold a number of transcriptions of individual 1841 and 1851 household schedules, which were produced as proof of age by applicants for old age pensions after 1 January 1909. The personal-name indexes to the transcriptions are arranged by county.

Census content

Originally, government enumerators filled in the schedules, but from 1841 this became the responsibility of the householders themselves. Separate schedules were completed for the military, Royal Irish Constabulary and Metropolitan Police stationed in barracks, and for workhouse inmates.

From the outset, the Irish household schedules gave the name, age, occupation, and relationship to the head of everyone sleeping there on census night.

People's religious denominations were specified in 1831, 1851, 1901 and 1911, which can be extremely helpful because you will have to rely on parish records for details of vital events before centralized civil registration began.

Each person's county of birth and marital status were recorded in 1901 and 1911. In 1911, the length of a woman's present marriage, her total live-born children and how many were still living were added, though this was not obligatory for widows. You can even find out the date of someone's marriage from the surviving 1841 and 1851 schedules.

Absent family members and the names of those who had died during the preceding ten years were listed in the returns for 1841 and 1851 too.

Literacy levels began to be recorded in 1841. In 1901 and 1911, an individual's ability to speak English or Irish, and the nature of any disability were set down.

Landholding acreages were given in 1821, 1831, 1901 and 1911 and, in the last two censuses, the number of rooms occupied by each household, the total number of any outhouses, and windows, and the type of roof material used for the dwelling.

Earlier censuses in the United Kingdom

Incidental parish lists of householders survive for the four previous censuses of Great Britain in 1801, on Monday 27 May 1811, in 1821 and on Monday 30 May 1831. Their known whereabouts are listed by county in *Local Census Listings,*

1522–1930: *Holdings in the British Isles.* Many of the English and Welsh lists are deposited in county record offices. Usually only the head of household was named, together with the number and ages of any other occupants, though for 1821 you might be lucky and find their names too, and in 1831 details of their occupations.

For Scotland, there are some parish lists for 1821 and 1831 among the Old Parochial Registers, in the General Register Office for Scotland, among the kirk session records, which are in the National Archives of Scotland, in Edinburgh, and in local archive collections.

In Ireland, a religious census was conducted on the orders of the Irish House of Lords in March and April 1766. This was done by county, barony and parish, and the returns were then arranged in alphabetical order by diocese and numbered. Each Church of Ireland rector was to furnish a list of names of heads of household, indicating their religious affiliations and those of other members of the household (totals only), together with the names of any Roman Catholic priests and friars who were living and active in their area. Some rectors gave full details about every household, others merely the number of families within a particular parish townland. The surviving returns are searchable at **www.ancestry.co.uk**. The original papers are held in the National Archives of Ireland, and transcriptions can be examined in the National Library of Ireland, in Trinity College, Dublin, in the Representative Church Body Library, in Dublin, and in the Public Record Office of Northern Ireland.

Census surveys overseas

Similar population counts have been undertaken at frequent or irregular intervals in almost all countries, some, for the first time only in the twentieth century. When civil registration began later than the census, and church records are unreliable or absent, such dated lists assume great genealogical significance as proof of a person's place of residence, occupation, approximate year and place of birth, and provide clues to when he or she emigrated, immigrated or died.

India

You can search the surname index to a census return of Europeans living in the Presidency of Bombay on the night of 30 March 1851, at **www.bl.uk/collections/asiapacificafrica.html**

The records themselves are in the Asia, Pacific and Africa Collections of the British Library.

United States of America

In the USA, the first decennial federal census was undertaken by assistant US marshals on Tuesday 2 August 1790, in each of the states then belonging to the Union (Connecticut, Delaware, Georgia, Kentucky, Maine, Maryland, Massachusetts, New Hampshire, New Jersey, North Carolina, Pennsylvania, Rhode Island, South Carolina, Tennessee, Vermont, and Virginia). However, the county returns for each state are incomplete, and nothing is known to exist for Virginia, although it has been possible to reconstruct some of the missing schedules from a state census taken around the same time. The other dates were

- Monday 4 August 1800
- Monday 6 August 1810
- Monday 7 August 1820
- Tuesday 1 June 1830
- Monday 1 June 1840
- Sunday 1 June 1850
- Friday 1 June 1860

- Wednesday 1 June 1870
- Tuesday 1 June 1880
- Monday 2 June 1890
- Friday 1 June 1900
- Friday 15 April 1910
- Tuesday 1 January 1920
- Tuesday 1 April 1930 (actually began on 2 April).
- Tuesday 1 October 1929 in Alaska

The date was often notional, as enumeration might be spread over several months or migrants might be recorded more than once, at different places.

Once the returns are over 72 years old, they are made available to the public, so at present you can examine them as far as 1930. Most of the 1890 returns were destroyed, and just over 6,000 schedules are known to have survived out of a total population of almost 63 million. The extant returns mainly concern the Western growth areas, and you can find out which these are at www.archives.gov.

Microfilm copies of all the federal returns up to 1930 can be inspected in the National Archives Building in Washington, DC, in its regional facilities (www.archives.gov/locations); surviving state copies in state archives; the third, county copy, in county archives or libraries, and in family history centres. Study *Your Guide to the Federal Census* by K. W. Hinkley, for details. The returns are arranged alphabetically by state or territory and then by county. Unfortunately, as political boundaries changed over time, you may need to consult *Map Guide for the US Federal Censuses, 1790–1920*, by W. Thorndale and W. Dollarhide, to be sure you are looking in the correct county. This book is invaluable, as it not only overlays later county boundaries but tells you which federal census returns survive or were lost. Online links to ten-yearly county census maps from 1850 up to 1910 are listed at **www.cyndislist.com**.

Indexes, digital images and transcriptions

The schedules for 1790 have been published. Where the returns for some places are lacking, householders' names have been imported from other contemporary sources.

Indexed digital images and transcriptions of all the census returns are available at **www.ancestry.com**. You can do 'Ranked' and 'Exact' searches, and simultaneous cross-searches of the British and Canadian (1851, 1901, 1906 and 1911) censuses too. Indexed digital images are accessible at **www.heritagequestonline.com** as well. Online access is free in the National Archives Building, in the Regional Archive branches of the National Archives and in the Library of Congress, in Washington, DC. You will need to obtain a special reader's identification badge or card to use these institutions. Indexed transcriptions of the 1880 census returns are freely searchable at **www.familysearch.org**.

If you are not following the online route, there are microfilmed personal-name indexes for each federal census up to 1850 to help you identify the correct returns. The indexes are arranged by state, then by county, and are widely distributed in the National Archives facilities, state archives, public and research libraries. In order to use them you must know your ancestor's full name, or that of the head of household and the state or county where he or she lived. The indexes give the name, age and birthplace (county) of each listed person. However, the index cards relating to the 1880 state schedules encompass only those households containing children aged ten or less, though families of a different surname in the same household were indexed too. The index cards for 1880, 1900 and 1920 employed the Soundex (phonetic) system. This system was also used to index the returns for 21 (mostly southern) states in 1910 and ten of the southern states in 1930. The Soundex index works like this: the surnames are listed alphabetically, starting with the first letter, followed by numbers representing the next three consonants, and ignoring any vowels. Under each surname, the forenames are then listed in alphabetical order, alongside the relevant census page and line numbers. Every householder's index card includes details about other family members who were enumerated with him or her in the census. Miracode index cards were adopted by some states in 1910, onto which the household schedule numbers rather than page and line references were written as a link to the original census entries.

Tips

- All the indexes are subject to omissions and errors, so it is worth checking every available index for a given census year to pick up any missing or incorrect references.

- Search for all likely surname variants and other possible permutations, especially when the Soundex system was applied, and drop prefixes such as 'Mac', 'O', 'De' and 'Von'. Try wild card * and single letter ? queries, or key in the forename and likely age or some other tag if the surname eludes you.

- You may be able to locate the city and town addresses of people in census years from directories of the period. The Library of Congress, and many public libraries and historical societies have extensive runs.

What the censuses contain

The households were arranged by county, and sometimes by town or district, and from 1880, street and house numbers or names were added, but the schedules only began to be individually numbered in 1930. Until 1840 the census schedules merely recorded the names of heads of household and the number, age-ranges and gender of free household members and the number of any slaves. Starting in 1820, other questions began to be asked, for instance about how many people in the household were engaged in agriculture, commerce or manufacturing, and in 1820 and 1830, how many members were not naturalized as American citizens. From 1840 the schedules also specified who was deaf, dumb or blind, insane or idiotic; in 1840, too, the schedules recorded the number and ages of any Revolutionary War or military pensioners in the household.

In 1850, the returns became far more expansive, as every free person was named, together with his or her age at last birthday and the county or country or birth, gender and colour (or race from 1920). The profession, occupation or trade of all males over 15 was given in 1850 and of all employed people from 1860, in addition to all that had been included before. Paupers and convicts now began to be identified as well. In 1900, everyone's month and year of birth were recorded although precise birthplaces were never given, making it difficult to trace the origins of migrants and immigrants.

Special uses of the American census returns

The early returns up to 1840 help you to distinguish between families of the same name, and set them in a specific locality. Although only the names of heads of household were recorded, you can work out the changing composition of each family and discriminate between different families headed by the same-named person using the given age-bands for the other hosuehold members. Unrelated visitors might eventually have married into the family, so they should not be ignored. The incidence of multiple marriages and of half- and step-brothers and -sisters was common too.

Examine the 1860 census returns, on the eve of the Civil War, and then look in the returns for 1870, and compare the values of someone's realty and personalty at each date.

With the opening of the Transcontinental Railway in 1869, coast-to-coast travel became possible, so people were able to travel further and faster if they could afford it. By studying a sequence of the returns, you should be able to plot migration routes from the given counties or states of birth.

When someone's name disappears, search for a local death and any probate records. The accompanying mortality schedules, recording deaths within the previous 12 months of the 1850, 1860, 1870, and 1880 censuses, will reduce the period to within nine years.

The stated lengths of residency in the United States, years of immigration and of naturalization are key links to ships' passenger lists, other immigration records and naturalization papers containing more personal background information.

table 1 what the American census returns can tell you

Census year	1850	1860	1870	1880	1890	1900	1910	1920	1930
Relationship to head of household				Yes	Yes	Yes	Yes	Yes	Yes
Marital status				Yes	Yes	Yes	Yes	Yes	Yes
Married within the previous year		Yes	Yes	Yes	Yes				
Age at first marriage									Yes
Length of current marriage					Yes	Yes	Yes		
Number of a mother's children and how many still alive					Yes	Yes	Yes		
Natal month if born within the previous year			Yes	Yes					
If attending school within the previous year	Yes		Yes	Yes		Yes	Yes (since 1 September 1909)	Yes	At school or college since 1 September 1929

(contd.)

Census year	1850	1860	1870	1880	1890	1900	1910	1920	1930
Value of real/personal estate	Real estate only	Yes	Yes						
Head of household or family member as property owner or tenant and if it was mortgaged. If the head was a farmer, if the property was owned, or rented or mortgaged.					Yes. Included Post Office address of the owner	Yes.	Yes.	Yes.	Yes. Value if owned or monthly rent. If lived on a farm.
Number of months unemployed within the previous year				Yes	Yes	Yes	Yes	Yes	If at work the previous day or the last regular working day
Whether an employer, employee or self-employed							Yes		

(contd.)

Census year	1850	1860	1870	1880	1890	1900	1910	1920	1930
Currently ill or disabled				Yes	Yes		Yes		
Soldier, sailor or marine during the Civil War, and whether Union or Confederate					Yes. 'UA' or 'UN'= Union Army/Navy 'CA' or 'CN' =Confederate		Yes		Yes, but broadened to all Wars (1861, 1898, 1899, 1900, 1914–18) and Expeditions (1916–17). 'CW'=Civil War Veterans
Widow of a Veteran					Yes				
Person's parents' birthplaces			If foreign-born	State or country of birth	State or country of birth	State or country of birth	State or country of birth	State or country of birth	State or country of birth

(contd.)

Census year	1850	1860	1870	1880	1890	1900	1910	1920	1930
Year of immigration						Yes, and citizenship status of foreign-born people over 21	Yes, and citizenship status	Year of immigration	Year of immigration
Number of years resident in the U.S.					Yes	Yes			
Already naturalized or applying for naturalization			If over 21, naturalized and qualified to vote		Yes	If naturalized ('Na') applying to be naturalized ('Al')/ or first papers lodged ('Pa')	If naturalized ('Na') applying to be naturalized ('Al')/ or first papers lodged ('Pa')	Yes. Year naturalized applying to be naturalized ('Al')/ or first papers lodged	If natralized ('Na'/ applying ('Al')/ or first papers lodged ('Pa')
Ability to speak English					Yes	Yes	Yes	Yes	Yes
Language spoken/mother tongue					Language spoken	Language spoken	Language spoken/ mother tongue of self and parents	Mother tongue if foreign-born	Mother tongue if foreign-born

Slaves

Until 1840, only the number of slaves in a household was listed, but in 1850 and 1860, a supplementary slave census was carried out. From these you can find out the names of slave owners, along with the number of their slaves of each sex, giving their ages, and whether black or mulatto. Free blacks began to be recorded in the 1850 and 1860 census, and after the emancipation of slaves in 1865, all African Americans were enumerated.

War veterans

Separate veterans' census schedules, giving the names and ages of Revolutionary War pensioners (including women) who were still alive in 1840, were written up on the back of the federal returns and under the name of the householder with whom they lived. A complete list of their names and ages was published in 1841, as *A Census of Pensioners for Revolutionary or Military Services*. This is widely available on microfilm. As many elderly veterans lived with married daughters or other kinsfolk of different surnames, these schedules are extremely useful. You should be able to trace their places of burial nearby and any surviving military and probate records.

Another, incomplete, series of microfilmed veterans' schedules dates from 1890, and is held in the National Archives Building. However, the schedules relate only to residents of states running alphabetically from Louisiana to Wyoming, about half of Kentucky, and of Washington, DC. The schedules, which were arranged by state or territory, and then by county or sub-division, concentrated mainly on Union veterans of the Army, Navy or Marine Corps or their widows. Each person's current postal address, former rank, company, regiment or ship, dates of enlistment and of discharge, and length of service were recorded, with a brief description of any medical disabilities. The names of deceased veterans were written alongside those of their widows. You can match up the numbered schedules with the (few) surviving federal census returns for that year, in which such people might be enumerated as living with married daughters or other relatives. Use the schedules to look for their service and pension details as well as their places of burial and any probate records.

Other American census surveys

The census surveys undertaken on Monday 1 June 1885 in some of the frontier states and territories (Colorado, New Mexico (including Arizona), Nebraska, Florida, North and South Dakota) partially compensate for the loss of the 1890 returns. You can search the indexed schedules at **www.ancestry.com**, and on microfilm in the National Archives Building or in any family history centre. The schedules set out by county, and locality, each person's name and relationship to the head of household, his or her gender and race, age, date and place of birth (state, territory or country), marital status, occupation, literacy level, any sickness or disability, and his or her parents' birthplaces. The accompanying agricultural and products of industry schedules tell you more about the nature and scope of people's farming and working practices.

Commencing in 1849–50, mortality schedules were compiled of deaths in the 12 months preceding the date of each federal census up to 1880, and prior to 1885. They are arranged by state, territory and county, and record each deceased's person's name, age, gender, month of death, his or her occupation, the cause of death and the duration of the final illness. The 1859/60 and later schedules specify his or her birthplace and marital status, and from 1869/70 onwards, his or her colour or race, and the birthplaces of both parents by state, territory or country. The schedules for 1879/1880 tell you where the fatal disease had been contracted, and how long the person had been resident in the area. Similar mortality schedules were filed alphabetically by county for the state census of 1885. The original schedules are preserved in state archives, the National Archives Building, and the library of the National Society of Daughters of the American Revolution, in Washington, DC, but indexes and printed copies are available in many libraries. The National Archives Building probably holds the best collection of microfilm copies, and you can also hire them to study in a family history centre.

The mortality schedules are a key genealogical resource, because they pre-date civil registration and are virtually a countrywide register of deaths. They make up for any shortfall or under-registration of burials by local churches, especially in remote areas and along the overland trails, and may tell you what happened to family members who were missing from the census itself.

Earlier censuses

Other colonial, state and local censuses were undertaken periodically from 1623 to 1918, usually as a pretext for taxation, urban planning or for military purposes, or to determine the need for more schools and teachers or for grain storage. They have been listed, with their whereabouts, in *The Source: A Guidebook of American Genealogy*, edited by L. D. Szucs and S. H. Luebking, *The Red Book: American State, County and Town Sources*, edited by A. Eichholz, and in *State Census Records*, edited by A. S. Lainhart. A number have been published.

General advice on tackling the census

Use the blank census forms at **www.familysearch.org** and **www.ancestry.co.uk** if you don't want to print or download the digital images or transcriptions.

The digital images of census pages are accessed in response to a specific personal-name, place-name or other index term. If you enter the wrong keywords or the spelling does not exactly match up with what was in the actual census schedule, the result is likely to be negative. Always try every permutation, and don't key in too much information, particularly about addresses. If someone's English was poor, the enumerator may have made an inspired guess when helping to complete a schedule. If you look at the image of an expected address, you may find that the handwriting was either too illegible or unclear to decipher people's names for inclusion in the index. Try the zoom-in facility to see what you can make of it yourself.

If you fail to find someone at an address, discover who was there and write down their full details in case they later turn out to be related to you. Your ancestor might actually have been recorded there too, but not in the way you imagined.

If you have no idea where your family was around a census year, the given address on a birth, marriage or death certificate of another member of the family might help to pinpoint their whereabouts. However, the online indexes should minimize the chances of this happening.

In Wales, people's names may have been recorded differently in a sequence of census returns. Try reverse-name index searches. The patronymic naming system, still prevalent in some remoter rural communities in the nineteenth century, particularly in the

West, adds to the complication. As populations were relatively small and scattered around the countryside, such individuals should be readily identifiable from their named farmsteads and localities, ages and birthplaces, and from the names of the other people in the same household.

There are numerous folk whose names do not seem to feature at all in the census. Where were they? Were the household schedules not filled in, lost or incorrectly copied up? Any empty houses should be identified in the returns. Certain households might have been overlooked, particularly in densely populated urban neighbourhoods and 'rookeries'. Another possibility is that a bogus name was assumed to conceal a person's true identity. Immigrants often changed their names, so a surname which initially seems British may actually be a translation or some other version of a European name. Some census returns are missing altogether, those for 1861 being notoriously incomplete.

By relying solely on a street- or personal-name index to take you straight to the household entry of your family, you risk overlooking their neighbours, so inspect the schedules of adjacent and nearby households.

The reliability and accuracy of given information depended on the honesty and knowledge of the heads of household. For instance, an illegitimate child might be euphemistically described as a 'nephew' or 'niece'. The census will not tell you how long a lodger or boarder had been in a particular household. A 'visitor' usually indicates someone staying overnight or slightly longer.

Large gaps between children's ages may indicate that some of them had already left home, were temporarily absent or had died.

The ages and birthplaces of aunts and uncles may point to the place of origin of a direct ancestor who was already dead by the time of the census, or whose whereabouts are unknown. Inspect the returns for the same year of the given birthplaces for other relatives, and the returns of those places for the years closest to the birth years to see which family members were there.

When a person was enumerated a long way from his or her place of provenance, the nearest town might be given as the birthplace, because the head of household or the enumerator could not spell an unfamiliar or strange sounding name. Place-names might be written down phonetically, reflecting the local dialect. Try pronouncing the name. If the dialect spelling defeats you altogether consult a gazetteer. The capital letter should at least be recognizable.

When you are searching the indexed digital images of the returns at **www.ancestry.co.uk** or **www.ancestry.com**, try a total index search of all the available returns for the United Kingdom and the United States, as this may pick up family emigrants, and people who returned home. If you include the available indexed digital images of the Canadian census returns of 1851, 1901, 1906 and 1911, at **www.ancestry.ca,** you may find cross-border migrants.

08

other ways of finding your ancestors' whereabouts

In this chapter you will learn:
- what name lists and directories are available
- how to use maps and associated material effectively
- what other local records can help you.

There are plenty of other sources which can help you fix where people were at specific dates, and here are some of the more useful ones.

Registers of voters

Registers of voters in England and Wales have been published since the late seventeenth century. Starting in about 1696, poll books were printed after each parliamentary election, and listed the names, addresses and qualifying properties of entitled forty-shilling freeholders, together with the names of the candidates for whom they had voted. However, in boroughs, there was no fixed qualification, though it was usually linked to ownership of land by men over the age of 21, or to property assessed at £10 a year. For details of the dates and whereabouts of copies of the poll books, consult **www.familia.org.uk** for library collections in the UK and Ireland, and *Poll Books and Lists, 1696-1872: A Directory of Holdings in Great Britain*, by J. Gibson and C. Rogers.

In 1832, the qualification was widened to include certain copyhold and leasehold property, which meant that many tenant farmers and shopkeepers became enfranchised. Later statutes, in 1867 and 1884, extended the right to vote even further, until virtually all men over 21 were included, as were naturalized aliens after 1870. The ballot became secret in 1872, the year in which the last poll book was published.

Electoral registers have been printed annually since 1832, except for 1916, 1917, and between 1940 and 1944. The borough parliamentary and local government electoral registers were combined in 1878 and in 1885 for the shires.

The earliest registers are obviously selective, and not until 1918 were women over 30 able to cast a parliamentary vote, their age limit being reduced to 21 in 1928. However, the names of female occupiers qualifed to vote in local elections were listed after 1869. In 1918 the property qualification was abolished, and all that was required was six months' residence or occupation of business premises in the electoral district with an annual value of £10. Since 1951, people reaching the minimum voting age during the forthcoming year have been listed too, and starting in 1971, the registers have included their actual birth dates, after the age threshold was lowered to 18 under the Representation of the People Act 1969.

The most complete series of electoral registers for the United Kingdom is held in the British Library, in London, many of which are on microfilm. They are listed in *Parliamentary Constituencies and their Registers since 1832*, by R. H. A. Cheffins. The survival rate of the earlier editions is patchy, but there are complete sets for the whole of the British Isles for 1937 and 1938, and from 1947 onwards. Copies of electoral lists of Irish voters are also held in the National Archives of Ireland. Some copies of older electoral registers can be searched locally in record offices and libraries. For library holdings in the UK and Ireland, visit **www.familia.org.uk**, and look in *Electoral Registers since 1832; and Burgess Rolls*, by J. Gibson and C. Rogers, for a county by county list of their other whereabouts.

The currency of the registers may span three years. The qualifying date for inclusion now lies in October, although the register is not published before December, or as late as the following February in past times, and is valid for a full year, when it is replaced by the next edition. During this time listed voters might die or move away, and newcomers take their place.

To 1915, the electoral registers were arranged by parliamentary constituency, ward, polling district, township, and type of voting qualification. Constituency boundaries changed from time to time, so the electoral division covering a specific address might vary. All such alterations up to 1971 are shown, with the use of maps, in *Boundaries of Parliamentary Constituencies, 1885–1972*, by F. W. S. Craig. The names of voters were listed alphabetically with their actual and qualifying addresses and electoral numbers. After 1918, the registers were organized alphabetically by street or road name under each township, and then alphabetically by voter's surname, making them more difficult to use. However, you can see from the entries how many of your family were living together and qualified to vote, or were in the same neighbourhood at any one time, though relationships were never given.

After 1918, men aged 19 or 20 and serving in the Armed Forces, were separately listed as 'absent voters' in their home parliamentary constituencies. The names of graduates were set out under their respective universities, until university representation was abolished in 1948.

Directories of names

A useful directory of addresses around a census year is the *Return of Owners of Land of One Acre and Upwards*, published in 1875 for England and Wales, in 1874 for Scotland, and in 1876 for Ireland. Copies can be found in many libraries. The county listings set out alphabetically each landowner's name, the address of the property, its size and nature, and its gross estimated annual rental. The returns are useful because they also reveal the whereabouts of absentee owners.

Trade and commercial directories were published as an outlet for those who wished to circulate and advertise their services and contact details, and to help strangers find their whereabouts.

Directories began to emerge in the late seventeenth century, and at first were mainly confined to naming public officers, rich private residents and merchants. Within the next 150 years almost every county, city and large town had been covered. Among the most prominent was the annual *Post Office London Directory*, which dates from 1800. The first telephone directory was issued in 1880, and updated annually from the mid-twentieth century. A full set of these is held on microfilm in the BT Group Archives, in London, where there is a public search room. The UK phone books between 1880 and 1984 are gradually being uploaded at **www.ancestry.co.uk**.

You can discover the background history, function, dates of publication and scope of known directories from *Guide to National and Provincial Directories of England and Wales, excluding London, published before 1856*, by J. E. Norton, *British Directories: A Bibliography and Guide to Directories published in England and Wales (1850–1950) and Scotland (1773–1950)*, by G. Shaw and A. Tipper, and *The Directories of London, 1677–1977*, by P. J. Atkins.

Good runs of London and provincial directories are held in the Guildhall Library, in London, and in the library of the Society of Genealogists. Local record offices and libraries generally have available at least some old directories for their own areas. Visit **www.familia.org.uk** for information about library copies. Scottish directories were compiled less often, but may be inspected in the National Archives of Scotland, and in regional archives. Those for Ireland are in the National Archives of Ireland, and in the National Library of Ireland, the first city directory (for Dublin) dating from 1751, and the earliest provincial directory from 1769, though they each became more common from the 1820s. For information about deposited Irish directories, search the National Library of Ireland's books and periodicals catalogue at **www.nli.ie**.

At least one digital copy of a directory for each English and Welsh county and city between 1750 and 1849, and for every decade between 1850 and 1920 is being made available at **www.historicaldirectories.org**. Use the map and click on the relevant county to find out what has been uploaded so far. Digital copies of a number of UK directories are searchable at **www.ancestry.co.uk**, and between 1852 and 1905 at **www.thegenealogist.co.uk**. Facsimiles of many directories are available on CD-ROM, microfiche or in book form. Visit **www.british-genealogy.com** for a list of what is available for each county.

How the directories were compiled

The publishers generally relied on local agents to collect the requisite information.

The range and quality of the directories were dependent on the purpose of the compiler, the integrity of his agents and the perceived needs of their targeted readership. Each new edition was invariably at least six months or a year out of date, and a number were often little more than reprints. Although rival publishers regularly lifted from each other's work, you will often find entries about different people in rural directories covering the same districts. Some of the stolen names and addresses were taken from an earlier edition, so their reliability may be questionable.

Provincial directories

The county directories were usually arranged alphabetically by administrative divisions (called hundreds, wapentakes, rapes or sokes), and then alphabetically by their constituent parishes, towns, villages and hamlets. Some directories concentrated on a single city and its hinterland, whilst others combined several contiguous counties.

After a brief introduction, came a list of the names, ranks and professions of private householders, with their addresses. The names and addresses of craftsmen, tradesmen, shopkeepers, farmers, hoteliers, lodging-house keepers, and publicans were usually listed alphabetically.

As might be expected, the directories of larger towns and cities were much more informative. The first to be published, for the City of London in 1677, was succeeded by regular editions from 1734. The earliest provincial town to be covered was Birmingham, in 1763. These directories often encompassed the surrounding countryside, so check the table of contents at the front of each book for a list of places which were included.

London directories

The *Post Office London Directory* was much bigger, especially from the middle of the nineteenth century. By then, it was divided up into sections:

- the 'commercial directory' listed alphabetically the names, addresses of people in the professions, or engaged in a trade or craft;
- the 'court directory' set out both the town and country seats of private residents;
- the 'official directory' included the names of people in government or legal offices;
- the 'street directory' arranged the principal London streets and roads in alphabetical order, with the names and occupations of householders by house number and showed road intersections;
- the 'trade and professional directory' was alphabetically classified, and cross-referenced to related occupations. Where dual occupations were carried on by the same person, there was usually one, asterisked, entry, with an explanatory note;
- the 'law directory' contained the names and official addresses of judges and legal staff in London and the provinces, including the police, barristers, solicitors and attorneys, proctors, notaries public, patent agents, district registrars of births, marriages and deaths, sheriffs and their officers, shorthand writers, law booksellers and stationers;
- the 'parliamentary directory' listed peers and members of the House of Commons, their country and town residences, constituencies and clubs, with a corresponding index of constituencies;
- the 'city, clerical and parochial directory' recorded the names of civic officials, the addresses of parish churches and other denominational places of worship, the names of officiating ministers and parish clerks, the titles of Poor Law Unions and the names of their officers;

- the 'banking directory' outlined the registered names and offices of banks in London and throughout the United Kingdom.

A map, on the scale of four inches to the mile, was generally attached for use with the street directory, to help the reader find his or her way around. There was also a section for 'too late entries' consisting of details from forms returned after the fixed deadline.

Similar directories were produced for the cities of Edinburgh and Dublin.

United States of America directories

Electoral registers of American citizens and naturalized aliens who registered themselves to vote are probably more difficult to find. However, local and city directories can make up for any defects in or lack of census returns. If you are lucky, they will not only list all adults names and addresses, but also their ages, places of employment and lengths of stay in the state, county, electoral ward or district. The city directories frequently contained a street map, and when street names were altered, these were updated in the following year's edition.

County and regional business directories date from about 1800 onwards, but they were published less often than their city counterparts. Generally, the lists of residents will give their names, lot and range numbers, their occupations, land acreages and the address of the nearest post office. A widow's late husband's name might be mentioned too, and the directories for smaller communities might even include dates of local births, marriages and deaths, so they are extremely useful not only for locating people in time and place, but are an invaluable substitute when there were no records of civil registration.

Copies of local directories are held in state, county or city archives, libraries and museums. Look in *Bibliography of American Directories Through 1860*, by D. N. Spears, for details of early editions. A number have been uploaded into **www.ancestry.com**, and if you visit **www.cyndislist.com** this will provide you with other website links for specific localities, and **www.uscitydirectories.com** will tell you the whereabouts of printed, filmed and online city editions. Click on the map and select the state in which you are interested. Study *Telephone and City Directories in the Library of Congress, A Finding Guide*, by B. B. Walsh for details of its holdings. The Library of the

American Antiquarian Society, in Worcester, Massachusetts, has an excellent set of directories, which is fully catalogued at **www.americanantiquarian.org/directories.htm**, but the most comprehensive runs belong to the Library of Congress and in the microfilmed collection in the Family History Library. Visit the library catalogue at **www.familysearch.org** for details of copies you can hire in to search in a family history centre.

What you can learn from directories

Directories provide fascinating insight into the changing social and commercial structure and fluctuating size of communities over time. You can trace an individual's continuity of residence, change of fortune, occupation, approximate year of death, a family's arrival or migration elsewhere and the wider distribution of your surname. However, directories can be frustrating to search as they listed only the names and addresses or business premises of householders, and not every one at that. Often it is an agricultural labourer, a domestic servant, seasonal worker or lodger you want to find, and these are the very people who were excluded. Some addresses were omitted altogether, and people did not always live where they worked. When street names or numbering were altered, this can also present difficulties. Most directories contained a throwaway map, and that is exactly what happened: they were generally thrown away.

Professional and trade directories

You can find the foundation dates and contact details of the various professional bodies and trade organizations from the current editions of *Trade Associations and Professional Bodies of the United Kingdom and Eire,* and *Directory of British Associations and Associations in Ireland.*

Good collections of professional directories are held by the Guildhall Library, and by the Society of Genealogists. Some professional and trade directories are searchable at **www.find mypast.com/HomeServlet**.

Each professional or trade organization fixed the terms and conditions of qualification for membership and fellowship and established a set code of conduct. The preface will normally give an outline of the basis of membership. The directory entries were usually arranged alphabetically and summarized each member's higher academic and professional training, a short career history and his or her current address. When someone's name disappears, look at the end of the volume for a list of deceased members, resignations and retirements. Parentage was not usually included in the directories, nor the date of birth, but these might be obtained from the records of the professional organization, the place of higher education or formal training.

You can find details about the various professional and trade bodies and their publications in America from *The Directory of Directories*, by J. M. Ethridge and C. A. Marlow.

Maps

The electoral registers and directories of names can be used in conjunction with contemporary maps and town plans to pinpoint exactly where your ancestors lived. There are three main types of UK maps of special genealogical interest: Ordnance Survey maps, Tithe maps and apportionments, and Valuation Office record sheets.

Ordnance Survey maps and town plans

A military map of the Highlands of Scotland was compiled between 1747 and 1755, and it was soon realized that similar maps, with an accurate triangulation, were required for the rest of Britain, which could be published for general use. In 1801, the Ordnance Survey, set up in 1791, began to issue a series of official maps for England and Wales based on a standard scale of one inch to the mile. The last, in 1873, was of the Isle of Man, when a thorough revision was commenced. Scotland was first mapped by the Survey in 1847, on a scale of six inches to the mile.

Facsimiles of the first edition have been published commercially, and copies of the original maps may be studied in county record offices and local studies libraries, as well as in the special map collections in the National Archives, the National Library of Scotland, in Edinburgh (**www.nls.uk/collections/maps/subject info/ord_survey.html**), the British Library, and in the Bodleian Library (**www.bodley.ox.ac.uk/guides/maps**).

The maps are immensely useful in showing place-names and the distances between towns, villages and hamlets. They mark out contours, trigonometric points, topographical features, man-made landmarks, canal, road and railway networks, but they are not sufficiently detailed to enable you to pick out individual field-names and boundaries.

For these, you will need to use a larger scale map. In 1840 and 1853, new Ordnance Survey maps and town plans began to be produced, using scales of six inches and 25 inches to the mile respectively. You can search copies for some census years both in the Family Records Centre and in the National Archives.

In Ireland, a similar Ordnance Survey county mapping project was commenced in 1824 and completed by 1842, and a revision began in 1846. The scale was of six inches to the mile, but a later series went up to 25 inches to the mile. You can examine copies of the maps in the National Archives of Ireland and in the Public Record Office of Northern Ireland.

Tithe maps and apportionments

From early times, at each annual harvest, parishioners in England and Wales contributed a tenth (tithe) to the tithe owner of what had been grown or nourished on their land or was a product of their labour during the year. The tithe owner was usually the parish priest, but it might by a layman (or 'impropriator'), or shared between several people or institutions. From the sixteenth century onwards, when enclosure of common land took place at the behest of the lord of the manor, or by a consensus of the chief landowners, the tithe was often commuted at the same time to a money payment. After 1750, enclosures were more frequently effected by private acts of parliament, and after 1801, by public general acts. You can find a list of these in *A Domesday of English Enclosure Acts and Awards*, by W. E. Tate, and in *A Guide to Parliamentary Enclosures in Wales*, by J. Chapman. The tithe was converted to an annual rent charge by the remaining 11,800 or so parishes after the Tithe Commutation Act of 1836.

Between 1836 and 1852, specially appointed Tithe Commissioners and their assistants travelled to every relevant parish, hamlet and township to confirm voluntary agreements between local landowners about commutation, or to draft and impose a compulsory award. This was the first large-scale survey of landownership and occupancy to be undertaken in Great Britain. A complete list of places can be found in *The Tithe Maps of England and Wales, A cartographic analysis and county-by-county catalogue*, by R. J. P. Kain and R. R. Oliver. The

Commissioners drew up maps on which were set out the boundaries of each piece of private property. The resulting rent charge assessments were based on the size of the property and a seven-year average of the price of wheat, barley and oats. The occupiers were the tithe payers, but the landowners were ultimately responsible if the occupiers demurred. The 'first class map', so-called because it was sealed and signed by the Commissioners, and the accompanying apportionment schedules, were lodged with the Tithe Office. More than 1,900 of these can now be inspected with the rest of the Tithe Office maps in the National Archives. A copy of the working record sheet was passed to the bishop's diocesan registrar in case of any dispute about payment and a third copy was placed in the parish church. These last two copies are now usually available in county record offices. Any later revisions or revaluations were appended to the original maps and schedules. A complete set of Welsh tithe maps and apportionments is in the National Library of Wales.

The dated maps were not all drawn to the same scale, but most were of about 25 inches to the mile, though they were not always accurate.

If you do not know exactly where your ancestors lived, it is best to look first at the apportionment schedules. These set out the date of the agreement or award, and then listed alphabetically, under headings, the names of the landowners, their chief tenants and plot numbers, the title or description of each premises, its state of cultivation, size in acres, roods and poles, and the annual rent charge. You can then match this up with the given plot number on the map. The entries were annotated with references to any subsequent annexed amendments of adjusted apportionments, for instance when land was taken to construct railway lines and embankments or to make way for suburban expansion.

The two documents show how a person's property was concentrated in one part of a parish or scattered about, whether it lay on the margins of the community or close to its heart. You can learn if your ancestor was an owner/occupier or the name of his or her landlord. The maps reveal the proximity of the plots to highways, footpaths and water, and adjacent tenants. You can discover what the land was used for, and how much was due from it each year.

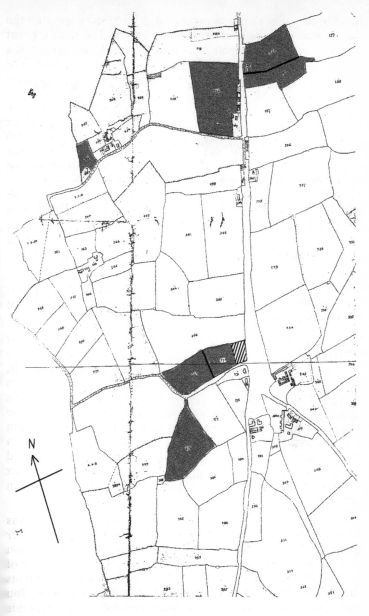

figure 11 tithe map of Great Finborough, Suffolk, in 1841
Meshech Chaplin farmed here until his death in 1849, aged 61 (reproduced by permission of Suffolk Record Office)

properties occupied by Meshech Chaplin

 Meshech Chaplin's house

In 1936, the rent charge was converted into a 60-year annuity, which was paid by the landowner, and further maps were commissioned. These too are in the National Archives. The annuity was abolished in 1977.

Because the surveys were undertaken close to the census years of 1841 or 1851, the maps can theoretically tell you exactly where your antecedents lived. Unfortunately, not every householder's name appeared in the apportionments, particularly if he or she was a sub-tenant or rented the property with several others.

The tithe material can be used in association with surviving manorial records. Their known dates and whereabouts can be elicited from the Manorial Documents Register, in the National Archives. Some of the catalogues to these are available at **www.nationalarchives.gov.uk/mdr**.

The manorial system dates back to at least the early Middle Ages, and continued until 1925, though some residual rights remain today. The records were written in Latin until 1733, except between 1653 and 1660 when English was used. Read *Using Manorial Records*, by M. Ellis, and *Welsh Manors and their Records*, by H. Watt, for more background information.

Scotland

The tithe survey between 1836 and 1852 did not apply to Scotland, where teinds (like the English and Welsh tithe) continued to be collected in kind or money from the proprietors of heritable property until it was stopped in 1925. Records of teinds may be found in the National Archives of Scotland, among family and estate papers, in the documentation concerning the settlement of disputes in the Court of Teinds, in Edinburgh, and in the Teind Commissioners' notes of adjusted payments.

Ireland

As in England and Wales, an annual tithe was taken in kind by parish priests of the Church of Ireland or by lay proprietors until the Tithe Composition Act of 1823. The Tithe Applotment Books, dating from about 1823 until 1837, covered every barony, civil parish and its townlands, and recorded the commutation of the tithe to a monetary payment, which was based on the average price of wheat and oats over the seven years preceding 1823. However, the rent charge proved to be virtually uncollectible, so in 1838 it was effectively absorbed into the landlords' rents. Upon its disestablishment on 1 January 1871, the Church of Ireland's right to collect the rent charge was lost and it then became payable to the Commissioners of Church Temporalities up to 1881, and thereafter to the Irish Land Commission.

The original books are in the National Archives of Ireland, although those for the six northern counties are in the Public Record Office of Northern Ireland, of which microfilm copies of available in the National Archives of Ireland. Microfilm copies and a county-by-county index to the incidence of each surname within each barony are also available in the National Library of Ireland. The indexed Applotment Books are searchable on CD-ROM and microfilm copies hired in to a family history centre.

The names of the occupiers (tenants) were listed, rather than the actual householders in each townland, and in many cases the names of their immediate landlords, who were usually lessees rather than freeholders. If your forebear was an agricultural labourer or weaver, he or she is unlikely to be mentioned. As they long predate the surviving Irish census returns, the onset of central registration of births, marriages and deaths, and in some instances parish registers of baptism, marriage and burial, the Tithe Applotment Books can help you to fix people in time and place, and provide a clue as to surname clusters and distributions in the early part of the nineteenth century. However, some parishes went unrecorded because the land was too poor, or were exempted because they were owned outright by the Church.

The valuers used local or common place-names which didn't always coincide with those in the Ordnance Survey maps. In 1830, therefore, a series of statutes tried to standardize the names and boundaries of townlands and parishes. Many were divided up, merged, renamed or altered, so may actually appear in the books, but under a different identity. Look in *A New Genealogical Atlas of Ireland*, by B. Mitchell, for civil parish boundaries.

Valuation Office records

A general land valuation of England and Wales was also undertaken between 1910 and 1915. This was in readiness for a proposed (abortive) Increment Value Duty which was to be collected whenever the ownership of private property changed.

The country was divided up into 118 valuation districts, then into income tax divisions and civil administrative parishes. The record sheets of the income tax districts, and the companion sets of field books, are in the National Archives, though there are some gaps. The working record sheets are in county record offices, and for Wales, in the National Library of Wales. A set of indexes and maps in the National Archives will help you to identify the number of the correct sheet.

The scale of the sheets, which were actually Ordnance Survey maps dating from 1880 to 1915, was determined by population density, but was generally on a scale of six inches to the mile. Each hereditament (premises) was demarcated, shaded in and allocated a unique number in red ink, except for exempt Crown property and any land owned by statutory and public utility companies such as for railways and canals.

The complementary civil parish field books were arranged sequentially by hereditament number, each of which was cross-referenced to its place on the appropriate numbered sheet. The numbers of any related properties were cited too. There is a street index to the London books, but otherwise you will need to find the appropriate sheet first, look for the hereditament number and link this to the corresponding entry in the field book.

The valuation officers used the parish rate books to extract the names and addresses of owners and occupiers, the size and rateable value of each property, and to note any unrated sites. The officers recorded in the field books the type of tenure (freehold, leasehold, yearly tenancy), annual rental, and any other annual financial liabilities attaching to each property. If a property had been bought less than 20 years before 30 April 1909 the purchase price was included, otherwise the calculation of duty was to be based on the difference between the property's assessable site value in 1909 and when the owner died, it was sold, leased, or any interest in it was transferred. A floor by floor summary of the layout and function of each room followed, with a list of any outbuildings, which, before 1912, were sometimes sketched out on an attached plan, particularly if they were farm buildings. The fabric of construction and roof materials of each building, and the approximate age and present condition of the premises were also written down, as well as details of any recent expenditure on improvements or extensions, and the property's gross market value.

Valuation (Domesday) books were prepared by the valuation officers before the field books. These have been deposited in county record offices, together with many of their working papers and draft record sheets. However, the volumes covering the City of London and Paddington (Westminster) are in the National Archives. They duplicated the field books, except that the building descriptions were omitted. As the properties were listed alphabetically under the names of the landowners in the same way as in the tithe apportionments of the previous century, you can quickly see who was dominant and exactly where each of his or her properties was situated. The entries may also give more specific addresses for non-resident owners and tenants.

Because the record sheets and books relate to the years immediately leading up to the First World War, they tell us about contemporary town and village layouts, urban and rural housing conditions and the estimated or recent sale values of local property. The precise locations of buildings can be utilized to resolve any problems presented by later changes of name or function. They form a bridge between the tithe maps and apportionments of the 1830s, 1840s and 1850s and the communities we know today. You can link them to surviving photographic evidence, estate agents' sale particulars, sale catalogues and auction notices in the local press. Used in combination with the 1901 and earlier census returns, you can discover your family's length of occupancy of a particular premises, the number of people who lived there at specific dates, their business use, and whether your ancestors owned their property.

Scottish Valuation Office records

Scotland was divided up into 12 valuation districts by the Valuation Office in 1910, and the sheet maps and field books, compiled between 1911 and 1912, are now in the National Archives of Scotland, whilst microfilm copies may be inspected in local libraries and archives. You can also search the yearly Scottish valuation rolls up to 1989, in the National Archives of Scotland, too, beginning with those for 1855, though there are a few earlier ones. Most of the rolls are unindexed, making them unwieldy to use, as they are arranged by county or burgh, then by parish or city or burgh electoral ward, by street, door number or house name. However, the valuation rolls are helpful in indicating when someone began or ceased to live at a specific address or had died.

The Primary Valuation of Ireland and other valuation material

In Ireland, the Tenement Act of 1842 led to a countrywide valuation of every property as a prelude to an assessment of tenants' contributions towards the Poor Law Union relief of paupers. Indexed digital images of the county-by-county Primary Valuation of Ireland between 1847 and 1864 (also called Griffith's Valuation), can be searched at **www.originsnetwork.com**. An index to the Valuation is also available on CD-ROM, though the original printed county volumes and microfiche copies are unindexed. You can hire these to search in a family history centre.

The county valuation books are arranged by barony, Poor Law Union, civil parish and townland. They set out under headed columns a map reference number, the names of the householders and of their immediate lessors (landlords), followed by a description of the tenement, including its size, accompanied by the rateable value of the land and buildings. Where there were two or more householders of the same name in a townland, their fathers' names were inserted alongside in brackets.

An incomplete set of the valuation surveyors' original notebooks, house books, field books and tenure books for southern Ireland is held in the National Archives of Ireland. Those concerning the six northern counties are in the Public Record Office of Northern Ireland. They all contain map references, the house books noting the names of occupiers, the field books the size of each holding, and the tenure books the yearly rent and nature of each occupancy. This information should be sufficient for you to investigate any surviving estate papers or title deeds in the Registry of Deeds, in Dublin. The books also record any changes of occupancy between the original valuation and its final publication.

Because there are so few extant 1851 and 1861 Irish census returns, the Primary Valuation can prove invaluable in helping you to plot your surname's distribution and to find the precise whereabouts of individuals. Since neither the 1901 nor 1911 census returns revealed exact birthplaces, the Primary Valuation can also be utilized to show where a particular surname was found within a given county of birth more than half a century before, enabling you to decide where to start hunting for family baptisms, marriages and burials before the introduction of civil registration in 1864. The surname clusters and distributions in the Tithe Applotment Books and Primary Valuation may assist you in locating later family tenants of the same properties in the 1901 and 1911 census returns.

The subsequent current revision and cancelled land books, and Ordnance Survey maps, in the Valuation Office, in Dublin (**www.valoff.ie**), and in the Public Record Office of Northern Ireland, refer to any changes of ownership or occupancy after the Primary Valuation. A revaluation was undertaken every ten or 20 years. The land books can accordingly help you to establish approximate years of death, movements into or out of an area, or even the emigration of former owners and occupiers.

You will need to provide the county, farmland and name of the person or family concerned, and the relevant street name for information about city or town properties recorded in the Valuation Office. There is a computerized place-name index to the Northern Ireland Primary Valuation and later revision books in the Public Record Office of Northern Ireland.

United States of America

You can find out which maps have been uploaded by visiting **www.cyndislist.com/maps.htm**. Try **www.abcgenealogy.com/Maps** for online dated state maps.

After the Revolution, land could be acquired in the United States in one of three ways: by patent in a state-land state, by a federal grant in a public-land state, or as military bounty by way of a reward for meritorious service. The state-land records of petitions, warrants, surveys (also called plats), first grants and enrolled later private conveyances are held in state archives. These concern the original 13 colonies and the states derived from them (Connecticut, Delaware, Georgia, Hawaii, Kentucky, Maine, Maryland, Massachusetts, New Hampshire, New Jersey, New York, North and South Carolina, Pennsylvania, Rhode Island, Tennessee, Texas, Vermont, Virginia, and West Virginia). Visit **www.archives.gov/research/alic/reference/state-archives. html** for contact details.

The plats are especially informative, as they used metes to measure the distances, and bands to name the boundary features, which included natural and man-made landmarks and the names of adjacent owners or occupiers. However, the private land transactions between individuals were not always recorded in the county land books. The federal land entry books, and tract books for the Western states, providing a full property description, can be examined in the National Archives Building, and those for the Western states in the local Bureau of Land Management office. Indexed digital copies of many of the original federal land title records relating to the Eastern states between 1820 and the 1960s are searchable at **www.glorecords.blm.gov/ PatentSearch**. The tract books are held by the Bureau of Land Management, in Springfield. Many of the land entry books, tract books and local deeds have been microfilmed, and can be hired in to examine family history centres. You can also find references to federal land grants at **www.genealogybank. com/gbnk/keyword.html**.

Applicants for federal land were required to show proof of American citizenship, so their petitions may include a copy of their naturalization certificate or of their declaration of intention to apply for citizenship, as well as other personal information such as their age, birthplace, and similar details about other family members.

The heyday of military bounty-land grants was between 1788 and 1855, but such free awards had been made since the seventeenth century to officers and soldiers of the regular regiments. The amount of land was determined by the person's rank, and he or his heirs could present a state or federal claim. You can search the application papers in the National Archives Building, and some are accessible at **www.genealogybank. com/gbnk/keyword.html**. No federal grants were made after 1855. Read *Locating Your Roots: Discover Your Ancestors Using Land Records*, by P. L. Hatcher, for more information.

Fire insurance maps, prepared after 1790 to show the location of buildings, man-made structures and other business premises in cities and towns with populations of more than 2,000, were relied on by insurance companies to balance the financial risks of the properties they insured. The best collection is in the Library of Congress, especially the bound-up city volumes produced by the D. A. Sanborn Company between 1867 and 1970. You can hire microfilm copies using the inter-library loan system. Read *Fire Insurance Maps, Their History and Applications*, by D. T. Oswald, for more information.

Old Poor Law settlement papers

After 1662 and until 1834, migration between English and Welsh parishes was regulated by a series of enactments requiring newcomers to produce evidence that they could support themselves and their families. In order to obtain a settlement certificate, a migrant had to provide a potted history of his or her life before two magistrates. The last place of legal settlement was the parish to which the individual would be removed if overcome by sickness or destitution. Settlement was conferred by place of birth, apprenticeship, employment for a year and a day, marriage with a resident, occupancy of property worth £10, service as a parish officer or as a ratepayer. The settlement certificate was presented to the officers of another parish when the holder went there for employment or seasonal work. The examination papers, settlement certificates and removal orders were placed in the parish chest for safekeeping, and most surviving documentation has now been transferred to county record offices. You can search the catalogues to some of these at www.a2a.org.uk.

Additional name lists

Other dated directories of inhabitants' names were drawn up from time to time. Examples were the regular parish lists of names of assessed tax- and ratepayers, of parish paupers in receipt of outdoor relief, of householders liable to serve for a year's turn as parish officers or as jurymen in the county quarter sessions or county Assizes, of manorial tenants and their half-yearly rents, of able-bodied men between certain ages in each parish who were liable to serve in the county militia, of people taking Holy Communion, and of suspected and known Catholics and non-Communicants.

Because of the want of other records, the post-1831 National School admission and discharge registers assume great importance in Ireland. There are excellent collections of these in the National Archives of Ireland and in the Public Record Office of Northern Ireland. The registers record the name, religious persuasion and age of each pupil, when he or she first attended the school, the father's name, address and occupation, and the date and reason for leaving.

09

finding your way to the records

In this chapter you will learn
- how to identify and locate the whereabouts of useful local records
- how to read and understand old documents
- how to store your findings.

A great twentieth-century English genealogist, Sir Anthony Wagner, wrote that

The prospects of success in solving problems of genealogy depend on many factors, but chiefly, I think, on four: property, continuity, name and record. The possessors of property, other things being equal, are better recorded and more easily traced than those with none, and the more so the greater their possessions. Those who from generation to generation maintain a continuity, whether of dwelling place, of trade, or of anything else, are, other things being equal, more easily traced than those who break with family tradition. Some names are rare, some common and the genealogical advantage is all with rarity, whether the question be of surname or Christian name or the two combined or of a pattern of names of brothers and sisters recurring in a family. Finally there are areas, both geographical and social, where the records are good and full and others where they are poor … Sometimes all four factors are favourable, sometimes one or two or three, sometimes none, but the presence of any one may compensate for the lack of another.

(*English Genealogy*, 1983, p. 411).

This is as true today as when it was first written. Now, though, we have at our fingertips indexed digital images or online databases of many of the prime genealogical sources throughout the world. Some of these sources are so voluminous that they would otherwise have proved impenetrable, if we had not had at least a rough idea of where someone was at a particular time in his or her life.

Not every record is available online. There is no seamless personal-name index to those that are. Some of the online information is out of date or inaccurate, so the internet can be a minefield for the unwary. You cannot afford to ignore the original sources.

Seventh step

The next stage of your research will involve widely dispersed local records to which there are no fully comprehensive personal-name indexes or copies. You will have to rely on them for clues about family links through blood and marriage, where people lived and moved around, and how they earned a living.

This scope, reliability and variety of available supporting documentation will be important too. We are not all going to be lucky enough to have ancestors who were landowners, who stayed in one place and pursued the same occupation generation upon generation, or whose names were uncommon or who used the same family baptismal names time and again. You will come across records which don't answer all your queries, run uninterruptedly from start to finish, or go back as far as you need.

Study your updated family tree: have you found the answers to your original questions? Are you now ready to press on, or do you need to spend some more time among the civil registration indexes and census returns, or to try some of the other records already described? Are there any contradictions in what you have discovered? If so, how can these be explained? Do family members seem to have moved around rather a lot? Have a look at a map to see if this is reasonable in the given timescale, or were they similarly named people belonging to an entirely different generation or family? Are there still some niggling gaps? You will need to sort these out first before going any further.

Drawing up a checklist

Which line do you want to pursue? Restrict your research plan to one or two generations at a time. List, in no special order, sources you think should produce results. Read up about their purpose and likely content, the periods, places and sorts of people they deal with.

How can you gain access to this material? Is it indexed, has it been transcribed, is it available online, on CD-ROM, microform or in print? Will you have to examine original documents, or are they not open to the public?

Use a search engine or web directory to hunt for websites containing subject descriptions or uploaded digitized records, indexes and transcriptions. The printed book catalogues of the two copyright libraries of the British Library (**www.bl.uk/ catalogues/listings.html**) and Library of Congress (**http://catalog. loc.gov**) and the subject-index in your local library catalogue should help too. Always study the bibliographies and notes in books and articles for suggestions on further reading. Have a look at *British Genealogical Bibliographies*, and *British*

Genealogical Periodicals: a Bibliography of their Contents, by S. A. Raymond. Feature articles in the family and local history press also shed light on many sources and how to resolve some of the problems involved in using them. Most libraries will have copies of current and previous issues of journals. Look out especially for *Ancestors, The Local Historian, Local History Magazine* and *Local Population Studies.* For North American family historians, *Family Chronicle, Ancestry Magazine, Everton's Family History Magazine, Family Tree Magazine* and *Heritage Quest* are packed with articles about specific sources and research methodology, recent database launches, search tips and reviews. The Gibson guides, published by the Federation of Family History Societies, focus on the background history, content, dates and whereabouts of many prime genealogical records.

You should now be able to prune and prioritize your list. Ideally it should consist of no more than ten research items. If you plan ahead thoughtfully, you will save yourself valuable time, money and effort. Review your findings and add new facts to your pedigree chart after you have completed each task.

Employ a simple storage system for your results, and regularly file them away. Always back-up anything you save on the hard drive and store it well away from your computer. Revisit your working notes for information that might have been discarded, in case it turns out to be relevant after all.

Finding historical documents

We all create and save records. A hoard of old records which are no longer in active use are known as archives.

Records are usually kept in their original arrangement, so for ease, they generally run chronologically by date. Over time, the sheer volume of accumulated material may give rise to heavy weeding and only selected items will be chosen for permanent preservation and the rest will be disposed of elsewhere or thrown away. Increasingly, records are now being created electronically from the outset, so their storage and retrieval problems will be different.

Always make sure you know what you are looking for and that you are in the right place to find it. Do you know the precise whereabouts of the archive office or library where the material is kept, and how to get there? What are the opening hours, and is there extended opening on certain days? Will you need to obtain a reader's ticket or card, and if so, what form of personal identification is necessary?

The annual editions of *Genealogical Research Directory, National and International* contain the addresses of archive offices and major libraries and historical societies throughout the world, whilst *The Family and Local History Handbook* focuses on those in the United Kingdom and Ireland. Look in *Record Offices: How to Find Them*, by J. Gibson and P. Peskett, for hours of opening, search regulations, and maps of repositories in the United Kingdom. *The ASLIB Directory of Information Sources in the United Kingdom* lists alphabetically by place of deposit the whereabouts of a lot of privately held material, and is helpfully indexed by subject too. Consult *The Genealogist's Address Book*, by E. P. Bentley, for American archive offices, and many Canadian and overseas listings. This is also available on CD-ROM.

There is a lot of preparatory work you can do online. You can access many of the websites of local, national and international record repositories with manuscript collections via **www.nationalarchives.gov.uk/archon**. A seamless catalogue of many of the records in English and some Welsh county record offices is at **www.a2a.org.uk**, and for Scotland, visit **www.scan.org.uk**. To search for catalogue references to privately held documents click on **www.nationalarchives. gov.uk/nra**, for Scotland, use **www.nas.gov.uk/nras/register.asp**, and for Ireland, **www.irmss.ie**. Try **www.archiveshub.ac.uk** for descriptions of UK university and college archives. Copies of many of the key family history sources are available in local libraries, to which **www.familia.org.uk** serves as the gateway for the United Kingdom and Ireland. If you want to know what might be available in UK museums, consult the directory at **www.museums.co.uk**. Look at **www.kinhelp.co.uk/arcnlib.html**, for details about Scottish libraries, archive and heritage centres, county museums and local studies departments. The Irish Family History Foundation website, **www.irish-roots.net**, is the conduit for details about holdings in the government-approved county heritage and genealogy centres in both the Republic of Ireland and in Northern Ireland, and you can find similar information at **www.nationalarchives.ie/genealogy/centres.htm**. For links to the websites of some of the major genealogical institutions in the United Kingdom, go to **www.familyrecords.gov.uk**. Look at the various ongoing projects to create free genealogy websites via **www.worldGenWeb.org**, and select a region of the world.

For the USA, visit **www.archives.gov/locations** for links to the websites of the regional National Archives facilities, **www.archives.gov/research/alic/reference/state-archives.html** for state and historical society archive collections, and **www.publiclibraries.com** for similar links to libraries. For links to the websites of county courthouses, their contact details and resources, use **www.genealogy.com/00000174.html** or **www.cyndislist.com/courthouses.htm#States**.

If you are interested in learning more about what is available in Canada, try **www.archivescanada.ca/** for links to the websites of provincial and territorial archives, and for similar links to provincial and regional libraries visit **www.collections canada.ca/gateway/s22-200-e.html**. Use **www.collections canada.ca/amicus/index-e.html** to search the catalogues of more than 1,300 libraries throughout Canada, and **www.collections canada.ca/genealogy/022-501, 005-e.html** for a directory of online genealogical databases and catalogues in libraries and institutions all over the country.

A complete list of addresses and contact details of family history centres of the Church of Jesus Christ of Latter-day Saints worldwide is at **www.familysearch.org**.

Some practical points

Here are some recommendations about visiting an archive office:

- Will you have to book a seat ahead of your visit? If you want internet access, or a microform reader, you may need to reserve a work station. Will it still be available if you arrive late? Are there any other rules and regulations you should be made aware of?
- If you have special needs, check if there are any designated parking facilities, ramps, lifts, and adapted research equipment which you can use. If the staff know you have a specific problem, they will generally go out of their way to help.
- Do go fully prepared, but don't take too much stuff with you. Use a pencil at all times, if laptops, digital cameras or Dictaphones are not allowed.
- Never bring any original material into a research institution in case of theft.
- It is not recommended that you take a friend. The chances are their interest in your family will not be as riveted as yours, and they can become a distraction to you and other readers.

- Try not to be too ambitious. Take frequent, short, breaks to offset mental fatigue and eye strain. The mind switches off unawares and you may suddenly find yourself gazing mindlessly at a screen or document. Stop, take a walk, have a coffee, browse the bookshelves, and come back refreshed. Revisit the last few screen shots or pages. You will be amazed at how new this information will seem.

- Don't be too hasty. If your expectations of your ability to quickly process and absorb the contents of documents are not met, and you start to run out of time, slow down, rather than panic. There is always another day. If you work carefully and steadily, your day will be far more productive. Plan a two-day visit if you can, and ask if any documents you have not finished with can be held over for you for collection the next morning.

- If you are using the internet in a public place, and you are asked to subscribe to use a website or to log on giving your credit card or voucher numbers, never leave the computer unattended, and always remember to log off as soon as you have ended your session.

- Note down exactly which sources, periods and names you have examined, even if the outcome was negative. This will prevent you covering the same ground again.

- If you do any document copying yourself, make sure each copy includes its full archival reference, so that you can find the item again if you need to.

Handling old documents

- Manuscripts are unique and irreplaceable. Many will be very old, fragile and faded, and may not have seen the light of day for a long time. They were never intended for frequent handling. They are preserved in controlled storage conditions so they deserve your utmost respect.

- Be sure you have enough room to spread out any large documents and use the provided weights to keep them flat. Foam wedges are often available to support the tender spines of heavy volumes.

- Some record offices will lend you white gloves to wear when handling old documents. Never lean on a document, touch it more than you have to, mark it in any way or write your notes on top of it. Never lick your fingers when turning a page or handling a document, and look away if you need to cough or sneeze. Don't eat or chew anything as you work, either.

- Special pencil sharpeners are generally supplied to avoid the risk of graphite rubbing off your fingers onto a manuscript, and erasers are forbidden.
- Place a long strip of clean white paper under each line when reading a lengthy, repetitive script with no punctuation. Always turn a document over to see if anything was written underneath, and uncurl folded corners for the same reason.
- When you have finished, replace the document exactly as you found it.

Problems reading old handwriting

Our styles of handwriting have changed dramatically over time, and they will vary from place to place and between official, legal and more informal documents.

By working gradually back in time, your eyes should become attuned to the different ways in which letters and words were written in the past, although some nineteenth-century documents can pose more problems than Tudor ones. There have been good and bad scribes and poor writing implements in every era. Spelling was haphazard or phonetic until standardized by Samuel Johnson's *English Dictionary* in the mid-eighteenth century, so a single document might yield up several versions of a person's name, and you may be forced to pronounce some words to see what was intended.

The clerks in the various central government offices and law courts evolved their own styles of handwriting, abbreviations and shorthand. Words that were used a lot were often truncated by contractions or suspensions to save time and space, especially in formulaic documents. Contractions were indicated by a horizontal line drawn over the top to show where vowels or letters in the middle of a word had been omitted. Where only the first few letters of a word were written, a curved line over or through the last letter, or a flourish or full stop was used to represent the suspended letter. Words might run together, contain double vowels or letters in superscript. Some letters were interchangeable, such as 'c' and 't', written in a different way, like the reverse 'e' and the long 's', or are now difficult to distinguish, like 'u' or 'n'. Arm yourself with an alphabet of old capital and lower case letters from a palaeography handbook as a means of reference.

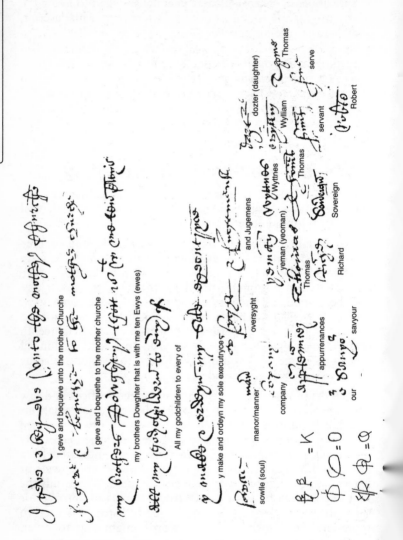

I geve and bequeve unto the mother Churche

I geve and bequethe to the mother churche

my brothers Dowghter that is with me ten Ewys (ewes)

All my godchildren to every of

y make and ordeyn my sole executryces

oversyght · and Jugemens

sowile (soul)   manor/manner   company   appurrenances   our   savvour

yeman (yeoman)   Wyttnes   Sovereign

Thomas   Richard   Thomas   Wylliam   Thomas   serve   Robert

servant   dozter (daughter)

figure 12 samples of handwriting, showing capital letters and small characters, common contractions, abbreviations and suspended letters, found in sixteenth- and seventeenth-century documents

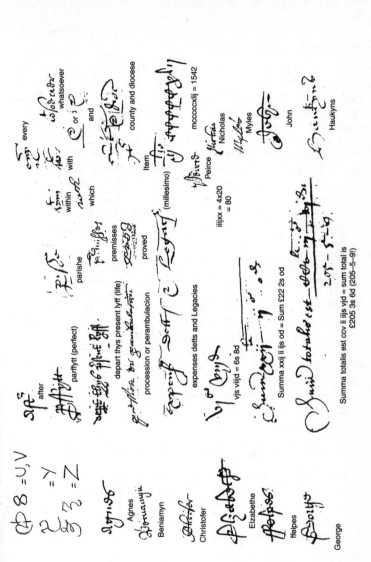

8 = U, V

= Y

= Z

after

parfytt (perfect)

parishe

premisses

proved

every

whatsoever

@ or i

and

within

which

county and diocese

Item

mccccxlij = 1542

(millesimo)

Peirce

Nicholas

Myles

John

Haukyns

iiijcx = 4x20 = 80

depart thys present lyff (life)

procession or perambulacion

expenses detts and Legacies

vjs vijd = 6s 8d

Summa xxij li ijs od = Sum £22 2s od

Summa totalis est ccv li iiijs vijd = sum total is £205 3s 6d (205–5–9I)

Agnes

Beniamyn

Christofer

Elizabethe

ffelpes

George

Local, vernacular, handwriting styles were much more varied and largely depended on the standard of literacy of the authors. Vernacular handwriting began to evolve during the late fifteenth century, and you will come across it especially in parish registers and other parochial records.

You can gain valuable practice by reading facsimiles and transcriptions of a wide range of documents, which will help in building up your expertise as well as telling you their likely content and the whereabouts of names, places, dates and other significant information. Try your hand at the online examples of documents at **www.nationalarchives.gov.uk/palaeography**, in *Palaeography for Family and Local Historians*, by H. Marshall, and in *Examples of English Handwriting 1150–1750*, by H.E.P. Grieve. For Scotland, try **www.ScottishHandwriting. com/content** for tuition. There is also a self-help pack, *Scottish Handwriting 1500–1700*, by A. Rosie. You might find *Understanding Colonial Handwriting*, by H. Stryker-Rodda, helpful too.

If you are attempting a word by word, line by line, transcription (exact copy) of a document, leave blanks for difficult words to which you can return later. If a specific word is awkward to decipher, its context may help. See if it crops up elsewhere in the same document where it might be more clearly written or its meaning is more obvious. Use a magnifying sheet, enlarge or reduce the screen magnification, or adjust the lighting over your seat. If this fails, try to construct the word letter by letter by picking each one out in other words, and set aside spaces for those you cannot identify. Eventually you should be able to guess what the word was supposed to be. Another approach worth trying is to write a word as you see it, because this may help you understand how it was formed. As a last resort, ask a member of staff to assist you decipher the odd tricky word.

A printout or a photocopy will be less stressful to pore over at leisure, particularly when your time is limited in a record office.

Meanings of words

You may need to look up archaic or obsolete words in a specialist glossary or dictionary. Regional dialect words were often written phonetically, especially when describing domestic furniture and work tools, for instance in wills and probate inventories. You may have to seek a local dialect dictionary to sort these out. For Scottish words, look at **www.scan.org.uk/ researchrtools/glossary.htm** or **www.dsl.ac.uk/dsl/**.

163

finding your way to the records

09

Understanding Latin documents

The law courts developed their own jargon and terminology. You can therefore usually predict where stock phrases, names, relationships, dates and other core information are likely to appear in legal documents. This can be indispensable when they were written in cramped, abbreviated Latin, which was the language of legal records until 24 March 1732/3, except between 1653 and 1660, when English was used. Probate acts, grants of letters of administration and manorial documents were also written in Latin.

It is a good idea to read printed examples in translation first, if Latin is not your strong suit. Try the exercises at **www.national archives.gov.uk/latin/beginners/** and in *Latin for Local and Family Historians*, by D. Stuart. A rudimentary knowledge of Latin vocabulary and grammar is helpful, but you should be able to get by with a Latin dictionary, such as that in *Introduction to Latin for Local History*, by E. A. Gooder, and a Latin glossary. Often the clerk's own grasp of Latin was shaky, or there was no Latin equivalent of an English word, so these were given Latin endings.

Be careful with proper names in Latin. You can find a list of Latin proper names and their English equivalents in *The Record Interpreter*, by C. T. Martin. In Medieval documents, people might be referred to by their place of origin, residence, occupation or paternity rather than by hereditary surnames. Such personal tags might change from one document to another, especially before the fifteenth century, when surnames were by no means fixed.

Working with numbers

The Arabic numbers that we use today were not common in English and Latin documents until the late sixteenth century. If you look at wills, manorial records and taxation lists, you will see that dates were rendered in full or as Roman numerals. Sums of money were expressed using Roman numbers too, and 'li' or 'l' (short for 'libras'), 's' (for 'solidos'), and 'd' (for 'denarios') were written after them in superscript to signify pounds, shillings and pence or smaller values as appropriate. A score was indicated by 'xx' in superscript above the number to be multiplied. When numbers ended with digits, each one was dotted, and the final one written as 'j'.

You can convert given money values to their modern equivalents by visiting **http://eh.net.hmit/,** and for Scottish currency, use **www.scan.org.uk/researchrtools/scots_currency.htm**. *How Much is that Worth?*, by L. M. Munby, is another useful guide.

The dating of documents

Before 1 January 1752, the first day of the year in England, Wales, Ireland and the Dominions was 25 March (Lady Day), according to the Julian calendar. In 1582, Pope Gregory Xlll introduced a new calendar, which was more readily adopted by European Catholic States than Protestant. Scotland started using the Gregorian calendar on 1 January 1600. The two co-existing calendars gave rise to much confusion.

If you find a baptism entry in January 1741, and a burial of an identically named person in October 1741, don't be lured into thinking the two concerned the same individual. These dates were written according to the prevailing, Old Style (Julian), year. When converted to the New Style (Gregorian) calendar, you will see that the dates actually fell in January 1742 and October 1741. It is important that you write down any dates as you see them, and convert them later, and indicate any events which happened between 1 January and 24 March before 1752 as being in 1741/2, in 1741 Old Style, or in 1742 New Style, for example, to remove any doubt. Be careful, though, when searching the International Genealogical Index, the British Isles Vital Records Index, and any other indexes and transcriptions, because some of the dates may or may not have been altered to our modern calendar.

The Religious Society of Friends rendered days and months in numbers, Sunday being the first day of the week, the whole of March being the first month and February the twelfth until the calendar was changed in 1752.

Many legal and official records were dated by regnal year. This starts on the date of each new monarch's accession and goes up a number with each anniversary, ending on the day of death.

Deeds and charters were often dated by the number of days or day in the week before or after a fixed religious festival or saint's day, whilst others were tied to a movable feast such as Easter or Trinity. You can decode these by consulting the tables in *A Handbook of Dates for Students of English History*, by C. R. Cheney, and revised by M. Jones, or a perpetual calendar.

Interpreting your findings

Always write down information gleaned from documents as you come across it and keep to the original spellings, even if in Latin. Sometimes the context in which certain things were written was crucial to their meaning and interpretation.

It can be helpful if you write people's names in block capitals, as they can be more easily picked up in your notes. Leave given family relationships as described, such as 'my son' and 'his son' to avoid any later misunderstanding.

Don't read into a document what isn't there. It may not tell you all, or indeed, anything, about what you want to know, or may be tantalizingly ambiguous. Its contents should be capable of corroboration or amplification by other contemporary sources. However, none may survive to do this. You will then have to evaluate its accuracy and honesty for yourself. Who created the document? What was its purpose? Who was it for? What was the author's standpoint, as official recorder, participant, litigant, witness or as someone's representative? How close was the writer to the date, the people or the event or activity described? Was the document a later copy of a lost original? Did it form part of a larger set of papers? The answers could be important and revealing.

Filing and storage systems

Ask yourself if a total stranger could understand your filing scheme unaided, and if you can quickly and simply retrieve your notes. Adopt a simple system, and stick with it.

Never throw away negative results or information that initially seems useless. It might become relevant later on.

It is best to use file paper of the same size, with a margin for any extra comments and punch-holes for easy filing in a ring-binder, with a search log at the front. You may want to arrange your material in source order, with the most recent at the top, perhaps with a special section at the end for temporary discards or nil outcomes. Coloured dividers will help too, to separate one type of document from another. Keep a discrete correspondence log, with the latest dated letter at the top. You can purchase research logs at **www.familysearch.org**.

You may prefer to buy family group sheets to record known facts about your ancestors. Each sheet will include one set of parents and their children. The group sheets are linked to each other by number. Family history worksheets are available too. Look for these at websites such as **www.familysearch.org** and **www.ancestry.co.uk** or in family history bookshops. The main limitations of worksheets are that they make little or no allowance for any idiosyncrasies. For instance, an illegitimate child's surname might not be given in a baptism entry, but as the parish register worksheet is arranged in headed columns, you may be tempted to write in a name which was not actually correct. You also alter the way in which an entry was originally written when you rearrange it in columns.

Another alternative is to devote a card to each person in your family, filing them alphabetically by surname and forename in a storage box, with the latest same-named person's card at the front. The cards are uniquely numbered and cross-referenced to parents' and spouses' names, and leave room for lots of biographical notes, but they are fiddly to work with when you want to extract facts to put on your family tree.

You might choose to feed your data into a computer, perhaps using one of the many commercial software programs on the market (such as Legacy or CLOOZ). Look for the regular published reviews of current packages and ask around for advice and comparisons from other family historians who have tried them. Software packages are more versatile than card indexes and loose bits of paper. You can edit, update, delete, amend and move your information around, create pedigrees in different layout styles, merge text, pictures and tables, save, copy, download, print, and share your results with others online. If you have a scanner, you can import copies of documents, photographs and other items to build up a family scrapbook. Always back-up your material on a disk, and never throw away your original notes. Word processing may be the answer if your handwriting is difficult to decipher.

It is worth investing a little money to ensure the safe preservation of precious family archives and photographs. Acid-free high-strength corrugated self-assembly archival boxes are ideal for housing loose documents. Try to buy boxes large enough to avoid having to fold up documents, as this causes damage. Transparent acid-free or Melinex sleeves should be used to stow away photographs, newspaper cuttings and other flat items, to prevent or forestall their deterioration and remove the need for handling. The sleeves can then be placed in an album.

Keep your boxes and albums in dark, cool, dry conditions, under cover and above floor level, away from direct heat and sunlight. Good ventilation is also important as it stops the development of mould.

Never place original material in airtight containers, and avoid using polythene bags and brown envelopes. Polythene sweats and will lift the ink and print from the very things it is supposed to protect. As envelopes degrade they deposit a brown stain, which will irreversibly spoil their contents. Remove any rusty clips, elastic bands and pink tape and replace them with brass clips and white tape if you have to.

Torn, frayed or damaged material should be repaired only with wheat starch or special archival tape rather than with glue or sticky tape, neither of which is durable and can lead to further damage. If in doubt, seek the expert advice of local record office staff about suppliers in your area, or about the most suitable conservation methods for your treasures.

10

searching parish registers in England and Wales

In this chapter you will learn:
- what parish registers are and where to find them
- what indexes and copies are available
- how to interpret parish registers.

The census returns between 1851 and 1901 tell you approximately when and where people were born. If a birth occurred after 1 July 1837, you should be able to trace it amongst the indexed civil registrations. Sometimes, however, births went un-notified or prove impossible to find.

Especially before 1874, some parents registered their child's birth or had it baptized, but not both. A birthplace was not necessarily the parish of baptism, and the census returns did not indicate a person's religious denomination either. However, if you know where your ancestor's parents usually lived, start by looking at the baptism registers of the Established Anglican Church of England, and if these are unproductive, move on to the registers of nearby nonconformist chapels. Baptism did not invariably happen immediately after birth, unless the child was sickly and was baptized privately. It might be delayed until the family was complete, so that all a couple's offspring could be baptized together years after the birth of their eldest child – so the given year of birth is no guarantee of the year of baptism.

The formal registration of baptism, marriage and burial became compulsory in September 1538. Every church was to keep a written weekly record, which was read out during Sunday services. The registrations provided proof of age, parentage, rights of inheritance and lineage, and could be used to establish that a person was the monarch's native-born subject.

Although parish registers were made mandatory in 1538, in practice very few survive without interruption from that date, but where they do they represent almost 470 years of continuous record-keeping. There are a number of reasons for their loss or breakdown of recording, which was widespread. In 1598, a canon issued by the Province of Canterbury ordered parish officers to purchase a special parchment book into which all the earlier baptisms, marriages and burials were to be copied up, particularly those after the start of the Queen's reign in 1558. Many of the older books were then discarded and the first 20 years of record-keeping were thus lost forever.

The registration of baptisms, marriages and burials was disrupted during the Civil War and Commonwealth period between 1643 and 1660.

From 1645 to 1660, parishioners' births and deaths were noted as well as their baptisms and burials, and between 1653 and 1660, only couples' publications of intent to marry, rather than the dates of the weddings themselves. This was because during this period they were civil ceremonies, performed by local magistrates rather than by priests. In 1653, a special officer, called a 'parish register', was elected by the parish ratepayers, and given custody of the books, when the Presbyterian Church became pre-eminent. Some register books were removed from churches into private homes, and were not returned at the Restoration of the Anglican Church in 1660, and so vanished. Many registers therefore have gaps spanning almost a generation. After 1660, the restored Anglican clergy often wrote up retrospective details of baptisms, marriages and burials during the hiatus years, possibly as evidence of parishioners' ages and paternity for purposes of inheritance. Some of these entries related to nearby churches as well as their own.

Many family histories grind to a halt in the mid-seventeenth century because of this erratic record-keeping and under-registration. You will have to turn to other contemporary parish and community sources for clues about residential continuity and the relationship of people to those of the same surname recorded in a particular parish before 1643.

Another reason for missing baptisms, marriages and burials may be explained by the Act of Toleration in 1689. Under this statute, dissenting congregations were permitted to erect their own places of worship, and began to keep their own records. However, from 25 March 1754, after an act of 1753, the marriages of everyone, regardless of creed, became obligatory in the Anglican Church until 30 June 1837. Only Quakers and Jews were exempted and allowed to continue to perform and record their own weddings.

The extent of registration was also affected by a tax on births, marriages and deaths, imposed between 1694 and 1706, and by a Stamp Duty on baptisms, marriages and burials between 1783 and 1794. These inevitably led to non-baptism, the description of dead people as paupers to avoid payment, and in the earlier period, to the increased incidence of clandestine marriages.

Church baptisms and marriages are still registered today. However, since 1853 (1852 in London) there have been fewer interments in most urban and many rural churchyards for reasons of public health and hygiene, so the entries in the burial registers represent only a sample of the true total of local deaths. The vast majority of these later burials have been recorded in the registers of the local authority or private company responsible for the cemetery concerned, or from 1902, the crematorium.

Where to find parish registers

The parish registers have not been deposited centrally, nor is there a union personal-name index to them. Originally stored in a designated locked chest in the church for safekeeping, when full, most registers are transferred to the local county record office, the incumbent retaining those which are still in use.

The Phillimore Atlas and Index of Parish Registers, edited by C. R. Humphery-Smith, contains a set of county parish maps for England and regional maps for Wales, showing the earliest recorded date in each surviving register. The index tells you their whereabouts at the time of publication, and about any indexes, copies and other finding aids. Most record offices have published guides to their current holdings. A phone call will give you up-to-date information.

Because of their fragile state and heavy use, many original church registers are no longer accessible to the public and can only be viewed on microform. If your ancestors came from a different part of the country, it may be easier to inspect microfilmed or hired-in microfiche copies of parish registers at a family history centre (see **www.familysearch.org**). Copies of local registers may be held in libraries (see **www.familia.org.uk**).

If you want to examine register books which remain in a church, you will need to write to the incumbent for an appointment. Always enclose a stamped self-addressed envelope with your request. Addresses of Anglican clergy can be found in *Crockford's Clerical Directory* or *The Church of England Yearbook,* but do not write to the named priest, who may have moved on to a different parish. There is a fixed scale of fees for searching the registers. If you are unable to inspect them yourself, he or she may be willing to do it for you, although they are not obliged to do so. The fee for this service will be different. An offer of a reasonable donation to church funds may be welcomed as an alternative. Always clarify in advance how much you are likely to have to pay. An urban register crammed full of scrawled yearly entries will take much longer to hunt through than a rural volume, so you may have to limit the period to be scrutinized. Always write and thank the incumbent for his or her help.

Indexes and transcriptions

Digital images of parish register indexes and transcriptions are in their infancy at present, but it is worth keeping an eye on the following websites for progress reports:

- **www.familyhistoryonline.org.uk** is run by the Federation of Family History Societies and is uploading parish register, marriage and burial indexes and transcriptions up to at least 1837 compiled by member societies. Access is free to the name indexes, but you will need to pay to view the full images;

- **www.freereg.rootsweb.com** is a database of baptisms, marriages and burials. Click on a specific county and place to find out what is presently available. Searches are by surname and by county, and you can select a period;

- the Online Parish Clerks Project is focusing on granting free access to indexed transcriptions of parish registers and records, county by county. Use a search engine to find out what is now online for your county.

Details about baptisms and marriages have been extracted from many of the microform copies for integration into the International Genealogical Index (IGI), which is produced by the Church of Jesus Christ of Latter-day Saints. The names of living people, anyone born less than 110 years ago or married more recently than 95 years ago are excluded. The index was first published on microfiche in 1968, when it was known as the Computer File Index, and more entries were added to the 1976, 1978, 1981, 1984, 1988 and 1992 microfiche editions. These are arranged by country, then by county for England and Wales. The 1992 edition, and later addenda up to 2000, is on CD-ROM too. An accompanying list of the places, periods and events covered is attached to every version.

You can search the latest edition of the Index at **www.familysearch.org**, and it is updated every week. From 1992, the International Genealogical Index has included unauthenticated information supplied on family group sheets by Church patrons. Since 1990, anyone may submit information, and suggest corrections, using a GEDCOM file. This has led to lots of duplication, overlap and contradictions. The British Isles Vital Records Index (BIVRI) is only available on CD-ROM at present, and is restricted to extracts from vital and parish records. To find out which English, Welsh, Scottish and Irish, birth, baptism and marriage extracts have been included in the second, 2002 edition, and their date coverage, visit **www.genoot.com/ downloads/BVR2/index.html**.

The entries are extracts, not full transcriptions, nor is every parish or every entry from a register included in either index. Because the indexes contain only a limited amount of information you should always treat them merely as research tools and examine the original register for full details, and to verify what you have found. As the indexes contain few burial entries, if you ignore the burial registers, you will risk establishing false matches with 'ancestors' who actually died young.

In spite of these caveats, they are an amazing time-saver, have completely transformed our success rates in tracking down the movements and whereabouts of ancestors worldwide, and have thrown up family linkages and surname distributions which might otherwise have lain undetected. The IGI and BIVRI can also help you to identify the correct entry or eliminate a few of the birth registrations of children of the same name in the same year and/or district, or to find a wife's maiden name by keying in her first name and her husband's full name. You may even turn up an ancestor's marriage whose date and place you might otherwise have been unaware of.

You can trawl both databases for the births or baptisms of an individual and his or her siblings, the baptisms of children of a particular marriage, and for details of every indexed extract from a specific given batch or film number. This facility is helpful if you don't know the names of your ancestor's siblings, the surname is a common one, you want to know who else was in the same parish at that time, or to see if there were any naming patterns at work. However, each database will only respond to your exact commands, so if the names of the same set of parents were written in one entry as 'Jn and My', in another as 'John and Mary', and in yet another as 'John and his wife', you will have to try each of these to be certain you have retrieved everything.

Welsh surnames pose a particular problem, as they were not fixed, even as late as the nineteenth century, and the pool of surnames was small because given names were cutomarily used. For instance, 'John Thomas' was John son of Thomas, and his own son Hugh might be known as 'Hugh John Thomas' or 'Hugh John'. His siblings might be similarly and variously described. In earlier parish registers, these strings of male names were frequently separated by 'ab' or 'ap', which eventually gave rise to surnames beginning with 'B' or 'P' such as Bowen and Powell, whilst 'Elin verch William ap Llywelyn' indicated that Elin was the daughter of William, who was the son of Llywelyn.

You may therefore have to try a number of permutations to retrieve their entries. Some of the middle names might have been dropped during indexing too.

If you are searching a microfiche edition of the IGI, the information is identical to what is included online or on CD-ROM, but what you see is what you get. The alphabetical entries run chronologically by date under each surname and forename, and note the name of the parents or spouse, their sex or family relationship, the type of event, its date, and place, with the encoded dates and places of any Church temple ordinances that had been performed with living relatives as proxies, and the batch or film number from which the information was taken. A standard phonetic surname index was employed, cross-referenced to the original spellings where appropriate. Similar sounding, though distinct, surnames might thus be wrongly grouped together. Given names appear strictly alphabetically as they were written in the records, for example as 'William', 'Willm' and 'Wm'. Some names were originally written in Latin, so William will also be listed as 'Gulielmus' and Giles as 'Egidius'.

For Wales, two microfiche copies of the indexes were produced, one of which was arranged by family name and the other by given name. The extracted entries of baptisms after 1813 are straightforward, because family names were written in special columns in printed registers, but for earlier baptisms, the indexers sometimes mistakenly assumed that the child took the name of the father as his or her family name, ignoring the longer patronymic string. If you know someone's approximate year and parish of birth, it may be simpler to search the given name index. Conversely, if you know the father's identity the family name index would be preferable.

The first fully comprehensive copies of registered baptisms, marriages and burials were those sent annually from each English and Welsh parish to the diocesan registrar. Sometimes duplicates were prepared for the archdeacon. The bishops' and archdeacons' transcripts date between 1598 and about 1936, though some started earlier than this, and the majority end in the mid- or late nineteenth century. The surviving bishops' and archdeacons' transcripts are now in county or diocesan record offices. There is no unbroken run for any diocese, nor were there any returns from 1646 until 1660, when the Church courts were suspended. Returns of marriages were discontinued in 1837, when civil registration was introduced. In Wales, bishops' transcripts exist only from 1661 onwards, and you can inspect them in the National Library of Wales, but many only date from the late eighteenth century or are deficient.

At first, the reporting year began at Easter, but from 1603 it became fixed at 25 March. The transcripts were generally arranged in parish bundles and chronologically by year, although some archdeacons' transcripts and register bills were organized by year, then by deanery and parish, which is handy if you know when an event occurred but not precisely where. Be careful to note any gaps, though. The transcripts may pre-date, be easier to access or read, and often complement the registers. The churchwardens or parish clerk might rectify errors and omissions in the registers or add extra information, but they might miss out, truncate, transpose or combine entries, so are not totally trustworthy. The spelling of surnames and forenames might be changed too, and dates and occupations vary from what was in the register itself. You may have to turn to other sources to decide which of the two conflicting versions was correct.

Probably the best collection of transcribed copies and indexes of English and Welsh parish registers is in the library of the Society of Genealogists, and some can be borrowed by members. Use the library catalogue at **www.sog.org.uk** for details. Its published catalogue, *Parish Register Copies in the Library of the Society of Genealogists*, is included in *The Phillimore Atlas and Index of Parish Registers. The National Index of Parish Registers: Parish Registers of Wales*, edited by C. J. Williams and J. Watts-Williams, lists the whereabouts of Welsh originals, copies and indexes.

The contents of parish registers

At first, the baptisms, marriages and burials were written up in one book, but from 25 March 1754, marriages were recorded in a discrete printed volume, and baptisms and burials were registered separately after 1813.

Until 1812, the baptism registrations reflected the whim of the parish clerk. At best they will tell you the date, the child's name, surname and parentage, the parents' place of residence (perhaps a particular farm, house or township), and the father's occupation, but at worst merely the exact date and infant's name. A baby's surname might be written either after his or her given name or parents' names, making searches laborious. When a child was illegitimate, you may have difficulty working out its surname if those of both parents were given. Between about 1770 and 1812, baptisms in the diocese of York and from 1783 until the same year in the dioceses of Sarum, Bristol and Durham, and in the Archdeaconry of Berkshire, were registered not only with the names of the child and his or her parents, the date of birth, and birth seniority, but the birthplace of each parent, names and addresses of the two sets of grandparents, and the occupations of the father and both grandfathers were frequently specified as well. A single entry in these 'Dade' and 'Barrington' registers could thus establish a family's history a further two generations back beyond the child itself.

Since 1813, baptisms have been written up in pre-printed books, under headed columns. They record the exact date, child's forename(s), the names of both parents, the child's surname, parents' place of residence, father's occupation and the signature of the officiating priest. All you have to do is skim down the surname column for the one you want.

figure 13 baptism register of Great Finborough, Suffolk, 1813 and 1814. The birthdays of the three Chaplin children are included. Daniel and Shadrach were two of the older brothers of Meshech Chaplin. Shadrach's son, also called Shadrach, was the great-grandfather of Charlie Chaplin. He died in 1893, at Ipswich in Suffolk (reproduced by permission of Suffolk Record Office)

Tips

- Although baptism was supposed to be on the first Sunday after birth, or on the next Sunday thereafter, in the few instances where dates of birth were given, this rarely happened. Weeks, months or years might elapse, before several offspring were baptized together.

- Always search a broad period, so that you can pick up the baptisms of brothers and sisters as well as or instead of that of your direct ancestor, and in case your information about the birth year was erroneous. The eldest child was often baptised in the mother's home church, which was generally where she had been married.

- If you cannot find a specific baptism, examine the registers of parishes within walking distance (about a 14-mile radius). The given birthplaces might vary in different census years,reflecting your family's mobility.

- Not many families are likely to be traced through the register of a single parish from their inception to the present day, so have a map handy, or refer to the county maps in *The Phillimore Atlas and Index of Parish Registers*, and look in the registers of surrounding parishes, for of clues as to where yout ancestors came from.

- Try the International Genealogical Index and British Isles Vital Records Index for itinerant family members.

- A child born during the mother's previous marriage or out of wedlock will have a different surname. Wherever possible, the identity of the 'putative' or 'reputed' father was cited in order that the vestry meeting and parish officers could force him to pay for the child's maintenance. If the mother subsequently married the father or someone else, the child probably took his or her birth- or stepfather's surname, and the original identity was lost. Youngsters, who were brought up as part of the families of older married sisters, or childless relatives, might adopt their surname too.

- An absence from parish registers may suggest nonconformity. See Chapter 11.

- Where two entries recorded children who had been 'privately baptized' and were later 'received into the Church' or 'publicly baptized', a home baptism by a licensed midwife, physician, surgeon or priest was indicated. Some of the 'public baptisms' before the late eighteenth century involved Roman Catholics. Such registrations ensured legal proof of parentage and age at a time when they were subject to civil persecution.

- You will have a problem when there were several couples in a parish with identical names, whose childbearing periods exactly coincided, and who gave their children the same baptismal names. This often happened in rural areas where there were relatively few surnames. The registers usually identified the fathers as 'senior', 'junior', 'elder' or 'younger' or by their township, farmstead, house name or occupation. A search of the burial registers and family wills may eliminate a few and sort out the survivors and other siblings. When the tag was dropped, a parent's death may be inferred, but it was not always the older person who died first. Any posthumous offspring should be described as such. However, one of the couples might simply have gone elsewhere or had stopped having children. Look for forename patterns over preceeding and later generations for clues too. In the past, people seem to have drawn on a fairly limited pool of baptismal names. Sometimes the first son was named after the father, the second after the paternal grandfather, the third after the maternal grandfather and so on. A younger child might bear the baptismal name of a sibling who had died before he or she was born, or several living siblings be given the same forename to preserve the family's predetermined inheritance of certain property. When fathers' occupations were recorded, look for their continuity if you need to separate families with matching names. This isn't foolproof, as some work was seasonal, and lots of people earned a living in the countryside as labourers, or practised the same local trades, home industries or crafts. The eldest son was the most likely to follow his father's line of work, while his younger brothers might be forced to move somewhere else for employment.

- Parents often named their babies after the patron saint of the church, the saint on whose feast day he or she had been born, or after some other biblical figure, a national or local hero. Names might also be plucked from popular literature, a well-known myth or legend. By the early nineteenth century, surnames began to be used as forenames too, especially the mother's maiden name.

- If you extract every mention of your surname and its variants from the beginning of the registers, especially in rural parishes, you should be able to piece together entire generations and different family groups. You are likely to be left with some seemingly unconnected strays. Such people often turn out to have been returners or residents of nearby parishes.

Looking for a marriage?

When you have found the baptism of your ancestor's oldest known child, you can then begin the search for his marriage. Until 1929, a male was legally able to marry at the age of 14, and a female at 12, though parental consent was necessary until 21.

As many as a third of all marriages began with the bride already pregnant, and some took place after the child's birth. The wedding ceremony was usually held in the bride's church, though sometimes the nearest market town, which was probably no more than seven miles away, or an ecclesiastical centre, was chosen, especially if the groom had applied for a marriage licence.

Until 24 March 1754, the registered entries should tell you the precise date, forenames and surnames of both partners, and if the wedding was indeed by licence ('by Lic.'). Occasionally, however, only the name of the husband was written down. Where one party was widowed or belonged to another parish this might be mentioned as well.

From 25 March 1754, the details about marriages were copied into a printed book, so the entries up to 30 June 1837 were uniform, whilst the later ones duplicate the central registrations. The names, current marital status, and parish of residence of the groom and bride, the date of their marriage, and whether it was after the reading of banns or by licence, were completed by their signatures or marks, together with those of at least two witnesses and the officiating priest. The witnesses might be the churchwardens, relatives or friends.

Banns published a couple's intention to marry. They were read out in their home churches during the services on the three preceding Sundays before the proposed wedding date. The dates of the banns and the names and parishes of the bridal pair were recorded in the registers of both churches. This might be done as part of the marriage registration, on separate pages in the same volume, or in a special banns book. If you cannot locate a specific marriage, have a look for the banns, because they will tell you where the other spouse lived, and thus where the ceremony took place. However, even if banns were read, marriage did not automatically follow.

The alternative to the publication of banns was for the groom to apply to the archdeacon, the diocesan registrar or his deputy for a licence to marry at a particular church within a specified period. The licence was produced by the groom to the parish

figure 14 marriage registration of George Chaplin and Susannah Bacon at Great Finborough, Suffolk, 1771. George was then a widower. The couple's nine children, born between 1773 and 1793 included Daniel, Shadrach and Meshech (reproduced by permission of Suffolk Record Office)

In the Archdeaconry Court of Suffolk.

The 27th day of October 1854

Appeared personally *Spencer Chaplin*

of the parish of *St Margaret in Ipswich* in the County

of *Suffolk* a Bachelor

of the age of 19 Years *but under the age of 21 Years*

and prayed a License for the solemnization of Matrimony, in the

Parish Church of *Saint Margaret in Ipswich aforesaid*

in the County of *Suffolk*

between him and *Ellen Smith*

of *St Nicholas in Ipswich aforesaid* in the County of

Suffolk a Spinster of the age of

19 Years *but under the age of 21 years* and made Oath that

he believeth that there is no impediment of Kindred or Alliance, or

of any other lawful Cause, nor any Suit commenced in any Ecclesiasti-

cal Court, to bar or hinder the proceeding of the said Matrimony,

according to the Tenor of such License. And he further made Oath

that he the said *Spencer Chaplin* —————

hath had his usual place of abode within the said Parish of *St Margaret*

in Ipswich aforesaid for the space of Fifteen Days last past. *And*

he further made oath that the consent of Shadrach

Chaplin the father of the said Spencer Chaplin and also the

(Signed) *consent of william Smith the father of the said Ellen*

smith hath respectively been obtained to such

marriage

Spencer Chaplin

Sworn before me

figure 15 Spencer Chaplin's marriage allegation, 1854
because both he and his bride Ellen Smith were under 21, their fathers, Shadrach
Chaplin and William Smith, were required to give their consent to the wedding
Spencer and Ellen were the grandparents of Charlie Chaplin
(reproduced by permission of Suffolk Record Office)

priest as his authority to perform the ceremony. The licences themselves rarely survive, but you can search the preliminary allegations and bonds, which date from the sixteenth century onwards, in the diocesan or county record office of the See where the wedding was planned. Have a look at *Bishops' Transcripts and Marriage Licences, Bonds and Allegations: A Guide to Their Location and Indexes*, by J. Gibson, for a complete list of their dates and whereabouts.

Common licences were granted by the Vicars-General of the Archbishop of Canterbury and of York for weddings in their provinces, when the couple lived in different dioceses, or wished to marry outside canonical hours, during Lent or other proscribed periods. The Faculty Office of the Archbishop of Canterbury dealt with weddings between partners from different provinces. Special licences were granted 'to marry at any meet and convenient place' and after 1753, these were only issued by the Faculty Office. You can search indexes to the marriage allegations filed in the Vicar-General's Office of the Archbishop of Canterbury between 1694 and 1850, and to those in the Faculty Office from 1701 until the same year, at **www.originsnetwork.com**. The indexes include any accompanying marriage bonds up to 1822, after which they were no longer necessary. The actual documents are held in Lambeth Palace Library, in London. The marriage licence allegations and bonds kept by the Vicar-General of the Archbishop of York after about 1660 are in the Borthwick Institute for Archives, in the University of York. There are published indexes to the allegations up to 1839, and to the accompanying marriage bonds as far as 1822. Indexed abstracts of allegations and bonds between 1567 and 1714 have been published by the Yorkshire Archaeological Society. Indexes to Welsh marriage allegations and bonds from 1616 up to 1838, in the National Library of Wales, are searchable at **www.llgc.org.uk**.

Although it cost money, a licence guaranteed privacy and was a quicker procedure than the reading of banns. Until 1822, the required residency period was four weeks in the parish where the wedding was intended. Later, this was reduced to 15 days. The groom and bride alleged under oath that there was no impediment in civil or canon law to their union, and confirmed that they were both over 21 or that parental consent had been given if either was still a minor. The allegations gave their current places of residence, marital status and occupation, and between 1822 and 1823, a certified copy of each partner's baptism entry was attached too. The groom's signed bond pledged a large sum of money as security for the truth of the allegations, and a friend or relative acted as his surety.

Clandestine and irregular marriages

Before 25 March 1754, there were three other ways of getting married, which were legal in common law, though frowned upon by the Church and the courts. One was by contract, whereby each party clearly stated their intention either to marry the other now or in the future and expressed their mutual consent in front of witnesses. 'Now' meant that the marriage was immediately valid rather than from the moment it was consummated. The second type of marriage was performed in secret (clandestinely) by an ordained priest in the presence of two or more witnesses. The third was an irregular ceremony in a church or chapel.

A number of city, urban and rural parishes earned a reputation for clandestine and irregular wedding ceremonies. The registers of such 'lawless churches', which claimed exemption from ecclesiastical control, contain far more wedding entries than baptisms and burials. A clandestine marriage dispensed with the need for banns or a licence, and was conducted in a church or chapel of a place where neither party lived, in a special room in a tavern or coffee-house or even within the precincts or vicinity of a prison. An irregular marriage took place in a parish where at least one of the couple was a resident, but again without banns or licence, or in a church other than where the banns had been read, or for which a licence had been granted but neither party was local or had not been living in the parish for the obligatory four weeks.

It has been reckoned that in the early eighteenth century between a quarter and a third of all weddings were contracted in such spots. As a result of the statute of 1753 (known as Lord Hardwicke's Act), marriages conducted in England and Wales were lawful only if according to Anglican rites, by banns or by licence, so contract, pre-contract, clandestine and irregular weddings came to an abrupt end. Similar marriages in Scotland were declared illegal in 1856, unless one of the parties had been a resident there for at least 21 days, so until then, many eloping English couples took advantage of the loophole and journeyed over the border to marry in places like Gretna Green, or sailed from Southampton to the Channel Islands, or from Heysham to the Isle of Man, where the 1753 Act did not apply either.

Many of the surviving registers, notebooks and indexes of clandestine marriages compiled by clergymen, marriage-mongers or register-keepers, are now available on microfilm in the National Archives, and in the Family Records Centre, and copies can be hired in to inspect in family history centres. It is planned to make indexed digital images accessible soon. Others found their way into other repositories, were filed as court evidence in legal proceedings, stayed in private hands or were destroyed. You can study printed and indexed transcriptions by M. Herber of clandestine marriages between 1680 and 1754 in the deposited records of the Chapel and Rules of the Fleet Prison.

The authenticity of a lot of the entries is questionable because they were subject to fabrication or duplication, pre-dated to legitimize a child or to claim a right of inheritance, were incomplete, or written up out of chronological order. Occasionally baptisms were included too. The professed wedding date, names and marital status of both parties, their places of residence and the husband's occupation were usually given, seemingly providing valuable clues as to where they came from, but some of the names and places were bogus to disguise their true identities.

To find the dates and whereabouts of register books of Scottish irregular marriage centres, visit **www.gro-scotland.gov.uk/famrec/hlpsrch/summrar/index.html**.

Tips

- If you find a marriage entry after 25 March 1754, but no baptisms of any children, it may suggest that one partner was nonconformist.
- Perhaps the wedding took place in a large city or town away from the prying eyes of neighbours, or because one of the couple was under-age and was unlikely to obtain parental consent. In an urban parish where the population was crowded and constantly shifting couples could lie about themselves and sit tight to fulfil the necessary residential qualification.

Marriage indexes

There are other marriage indexes you can find besides the extracts in the International Genealogical Index and British Isles Vital Records Index. Look at *Marriage and Census Indexes for Family Historians*, by J. Gibson and E. Hampson. There are two outstanding examples. Up to 1955, Percival Boyd and his associates compiled a marriage index for England containing almost seven million names in published material relating to 4,300 parishes, representing between 12 per cent and 15 per cent of the recorded marriages between 1538 and 1840. Not every county was covered, nor are the date-spans identical or unbroken for each place. You can search the index at **www.origins network.com** as well as details about what is included. The original volumes are in the library of the Society of Genealogists, to which there is a published list, and microfilm copies are available for hire in family history centres. There are double entries for each marriage. Just the year, surnames and abbreviated forenames of each couple, the place of marriage or licence issuing office were noted, so you will need to go back to the original documentation for full details. The spelling of surnames was usually phonetic: for instance, surnames beginning with 'Gn-' and 'Kn-' appear under 'N-', so caution is required.

The second research tool is Pallot's Marriage Index. If you have totally lost trace of your ancestors between 1780 and 1837, use this to discover if they were married in London. The index contains double entries for each couple's wedding, in all but two of the 103 City of London churches, making it a prime genealogical source. It also includes selected extracts from registers in other counties, and there is a less extensive baptism index for the same period. See **www.ancestry.co.uk** for indexed digital images of the cards themselves. The basic index is on CD-ROM. Details of parish coverage are listed there and in *The Phillimore Atlas and Index of Parish Registers*.

You can search indexed transcribed copies of more than 1,000 marriage registers at **www.thegenealogist.co.uk**. This website includes all the printed compilations edited by W. P. W. Phillimore and E. A. Fry, most of which end in 1812, leaving a gap of 25 years before civil registration.

Look out, too, for the ongoing project of the Federation of Family History Societies to compile county marriage indexes particularly from 1754 up to 1837, which will eventually be uploaded into **www.familyhistoryonline.org.uk**.

Tips

• If you know your ancestor's approximate year of birth, but cannot locate his baptism or marriage, search the above indexes for the weddings of females of the same surname and generation, who might be his sisters, as brides tended to marry in their parish of birth.

• You can draw on marriage indexes to plot your surname's distribution over time and place and to find stray references to family members who married away from home.

Having found your ancestor's marriage, you can then begin to hunt for his baptism. If you haven't been lucky enough to trace his marriage, tackle his parish of residence first, if you know this. You will need to cover a wide period if you do not have an approximate birth year to work from. If he died after 1813, the burial register will invariably record his age. However, in the past, people were frequently uncertain about their true ages, so you will still have to search several years around the estimated year of birth.

Family burials

Burial registers tend to be neglected by family historians, perhaps because they are thought to contain little of genealogical interest. Up to 1812, at best they can tell you the date, name, place of abode, occupation and age of the dead person. If he or she was under 21, the parents' names should be mentioned, and whether the individual was an infant. If you have ancestors who died and were buried between about 1770 and 1812, in the dioceses where Dade and Barrington registers were in use, you are likely to find their ages, cause of death and parentage recorded too. A woman's marital status was often disclosed, together with her husband's name. In Wales, married women were frequently referred to by their maiden names when they were buried. At worst, the burial registers will tell you merely the date and the deceased's name.

In times of crisis or during epidemics such as the 'pox' or plague, under-registration was inevitable, especially in thickly populated parishes. The reason for sudden increased mortality or interrupted recording was usually explained. Some late eighteenth- and nineteenth-century registers in and around the City of London set out the cause of death. Exact places of interment in the church or churchyard might occasionally be specified too. When the initial letter 'P' was written against someone's name, this signified a pauper's funeral, though it was probably done with latitude when there was a Stamp Duty on burials between 1783 and 1794.

By law, from 1667 until 1814, corpses had to be wrapped in sheep wool to buoy up the English woollen industry. Each burial entry was completed by a note ('by Aff') testifying that an affidavit had been sworn before a magistrate by a member of the defunct's family to this effect. The details about affidavits were sometimes accompanied by the person's name and relationship to the deceased. Where the burial registers are deficient, the affidavits can prove invaluable as they were sworn within eight days of the interment.

Some registrations mentioned people who were 'hurled', 'interred' or 'tumbled' into the ground. These are likely to relate to the burials of dissenters without Anglican funeral rites, of an unbaptized or excommunicated parishioner or of a suicide. Burials of executed convicted felons abound in the registers of towns where the county Assize Sessions sat.

After 1813, you will invariably find under headed printed columns, the date of burial, forename, surname, age and place of residence of the deceased and the signature of the officiating priest. The given ages were often unreliable, and marital status and family relationships were omitted. You may even discover a burial entry for which there is no corresponding civil death registration.

From 1853 (1852 in London) only churchyard burials were recorded in church registers. If you know approximately when and where a person died you may have to track his or her burial to a public or private cemetery. Until 1894, when local council authorities took over, most of the cemeteries were run by parish Burial Boards. The Burial Boards' registers are now in county record offices. These will tell you the date of each person's burial, his or her last place of residence, occupation, age and the relevant plot number, and whether the body was placed in consecrated or unconsecrated ground. The unconsecrated area was reserved for non-Anglicans. The location of many district council and private company cemeteries and crematoria are listed in *The Family and Local History Handbook*. For London, consult *Greater London Cemeteries and Crematoria*, by P. S. Wolfston, and revised by C. Webb, and *London Cemeteries, An Illustrated Guide and Gazetteer*, by H. Meller. You may not be able to inspect the registers yourself, and a fee may be charged for the disclosure of any information. Always obtain the plot numbers and ask for instructions on how to find a particular grave.

Burial indexes

The National Burial Index (see page 59) is well worth trawling. Indexed transcriptions of some cemetery registers are also searchable at **www.familyhistoryonline.org.uk**.

Boyd's London Burials, 1538–1853, contains 300,000 indexed names including those of Protestant dissenters who were interred in Bunhill Burial Ground after 1833. The index is searchable at **www.originsnetwork.com**, and on microfiche, whilst the original volumes are held in the library of the Society of Genealogists. The entries were largely restricted to adult males, and consist of the surname, forename, year of death and burial ground, and the person's age if known.

Tips

Don't leave burials out of your research plan. Burial registrations complement baptisms and marriages in a variety of ways:

- they round off a person's life, and may tell you how old they were at death;
- they may mark the end of one marriage and the availability of the surviving partner to enter a new one. Multiple marriages were very common in the past, as women often died in childbirth, leaving a widower needing someone to care for his younger children. A widow might be left without enough income to support herself and her offspring, so might marry a much older man, who perhaps already had a family of his own;
- they can clarify family relationships and eliminate other people of the same name;
- they may indicate where incomers or strangers came from;
- the given places of residence may provide clues to family continuity of occupancy, and the names of houses or farms to their latest date of construction;
- you may need to rely on them as a starting point from which to work your way back over someone's life if you have failed to find his or her marriage or baptism.

The date of burial should prompt you to look for a will or a grant of letters of administration.

Gravestone inscriptions

Wherever practicable, use burial registers in conjunction with gravestone inscriptions, as they often contain extra personal and family details. An inscription carved before 1813 may be the only evidence you have about someone's approximate year of birth.

However, because the majority of parish registers have been removed to county record offices, this may involve a special journey to an outlying churchyard or cemetery. Many churchyards have been cleared but it is worth enquiring whether a plan of the numbered plots and a copy of the inscriptions were made, and their present whereabouts.

It is worth asking at the county record office about any transcriptions in its collections, and use a search engine to find out what may be available online. A good collection of copies of headstone inscriptions is in the library of the Society of Genealogists (see **www.sog.org.uk**). There are published lists to its holdings too. Such transcriptions can be particularly helpful when gravestones are no longer legible or in place, or are set in a crowded or overgrown churchyard or cemetery.

No gravestone inscriptions are included in the National Burial Index, but the Federation of Family History Societies is creating a database of indexed transcriptions and images of gravestones, which are searchable by county and place at **www.family historyonline.org.uk**.

Headstones became popular and widespread from the late eighteenth century, using local materials. At best, an inscription will identify the occupants of the plot, their dates of birth and death, their places of residence and occupations, and their relationship to each other. Sometimes, occupations, activities or hobbies were represented by carved symbols. Don't forget to look for war memorials too. The Federation of Family History Societies, in collaboration with the Imperial War Museum, is currently compiling a national inventory of war memorials. See **www.ffhs.org.uk** for more information.

Inside the church, more elaborate memorials were used to commemorate the local nobility, gentry, wealthy landowners, and merchants. Many of the earlier inscriptions were written in Latin. A short printed guide to the church will usually translate them for you.

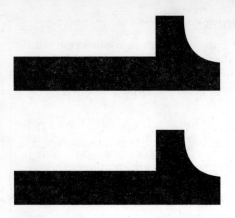

the nonconformists

In this chapter you will learn:
- how different religious sects broke away from the Established Church
- what non-parochial records you can search
- how the records complemen
  parish registers.

It is likely that we all have ancestors who were nonconformists for however short a time.

Since 1558, when England became a Protestant country, the Established Church has been Anglican rather than Roman Catholic. The first overt Protestant dissidents were the Puritans, many of whom, in the early and mid-seventeenth century, voted with their feet, and took ship with their priests to the Netherlands or to the English colonies and plantations along the Eastern seaboard of North America. Nevertheless, the baptisms, marriages and burials of nonconformists were still performed in local churches, because they were forced to meet in secret and were subject to civil and religious intolerance. They soon ramified into three discrete Movements: the General and Particular Baptists, the Presbyterians and Unitarians, and the Independents or Congregationalists, collectively called the Old Dissenters. In the mid-seventeenth century the Religious Society of Friends also broke away from the Established Church.

Between 1643 and 1660, the Anglican clergy were ejected and replaced by Presbyterian elders, After the Restoration of the Monarchy in 1660, many of the Presbyterian ministers were evicted. Some held informal meetings and performed secret marriages in the countryside, whilst others chose to emigrate.

From 1672, nonconforming preachers and householders were permitted to apply to the local bishop for a licence to 'teach' or hold meetings in their homes. A list of their names, addresses and denominations, taken from sources in Lambeth Palace Library, and from State Papers in the National Archives, has been printed in *Original Records of Early Nonconformity under Persecution and Indulgence*, by G. Lyon Turner. The Act of Toleration in 1689 went further, and henceforward Protestant dissenters could erect their own meeting houses or chapels for worship, so long as they were registered with the local archdeacon, bishop or county quarter sessions. This granted them official recognition and provided a place for people of the same religious persuasion to gather, take their children for baptism, marry and even bury their dead.

Although lots of chapels were established around this date, they did not all flourish. At first, most meeting houses served a wide radius, or were shared by different congregations. As the number of adherents increased, daughter chapels might be founded, although the births and baptisms might continue to be recorded by the mother chapel. Some preachers travelled around on circuit, whilst others became so popular that their fame attracted people from far afield, so births and baptisms might be registered many miles from home.

Some dissenters returned to the Anglican fold, or joined another denomination. Returners to the Anglican Church were frequently described in parish registers as 'Anabaptists' when they were baptized or buried. Where they had no burial grounds of their own, especially before the mid-eighteenth century, nonconformists were often allocated a separate area in the parish churchyard, where they performed their own funeral services. It can be difficult to distinguish from the parish registers alone who was and was not an Anglican. You may have to seek this information from sources such as the archdeacons' six-monthly parish visitation papers, in which were listed the names of known or suspected dissenters and non-Communicants. The records are in diocesan or county record offices, but they are not indexed.

Gradually, splinter sects, whose beliefs diverged from the mainstream, hived off to form their own meetings. Pre-eminent among the newer Movements were the Methodists. Until 1790, however, the Methodists generally continued to be baptized and buried by clergy of the Established Church, but worshipped in their own places.

Each denomination had areas of the country where its influence was particularly strong.

Nonconformists' registers

The first known surviving English Protestant non-parochial register dates from 1644, but few commenced that early. Moreover, when the Presbyterian Movement was predominant between 1645 and 1660, every birth and death was recorded in the church registers, rendering separate registration unnecessary. Similarly, under an act of 1694, when a tax on births, marriages and deaths was in force until 1706, these events were noted in parish rather than chapel or meeting-house registers. The advantage for nonconformists of mandatory registration was that such records could be produced in a court of law to prove paternity or age, whereas their own registers could not.

In 1840 and 1857, the Registrar General of England and Wales ordered the surrender by every nonconformist congregation of its registers up to 1837 for examination and authentication. Foreign Protestant congregations in England also submitted their registers for inspection and validation. The register books are now in the National Archives, and microfilmed copies of these, and of deposited but unauthenticated registers, can be searched there, in the Family Records Centre, and in family history centres, whilst county record offices invariably have microfilmed copies of the registers relating to their own areas. Microfilmed copies of the Welsh nonconformist registers are available in the National Library of Wales. It is planned to upload digital images of the deposited registers on **www.thegenealogist.co.uk** soon.

A large number of non-parochial registers were withheld, particularly by the Baptists. Some may still be found in local chapels, but most have been transferred to county record offices, denominational headquarters or libraries, or other places. The county by county editions of the *National Index of Parish Registers* list the dates and known whereabouts of many nonconformist chapel registers, indexes and transcriptions. An online database of the dates and present location of Welsh chapel registers is available in the National Library of Wales, and *Nonconformist Registers of Wales*, edited by D. Ifans, contains a complete survey of the Principality. The National Library of Wales holds an extensive collection of material generated by the Welsh Calvinist Methodists. Most denominations publish *Yearbooks*, giving the addresses of present-day chapels and meetings, so it is worth making contact if you cannot locate a specific chapel register, or want to collect information from a date later than 1837.

Tips

- The catalogue to the holdings in the National Archives (**www.nationalarchives.gov.uk/catalogue**) gives the title, foundation date and denomination of each chapel when the registers were surrendered, and the dates of the first and last recorded entries. However, the denomination might have changed several times, and the first given date might not be the earliest recorded. The foundation and first register entry dates may be many years apart too. Always examine the registers of all the known chapels within a 30-mile radius of where your ancestors lived to make sure you have missed nothing.

- The books were not uniformly preserved or kept up to date, and were subject to gaps and under-recording. Baptism entries might be jumbled up retrospectively amongst those of a later date, and burial registrations were often erratic or short on detail. Under-recording was least likely between 1785 and 1794, when the Stamp Duty on baptisms and burials was extended to nonconformist registrations. This was seen as a tacit acceptance of their records as legal documents.

- Because the registers were regarded as the personal property of the minister, he might carry them with him from chapel to chapel, so entries from entirely different parts of the country might be mixed up in his book.

What the registers contain

There are fewer entries than in parish church registers because the congregations were much smaller, making them quick and easy to search. Extracts from all of the centrally deposited and authenticated registers of births and baptisms are included in the International Genealogical Index.

The dated birth or baptism entries usually disclose the names of the child and his or her parents (including the mother's maiden name), where they lived and the father's occupation, so are more informative than their Anglican counterparts. The inclusion of the mother's maiden name makes it simpler to trace parents' marriages in the parish church registers after 25 March 1754, and the given places of residence tell you how far people travelled to have their infants baptized by their favourite priest, or in their nearest denominational chapel. They also provide invaluable clues as to where the parents themselves might have been baptized and married. Certain family names recur again and again in the registers, suggesting a long and close association with the local chapel, and the likelihood of marriages between families holding similar beliefs.

Don't forget that parish church registers might refer to the bodies of dead dissenters who were 'interred', 'hurled' or 'tumbled' into the ground. However, from the eighteenth century, congregations began to entrust or purchase land for their members' burials, but the registers were often deficient before 1864, when all burial grounds became legally bound to keep full records. After 1880, nonconformist ministers were allowed to conduct their own funerals in parish churchyards, which were then registered by the church. Extracts from many nonconformist registers are included in the National Burial Index.

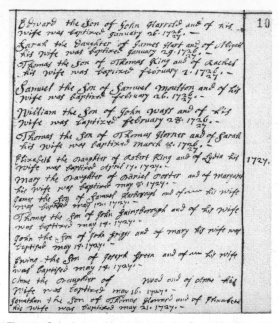

Figure 16 Thomas Gainsborough's baptism in the Great Meeting of the Independent Congregation in Sudbury, Suffolk, 1727. The family later assigned some of their land to the Meeting for use as a burying ground. John Gainsborough, the artists father, was a clothier
(reproduced by permission of The National Archives)

The non-parochial burial entries set out the date and name of the deceased, which was sometimes accompanied by his or her place of residence and age.

The registers of public burial grounds in large urban centres contain references to people of all sects. The most well-known of these were Bunhill Fields, and Bethnal Green Protestant Dissenters' Burying Ground, in London. You can search their registers, between 1713 and 1854 and 1793 and 1837 respectively, on microfilm in the National Archives, the Family Records Centre, and in family history centres. The registers of Bunhill Fields Burial Ground, in City Road, are indexed up to 1838, and you can trawl the database at **www.originsnetwork.com** for details of interments from 1833 up to 1853 in Bunhill Burial Ground (Golden Lane Cemetery).

Gravestone inscriptions

Monumental inscriptions may complement or fill gaps in the registers, many of which they pre-date. Transcripts of a number of these have been published, of which there is a good collection in the library of the Society of Genealogists (see **www.sog.org.uk**). The Federation of Family History Societies is gradually uploading indexed transcriptions, arranged by county, and then by place, at **www.familyhistoryonline.org.uk**. Use a search engine to find out what else is available online.

Two London birth registries

In 1742, a centralized birth registry was set up in Dr Williams's Library, in London, by elders of the Old Dissent. It was hoped that its certificates would become admissible as evidence of age and paternity in a court of law, and make up for the recognized deficiencies of local record-keeping. Anyone paying the requisite fee was welcome to register their children's births, and as it was not limited to Londoners, the resulting volumes contain details of the births of people from all over the British Isles and abroad. The earliest birth occurred in 1717, and there were more than 50,000 registrations before it was closed at the end of 1837.

Duplicate certificates were first completed locally and signed by the parents and by two witnesses, who testified the date and parish of birth. The names of the child, both parents and of the maternal grandfather were recorded, together with their places of residence, the occupations of the father and grandfather, and the name of the local Anglican clergyman. After 1768, the date and place of the child's baptism were frequently included too. The two certificates were then presented with the registration fee at the registry, where the information was copied up into the register. Each registration was dated and consecutively numbered, and endorsed on the duplicate certificates. When parents took the opportunity of registering their own births at the same time as those of their children, or their visit to the registry was delayed until childbearing was complete, the registration numbers of an entire family will follow in sequence. One of the two certificates was kept in the registry and the other handed back to the parents. The registers and certificates are available on microfilm in the National Archives and Family Records Centre, and can be hired in to search in a family history centre. The numbered entries are accessed by intial-alphabetical indexes, which are arranged in blocks of years. Extracts from 80 per cent of the certificates have been incorporated into the British Isles Vital Records Index.

A similar Wesleyan Methodist Metropolitan Registry was established in London in 1818. Its indexed registers cover more than 10,000 registered births between 1773 and 1838. You can inspect them on microfilm in the National Archives, the Family Records Centre, and in family history centres. Extracts from these certificates, too, are embedded in the British Isles Vital Records Index.

> **Tip**
>
> The registers are arranged by date of registration rather than of birth, so search the indexes for an extended period.

Religious Society of Friends

The Religious Society of Friends has its roots in the 1650s. The minute books of their fortnightly preparative, monthly and county quarterly meetings in England and Wales, include notifications of births, deaths and burials, and exchanges of marriage vows. The majority of the registers up to 1837 were surrendered for inspection and authentication in 1840 or in 1857, and you can search them on microfilm in the National Archives, and in the Family Records Centre, or hire them in to study in family history centres. It is planned to make indexed digital images available soon. The minute books of the Friends' meetings in Wales since the 1660s can be inspected in the Glamorgan Record Office, in Cardiff.

Indexes and copies

Before the minute books were handed in, separate county digests of births, marriages and deaths were compiled and indexed initial-alphabetically by surname. Microfilmed copies are in the Religious Society of Friends Library, in London (**www.quaker.org.uk**). If you want to examine them, unless you are a member, you will need to bring a letter of introduction with you, and you will also need to book a microfilm reader before your visit. There is a search fee. You can extract all the references to your surname and its variants from the seventeenth century up to 1837 in any chosen county before searching the minute books themselves. However, the birth and death digests are virtual copies of what you will find in the minutes, although the county marriage digests omit the names of the witnesses. Look in the digests under the surnames of both marriage partners for details of their parentage.

Also in the Friends Library are centralized registers of births from 1 July 1837 until 1959 (when birthright membership was abolished), deaths and burials to 1961, and of marriages between Friends throughout Great Britain to 1963. These are arranged chronologically by initial letter of surname. From 1843, the announcements of births, marriages and deaths in *The Friend* (discontinued after 1913) or *British Friend* may be better sources. There is also an index to about 20,000 names of Friends who died between 1813 and 1920, which was compiled from the *Annual Monitor*.

What the minute books tell you

The birth registrations record each child's name, when and where he or she was born, the names of both parents, their place of domicile, and the father's occupation. Retrospective details about early seventeenth-century births of founder-members might be enshrined in the minutes too.

The dated marriage entries set out the names and addresses of each bridal couple, their occupations, parentage and the places of residence and occupations of their fathers, followed by a list of names of everyone who was present, starting with their kinsfolk. The names of the witnesses are extremely helpful because you can often trace their family connections through the minute books, which were usually integrally indexed by the grooms' and brides' names, and they reveal who in your family was alive at a certain date. Quaker marriages continued uninterrupted after 25 March 1754, as they were exempted from Hardwicke's prescriptive Marriage Act of 1753.

The notifications of death were very comprehensive. In most instances they provide the dates and places death and burial, as well as the name, age, last place of residence, occupation and parentage of the deceased person. Husbands' names are included for married women and widows. You can thus gather information about two generations in your family from a single registration.

As Quakers were frequently interred in private gardens, orchards, or in a parcel of land designated as a Sepulchre, the precise location of their graves might be difficult to find. In 1717, headstones were denounced as idolatrous, so memorial inscriptions were rare before 1850, when the rule was relaxed.

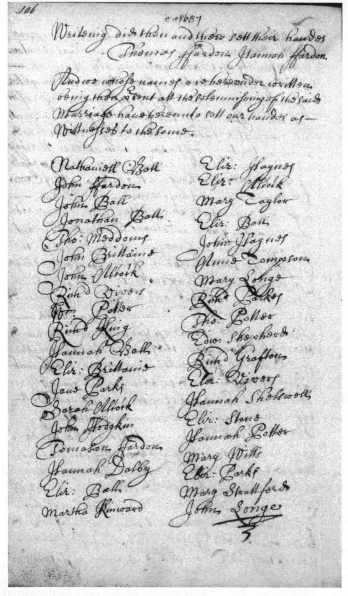

Figure 17 part of the register of Banbury Monthly Meeting of the Society of Friends, Oxfordshire, recording the exchange of marriage vows between Thomas Fardon and Hannah Ball, 1687. The couple's relatives were the first to sign as witnesses, with a number of other more distant kinsfolk, whose relationship to Thomas and Hannah can be traced in the other monthly minute books (reproduced by permission of The National Archives)

Tips

- Remember that days and months were numbered rather than named by the Quakers. Before 1 January 1752, the first day of the year fell on 25 March, which was also the first month, February being the twelfth, and Sunday was the first day of the week. The dates given in the county digests are exactly as they appeared in the minute books.
- Look in parish church registers for the baptisms of lapsed Quakers, for their marriages to non-Friends, and for their burials in churchyards, especially in the first 50 years after the reinforcing Burial in Wool Act of 1678.

You may find details about Friends' forthcoming marriages in the minutes of the men's and women's joint or separate preparative and monthly meetings. If one of the parties belonged to another meeting, a certificate affirming his or her fittedness for marriage was secured, and finally, a certificate recording the publication of marriage and lack of any objection was issued. Occasionally a couple's two or three minuted monthly notifications of intent and this certificate are the only extant records of a marriage, although they do not necessarily mean the ceremony actually took place. Sometimes it was discovered that someone had entered a previous engagement which had not been cleared by a written certificate of liberation.

When a Quaker was married by a priest or married someone who was more closely related than the fourth degree (i.e. they shared a great-great-grandfather), he or she was disowned. It was possible for the Friend to be re-instated later and should the non-Quaker partner join the Society, their children were regarded as birthright members. Even if this did not happen, the children's births might still be recorded. Any infants born during the period of disownment were not registered.

Embedded in the monthly and quartely minutes are testimonies about recently deceased Friends which will tell you more about their lives and reputations. The minutes of the London yearly meetings of county elders and representatives contain similar obituaries. Until 1796, minuted yearly meetings were also held in Wales. Copies of the indexed printed minutes of the yearly meetings between 1672 and 1906 are in the Friends Library.

Roman Catholics

If your ancestors were Roman Catholics, their baptisms, marriages and burials most probably took place in the Established Anglican Church until about 1791, because from at least 1581, their own religious practices were proscribed by a series of punitive laws.

As a result of a statute of 1606, Roman Catholics were obliged to be baptized and buried by the Church of England, on penalty of a hefty fine. Private Catholic baptisms were often peformed in a local nobleman's or landowner's house by his personal priest or chaplain, thereby avoiding the necessity of setting foot inside the church, and conforming with the law. However, Catholic landowners' children were invariably publicly baptized in the Established Church in order to protect their rights of inheritance, so local Catholic recusants may be difficult to tell apart from Anglicans in the registrations. Full Catholic emancipation did not happen until 1829.

Early Catholic records were carefully protected and thin on the ground to prevent their confiscation as incriminating directories of adherents. The first known extant register dates from 1657. Although rough notebooks, missals, pocket books and loose paper were used by private priests and house chaplains to write down details about baptisms, more formal recording became prevalent only from the mid-eighteenth century, especially after the passage of the first Catholic Relief Act of 1778, and from 1791, when their places of worship could be registered with the county quarter sessions and thus became legal.

Many of the Roman Catholic registers are still in private hands, though a small number up to 1837 were deposited with the Registrar General in 1840 and 1857 for scrutiny and validation. These mainly relate to congregations in Yorkshire, Northumberland and Durham, and can be searched on microfilm in the National Archives, the Family Records Centre, and in family history centres. Extracts from the authenticated registers have been incorporated into the International Genealogical Index.

A few registers from other counties such as Hampshire and Lancashire have been published by the Catholic Record Society. Look for lists of surviving records, their dates and whereabouts in *Catholic Missions and Registers, 1700–1880*, compiled by M. J. Gandy. There is a separate *Catholic Parishes in England, Wales and Scotland, An Atlas*, by the same author, marking out their boundaries. You can obtain the names and addresses of priests who have retained their registers from the current edition of *The Catholic Directory*, which is arranged by diocese and then by parish.

What the registers disclose

The register entries were generally composed in Latin, the dated baptisms setting out the name of the child, its parents, mother's maiden name, the parental residence and father's occupation. The child's date and place of birth and parents' birthplaces might be included as well, and the entries invariably mentioned the names of grandparents and godparents ('sponsors' or 'gossips'). Some baptisms were recorded retrospectively, and the spelling of surnames was idiosyncratic and often phonetic.

Marriages between Catholics may have been covert, or by licence in an Anglican church, after which a private ceremony was conducted by a Catholic priest. From 25 March 1754 until 30 June 1837, they were compelled to marry in the Anglican Church.

In the seventeenth and eighteenth centuries Catholic recusants were often buried in private land, although after 1791 graveyards were sometimes attached to their chapels and churches. The surviving registers of interments usually record the name, date of and age at death and when the deceased was laid to rest. Local Catholics who were allowed to be buried in the parish churchyard might be described in the registers as 'papists' or 'recusants'. Excommunicates could not be buried in a churchyard without a special licence from the bishop, so might be 'privately interred' at night, indicating the absence of Anglican rites. The Burial Act of 1852 legalized Roman Catholic burial grounds, and in 1880 funeral rites outside the Church of England were permitted in Anglican churchyards too.

Monumental inscriptions on headstones in churchyards prior to 1830 are likely to concern Catholics if they were incised with a cross or the monogram 'IHS', but thereafter their attribution is less certain.

12

parish registers in the rest of the British Isles, Ireland and the USA

In this chapter you will learn:
- what Established Church registers exist and their whereabouts
- what registers are indexed and available online
- what other denominational records you can examine.

The Channel Islands

The International Genealogical Index is worth trawling first for register extracts of baptisms and marriages of Channel Islanders. This will tell you in which parishes you should be looking for full information. Don't forget to find out from the accompanying list which parishes, events and periods are covered by the Index.

The first surviving parochial registration in Jersey dates from 1542, in Guernsey in 1563, Sark in 1570 and in Alderney in 1657, although there are a few earlier entries after 1628.

The Anglican Church registers in Jersey up to 1842 are kept in the Jersey Archive, together with copies of the Channel Islands Family History Society indexes to entries in these and in the registers of the Methodist, Independent and Roman Catholic congregations up to the same date.

In Guernsey, you can examine microfilmed copies of the registers of each of its ten parishes, of Alderney and of Sark in the Priaulx Library. Copies are also held by the Guernsey Island Archives Service, in St Peter Port. Details about Roman Catholic residents are preserved among the records of the Bishop of Portsmouth, on the mainland, and a transcript of the baptisms, marriages and burials of native Channel Islanders at the 'French Church', in Southampton, is in the library of the Society of Genealogists. This runs from 1567 until the eighteenth century.

It is worth looking for births, marriages and deaths of Channel Islanders between 1831 and 1958 in the indexed microfilmed copies of the Registrar General's Miscellaneous Non-statutory Foreign Returns, which you can inspect in the National Archives, in the Family Records Centre, or hire in to search in a family history centre. It is planned to upload digital images of these at **www.thegenealogist.co.uk**.

Isle of Man

In 1883, after the introduction of civil registration, the registers of all 17 ancient parishes and nonconformist chapels were called in and are now held in the Civil Registry, in Douglas. The earliest entry dates from 1607. However, the registers of Roman Catholic congregations have usually been retained by the parish priests. Indexed copies of deposited registers are on microfilm in the Manx National Heritage Library and Archives, and in the Isle of Man Family History Society Library, in Peel. You will need to employ a researcher to use the former institution; the staff can advise you about this. Extracts of the baptism and marriage entries have been included in the International Genealogical Index too.

The surviving bishop's transcripts, which were arranged by district, span the years between 1734 and 1767, and from 1786 up to the end of the nineteenth century, and are available in the Registry too. Filmed copies up to 1799 can also be consulted in the Manx National Heritage Library and Archives.

Until 1849, nonconformists had by law to marry in the Established Church. Indexed registers of their later marriages up to 1883 are in the Civil Registry with the later civil registration indexes and registers. You can hire in microfilm copies in family history centres.

The Isle of Man Family History Society has been very active in compiling personal-name indexes and transcripts of all the known local gravestone inscriptions, and you can search these both in their own library and in the Manx National Heritage Library and Archives. You can also examine them on microfilm in family history centres.

Scotland

In 1552, the General Provincial Council of Scotland ordered each parish to keep similar registers to those which had been introduced in England in 1538. The earliest extant old parochial register of the Established (Presbyterian) Church of Scotland dates from 1553, but most commence after 1616. Visit **www.gro-scotland.gov.uk/famrec/hlpsrch/opr-cov.html** for a list of start dates of births, baptisms, marriages, deaths and burials. You can also find the dates of earliest register entries from *The Phillimore Atlas and Index of Parish Registers*.

Registration was frequently spasmodic, particularly in remote crofting and fishing communities and the islands, and there might be lengthy intervals when there was no recording at all, especially of deaths and burials before 1855. This might be explained by the custom of taking the bodies of people back to their birthplaces or ancestral burying grounds, or by the presence of several graveyards in a parish. From 1661 to 1689, when the Established Church was Episcopalian, many Presbyterians were baptized, married and buried in secret, so there is likely to have been no recording, at least until the

Declaration of Indulgence in 1687. Further disruptions were caused in 1733, 1761 and 1843, when seceders refused registration of their children's births, and instead paid fines to the kirk session clerks. The Stamp Duty on baptisms, marriages and burials, in force between 1783 and 1794, led to more under-registration.

Digital images of the indexed registers and microfilm copies of the births, baptisms, marriage banns and proclamations of marriages in the Established Church of Scotland up to 1854 are in the General Register Office for Scotland, and can be consulted in regional archives and libraries throughout the country. See **www.kinhelp.co.uk/arcnlib.html** for a list. A register of 'Neglected Entries', compiled by the Registrar General's clerks, of births, marriages and deaths between 1801 and 1854 which had not been recorded in the old registers, is filed at the end of each relevant Old Parochial Register. The indexes and digital images are accessible at **www.scotlandspeople.gov.uk** as well, so you can go swiftly and easily from the indexed birth, marriage, and death registrations after 1855 to the census returns between 1841 and 1901 and then move on to the Old Parochial Registers. The indexes to the Old Parochial Registers are also available at **www.familysearch.org** and on CD-ROM. Registers later than 1854 are generally still in the relevant parish presbytery.

Tips

- If your surname begins with Mc- or Mac- be sure to check under both prefixes, as they are indexed separately.
- Look out for interchangeable capital letters such as 'Qu' for 'W', and for Gaelic forenames.
- Where both the birth and the baptism dates were recorded in the registers, the index reference is to the baptism date, and date of the proclamation of banns is preferred to that of a marriage.
- Only the first parish will be named in the indexes where several were joined together. You can identify which these were at **www.gro-scotland.gov.uk/files/registration-districts-from-1855.pdf**, the maps in *The Phillimore Atlas and Index of Parish Registers*, or from a gazetteer.

What the registers will tell you

The entries were recorded in Old Scots or in English. The most instructive registers concern births and baptisms. They nearly always contained both dates, the names of the child and its parents, the mother's maiden name, the parents' place of abode and the father's occupation. Even if its birth seniority was specified, this does not necessarily mean that it was the same mother throughout. The relationship of the godparents to the infant might also be stated.

The eldest son was customarily named after the paternal grandfather, the second after the maternal grandfather, and the third after the father, whilst the eldest daughter took the name of the mother's mother, the second that of the paternal grandmother, and the third daughter her mother's name, though there were variations. Some male and female first names were interchangeable, particularly in the Highlands, and Gaelic names, foreshortenings and forename variants were common, making positive identification hard.

Patronymics were often used instead of hereditary surnames in the Northern Isles up to the nineteenth century. Siblings might even be described by different surnames, although sharing the same father. From the eighteenth century, surnames, sometimes unconnected to the family, began to be used as baptismal names. Visit **www.scotlandspeople.gov.uk** for advice on surname and forename variants.

Until the nineteenth century, illegitimate infants normally took the known father's surname, so long as he acknowledged his patenity. Otherwise, the mother's name was used, and the children were legitimized if the parents subsequently married, whereupon the father's name was assumed. The kirk session registers, in the National Archives of Scotland or in the General Register Office for Scotland, recorded the outcome of any parochial investigations into the paternity of base born children so are worth exploring for more information.

Until 1834, all Scottish marriages were supposed to take place in the Established Church after the proclamation of banns on three successive Sundays or on a single day. The marriage or kirk session registers usually recorded these dates instead of the actual ceremony. The proclamations identified the couple's parishes of residence, perhaps the name of the bride's father, the groom's occupation, and if he was a minor (under 16), his paternity. If the couple lived in different parishes, the registers of one might note the proclamations and the other the date of their wedding.

The names of English Presbyterians appear in the registers between 25 March 1754 and 30 June 1837, when only Established Church weddings were legal in England and Wales. Edinburgh and Haddington, in East Lothian, were particularly popular marriage venues. Conversely, prior to 1754, Scottish Presbyterians in England tended to marry in Scots churches. Some of the registers have been deposited in the National Archives, at Kew. A list of Scots churches in England is held by the Presbyterian Historical Society, in London.

Irregular marriages

Up to 1939, irregular, but nonetheless valid, marriages were permitted in Scotland. These were

- by betrothal followed by consummation,
- by a mutual declaration of consent in the presence of witnesses,
- by cohabitation and repute (indicating mutual consent, but without the presence of witnesses), or
- without proclamation of banns, though taking place in the Established Church.

Since then, only unions by cohabitation and repute have been legally recognized, for which a decree of declaration of marriage is required from the Court of Session in Edinburgh.

Irregular marriages were conducted at Tolls, such as those at Lamberton, Mordington, Halidon Hill, and Coldstream, in the Scottish Border Country, and in matrimonial offices like Gretna Hall, in Dumfries and Galloway. See **www.gro-scotland.gov. uk/famrec/hlpsrch/sumrmar/runmar.html** for details of irregular border and runaway marriage centre records and their present whereabouts.

Irregular marriages were often recorded in parochial and kirk session registers, especially when a couple wanted to have a child baptized, or when one of the partners had died. The kirk session registers note the payment of fines for irregular marriages taking place without the proclamation of banns.

Burials and gravestones

Look for the dated accounts of fees received by the kirk session clerk for the hire of a mortcloth or pall to drape the coffins of parishioners over the age of ten. However, pauper families were not charged. The accounts partly compensate for the inadequate recording of burials.

Burial inside the church was forbidden in 1588, except of landowners and people claiming an ancestral entitlement granted by the kirk session. Until the eighteenth century, bodies were buried in the parish churchyard, but in the following century, non-denominational cemeteries began to be set aside in larger towns and burghs. The registers of these burial grounds were better kept. These are mostly held by the cemetery, municipal authority or parks department, but the General Register Office has a number before 1855. The Association of Scottish Family History Societies is currently compiling a national burial index from these records, which will eventually be made available to the public. The durable quality of Scottish granite and slate has ensured the survival of a surprising number of gravestone inscriptions from at least the sixteenth century, so where the registers are defective, these can be extraordinarily useful.

The Scottish Genealogy Society has an extensive collection of transcribed monumental inscriptions from all over the country and the outlying islands. Copies of many of these have been lodged in regional record offices and libraries. Consult the Family History Library catalogue at **www.familysearch.org** for microfilmed copies you can hire to search in family history centres.

The inscriptions usually recorded the deceased's dates of birth and death, occupation, trade or craft, which might be represented by carved symbols. His or her place of origin, croft, farm or township of domicile, parentage, spouse's name and parish of birth, and the names of any children might be added too. The word 'of' before a place-name indicated a landowner, 'in' a tenant, and 'at' a landless person. Women were invariably commemorated by their maiden names, which they retained throughout their lives.

Tip

If you fail to find your ancestors in the Old Parochial Registers, try the parish kirk session registers, some of which have been published. Microfilmed copies can be searched in the General Register Office for Scotland, including copies of those in the National Archives of Scotland. A complete list of kirk session registrations in the Old Parochial Registers, giving their dates, is available at **www.gro-scotland.gov.uk/famrec/hlpsrch/opr_app2.pdf**, and in *Detailed List of the Old Parochial Registers of Scotland*. Try **www.nas.gov.uk/catalogues/default.asp** for references to deposited material.

Dissenters in Scotland

When Roman Catholicism was outlawed in 1560, the Established Church in Scotland became Presbyterian, though from 1610 to 1638, and from 1661 to 1689, it too was displaced by the Episcopalian Church. Full religious toleration was restored in 1788.

If your ancestors lived in the Border Country it would be a good idea to search the registers of churches on both sides of the divide, especially after the Treaty of Union in 1707.

Unlike their English and Welsh counterparts, the Scottish nonconformist registers were never deposited centrally, although some dissenters' pre-1854 baptism, marriage and burial registers are in the National Archives of Scotland.

The Old Parochial Registers recorded people belonging to other denominations. For instance, the births, baptisms and banns of marriage of Episcopalians will be found there, especially after the two Jacobite rebellions of 1715 and 1745. The baptisms of many Methodists can also be traced in the registers of the Established Church of Scotland, rather than in their own records.

When nonconformist weddings were forbidden in 1661, many Scottish dissenters crossed over into England to marry until the 1753 statute put a stop to marriages outside the Established Church of England. Exceptionally, from 1712 until 1716, Scottish Episcopalians could be married by their own clergy provided that prayers were said for the Royal Family. When the prohibition on weddings in churches or chapels other than those belonging to the Church of Scotland was removed in 1834, the proclamation of banns was still required and recorded in the parochial registers. After 1939, the local registrar could perform such marriages on production either of a certificate showing that banns had been proclaimed or a licence from the county sheriff after the publication of a notice of the impending marriage.

The Religious Society of Friends

During the mid-1650s Quaker missionaries from Westmorland and Yorkshire started preaching in Scotland. In 1661, the Scots Quaker Act outlawed their meetings, and they became the subject of persecution, until the Act of Toleration in England in 1689 made tolerance fashionable, but not compulsory, in Scotland.

A comprehensive register of births, marriages, deaths and burials between 1622 and 1890, which were notified to the local preparatory and monthly meetings of Friends, is held in the General Register Office for Scotland. There is a microfilm copy of the register in the Religious Society of Friends Library, in London. A Scottish digest of the entries, also in the Library, runs up to 1837. This is arranged in initial-alphabetical order of surname and then chronologically by date. The birth and death entries are identical to what appeared in the original, but the names of witnesses to the exchanges of marriage vows were omitted – see **www.familysearch.org** for details of copies you can hire in a family history centre. A transcript of the minuted births to members between 1647 and 1874, proposals of marriage, 1685–1789, exchanges of marriage vows from 1656 until 1875, and deaths between 1667 and 1878, is in the library of the Society of Genealogists.

A central register of Quaker births throughout Great Britain from 1837 up to 1959, deaths to 1961 and marriages to 1963, is held in the Friends Library, too.

Roman Catholics

After 1560, and until the first Relief Act of 1792, Roman Catholics were subject to persecution in Scotland. The worst periods were after 1570, 1628 and 1688. Few Catholic registers survive from this era for obvious reasons. It was common for Catholics to attend church for Protestant worship and to take communion once a year to avoid being fined or otherwise penalized. During the early nineteenth century, large numbers of Irish Catholics arrived to work as railway navvies and shipwrights in the dockyards around the River Clyde, and in the cotton and textile factories in Glasgow, Paisley and elsewhere.

When the steamboat service started between Belfast and Glasgow in 1818, this gave added impetus to the recruitment of Irish labour, to the point at which the number of Roman Catholics was second only to membership of the Established Church of Scotland. Unfortunately, the registers and census returns do not tell us exactly where they came from, though their birth, marriage and death registrations after 1855 might provide a clue, as well as the online and other indexed Irish census returms.

Consult *Catholic Missions and Registers, 1700–1880*, Vol. 6, for details of the dates and present whereabouts of known Scottish records, some of which have been lodged in the National Archives of Scotland. Look in *Catholic Parishes in England, Wales and Scotland, An Atlas* for maps showing their boundaries.

As in England, the Roman Catholics resorted to private baptism ceremonies, although these had been prohibited since 1642. The parents then paid their dues to the kirk session, and held a second baptism service in the church.

The ban on nonconformist marriages in 1661 was directed largely at the Roman Catholic clergy, but couples might still have a second, private, wedding ceremony. The right to be married by their own clergy was specifically denied to Catholics under the Relief Act of 1792, and even when virtual full emancipation was granted in 1829, many of them continued to marry by cohabitation and repute.

The burials of Scottish Catholics probably happened in secret, and although they eventually opened their own burial grounds, no known records survive, so it is best to look for references in the registers of the non-sectarian cemeteries in the larger towns and burghs.

Ireland

Despite being a minority Movement, the Church of Ireland was paramount until its disestablishment on 1 January 1871, when its records were declared the property of the state, and were collected up for central storage.

The official keeping of parish registers of baptisms, marriages and burials began in Ireland in 1634. However, very few start so early, and most date after 1770, particularly outside towns. In

1922, a fire destroyed nearly a thousand registers of baptisms and burials up to 1870, and of marriages to 1845, which had been deposited as public records. This has left us with less than half the original total, fortuitously held back by the clergy when they were supposed to have been surrendered, plus any incidental copies made by priests at the time they were handed in, and extracts compiled by historians and genealogists before the fire. As the civil registration of non-Catholic marriages was not introduced until 1845, and of births, deaths and Catholic marriages not until 1864, the fire has held a disastrous impact.

There were no bishops' transcripts in Ireland, and few census returns exist before 1901. Mercifully, the 1901 and 1911 census returns recorded people's ages and counties of birth, albeit without specifying the precise places, and the 1911 returns indicated how many years each woman had been married. However, the given ages may be unreliable. Helpfully, the 1901 and 1911 censuses asked about each person's religious affiliation.

Once you know the approximate year and county of birth you can find the local distribution of your surname by trawling the International Genealogical Index, the British Isles Vital Records Index, the Primary Valuation of Ireland between 1847 and 1864, and the Tithe Applotment Books from 1823 to 1837. The IGI and Primary Valuation are searchable online. As with Scotland, the limited ranges of surnames and forenames mean you should exercise extreme caution when trying to identify the exact whereabouts of your ancestors.

Any changes to parochial boundaries can be frustrating, as you may need to hunt down more registers than you thought.

A list of all the known surviving Church of Ireland registers is held by the National Archives of Ireland and by the National Library of Ireland, and *Guide to Irish Parish Registers*, by B. Mitchell, will tell you their start dates and about any gaps. Extant deposited originals, microfilm and other copies can be inspected in the National Archives of Ireland, and in the Representative Church Body Library (**www.ireland. anglican.org/library/index.html**), in Dublin. The prior written permission of the incumbent or the Representative Church Body may be necessary before you can search or make copies of some of the filmed registers. Many of those relating to parishes in the six northern counties are held by the Public Record Office of Northern Ireland, though some registers still remain with local clergy. You can find details about Northern Irish parish registers from the *Guide to Church Records: Public Record Office of Northern Ireland*. The names and addresses of parish priests can be gleaned from the *Church of Ireland Directory*.

Indexes to many of the parish registers are held by local heritage centres, which can be searched on your behalf for a fee. You can find their addresses at **www.irish-roots.net**, and at **www.nationalarchives.ie/genealogy/centres.html**.

What the parish church registers reveal

Recording was often erratic, the handwriting poor, and the spelling of names inconsistent and phonetic.

You can expect the baptism entries to state the date, child's name, and those of his or her parents, and sometimes, the townland where they lived. From about 1820 onwards the father's occupation was included as well. The marriage registers contain the wedding date and the names of each groom and bride, and the parish of abode if one of them was a non-resident. Between 25 March 1754 and 31 March 1845, because all weddings excluding those of Quakers and Jews had to be performed in the Established Church of Ireland after banns or by licence, the entries were annotated accordingly. After this, all non-Catholic marriages were centrally registered. Details about the reading of banns are rare, and the marriage licence bonds were all destroyed in 1922, but indexes to the names of bondsmen, giving the date and intended place of marriage, are available in the National Archives of Ireland. A similar index covering the diocese of Dublin up to 1858 has been published as part of the *Index to Dublin Will and Grant Books*. The Genealogical Office holds abstracts of the marriage licence bonds which were filed in the Prerogative Court of Armagh between 1630 and 1858. Marriages were often mentioned in wills as well.

The burial registers usually provided just the date, name, age and townland of the deceased, regardless of his or her denomination, as few nonconformists had their own burying grounds.

Many of the headstone inscriptions have been transcribed and indexed. The extracts published in the *Journal of the Association for the Preservation of the Memorials of the Dead*, between 1888 and 1934, are separately indexed up to 1910 by personal- and place-name, and then integrally. Indexed copies of the printed inscriptions are held on computer in local heritage centres throughout Ireland. For Northern Ireland, visit the website of the Ulster Historical Foundation and Ulster Genealogical and Historical Guild at **www.historyfromheadstones.com**, though you will have to pay to use this. There are also extensive collections of transcripts in the Genealogical Office, and in the Society of Genealogists (**www.sog.org.uk**). Try the Family History Library catalogue at **www.familysearch.org** for details of copies you can hire in family history centres.

Other avenues worth exploring are the National School registers of admissions of primary school pupils after 1831, as their ages and paternity were disclosed, plus the father's address and occupation, and each child's religious denomination. In the Republic of Ireland, the registers are preserved in the National Archives of Ireland, or locally in the schools or by churches, whilst more than 1,500 such registers have been deposited in the Public Record Office of Northern Ireland.

Tracing nonconformists

Irish Presbyterianism has its roots in the migration of Scots from the mainland during the early part of the seventeenth century. The first presbytery was set up in 1642 by chaplains of the Scottish army stationed there to quell an Irish Catholic rebellion. As a consequence, the Irish Presbyterians were strongest in the Northeast of Ireland. However, its hold was weakened in the eighteenth and nineteenth centuries by the emigration of many adherents to North America.

Some of the Presbyterian chapel registers date from the late seventeenth century, although they frequently used the Church of Ireland for their baptisms and burials, especially when they had no burying places of their own. Until 1782, it was illegal for Presbyterian ministers to conduct marriages, so the Church of Ireland was their sole recourse. Their original registers may still remain locally, especially in the southern counties, but the present whereabouts of a particular register may be difficult to ascertain as so many of the Presbyterian congregations merged, moved or vanished. A number of the Presbyterian chapel registers of the six northern counties have been transferred to the Public Record Office of Northern Ireland, or to the Presbyterian Historical Society, in Belfast. The Public Record Office of Northern Ireland also has microfilmed copies of most of the locally held registers for these counties, and a list of those which have been deposited with the Presbyterian Historical Society. Irregular marriages of Irish Presbyterians during the years between 1754 and 1845 can be found in the registers of Portpatrick, in Wigtownshire, and in Gretna Green, both of which were reached by the short sea crossing to Scotland.

Like the Presbyterians, the early Irish Methodists were mentioned in the Church of Ireland registers rather than in records of their own creation. During the split in the Movement between 1816 and 1878, the Primitive Methodists continued to use the Established Church, whereas Wesleyan Methodist ministers began to keep registers of the baptisms they performed within their circuits. Many of the county heritage centres have online indexes to copies of surviving registers. A register of baptisms in Methodist chapels throughout Ireland between 1815 and 1840 is now the property of the Public Record Office of Northern Ireland, where it is searchable on microfilm.

The earliest records of Irish Baptists stem only from the 1860s and consist of their marriages and minute books recording the names of people coming into membership. There are no burial entries. Most of the registers are still kept locally or have been deposited with the Baptist Union of Ireland, in Belfast.

The Religious Society of Friends

The Quakers first had a presence in Ireland after 1655. Microfilmed copies of the minutes of their local monthly meetings, recording births, exchanges of marriage vows, deaths and burials, are held in the Friends Historical Library, at Rathfarnham, and for Northern Ireland by the Society of Friends Library, in Lisburn. Copies of the minute books kept at Rathfarnham can be hired in to search in family history centres, whilst the Public Record Office of Northern Ireland has copies of almost all the minutes of meetings in Ulster. Some of the minute books date from the seventeenth century. Indexed records of the births, marriages and deaths of Friends throughout Ireland between 1859 and 1949 are preserved in the Friends Historical Library.

Roman Catholics

In general, the Established Church of Ireland took over the old Roman Catholic parochial boundaries, so the Catholics had to create new ones. Their parishes were larger and more sprawling, and were often focused on the new prosperous Anglo-Catholic urban centres in the East, out of which, during the nineteenth century, new parishes were carved as the population increased. In order to identify which Catholic church served a civil parish look at the *Topographical Dictionary of Ireland*, edited by S. Lewis. County maps, showing Roman Catholic parishes and the date of their first known register entries, are included in *Tracing Your Irish Ancestors*, by J. Grenham, and in the *Guide to Irish Parish Registers*.

The earliest known surviving Roman Catholic register of baptisms and burials in Ireland dates from 1671. Many Catholic priests failed to keep any records about their congregations until the nineteenth century as a precautionary measure against their seizure. When the civil and religious restrictions were relaxed after 1793, and full emancipation was granted in 1836, Catholic registers began to flourish.

Computerized indexes to the registers are held by local heritage centres, but you cannot search these yourself. Microfilmed copies of the registers up to 1880, and some as late as 1900, are lodged in the National Library of Ireland and are listed at **www.nli.ie/new_what_res.htm**. You may have to seek the written permission of the parish priest before you can examine them. You can obtain their addresses from *The Catholic Directory*. Filmed copies of some registers can be hired for inspection in family history centres.

The Catholic registers were written in Latin or English, and relate almost entirely to baptisms and marriages. You can find out the date of each baptism, the infant's and parents' names, the mother's maiden name, where the family lived, and the names of the godparents or sponsors. The marriage entries noted the date, the names of the bride and groom and of at least two witnesses, but might also include the couple's (and witnesses') addresses, ages, occupations and paternity. The registers recorded marriage dispensations, which were required when the partners were blood relatives (**consanguinati**), and specified their degree of kinship as first cousins (second degree), second cousins (third degree), or whether the two families had been linked by an earlier marriage (**affinitatus**). This is helpful when you are trying to sort out family relationships in small communities. State registration of Roman Catholic marriages only began on 1 January 1864, and although forbidden to many outside the Established Church of Ireland after 25 March 1754, many of their own wedding registers survive. The registration of Catholic burials was uniformly patchy, especially before 1900, so you may have to rely on gravestone inscriptions as a substitute.

United States of America

In 1850, the ten-yearly federal census returns recorded for the first time people's actual state, territory or country of birth as well their ages, and in 1870 and 1880 the given birth months of infants born within the previous year. If someone's marriage had taken place in the 12 months leading up to the census years of 1850 through 1890, this too was noted, including the precise month between 1869 and 1870. In 1900 and again in 1910, the length of each woman's current marriage was specified and from 1890 to 1910 the number of her children. Age at first marriage was disclosed in 1930.

Dates and places of birth, marriage and death can also be elicited from the application papers of military veterans and their widows between 1775 and 1916.

It is worth looking at the indexed mortality schedules of the relevant state, territory and county for the 12 months preceding the 1850 and later censuses up to 1880, to find out the age, birthplace, and county of death of anyone in your family who had recently died, because this will at least localize your researches.

Unfortunately, the exact location of births, marriage and deaths, and people's religious denominations are lacking in the census returns. However, more information about places of birth and burial may be gleaned from civil registrations of marriages and deaths.

Because civil registration was introduced in some states only in the last century, particularly in the South, church, chapel, religious assembly and meeting-house registers assume great significance as a genealogical resource. However, the absence of any federal or state Established Church, coupled with the frequent movement of families inter-state and from one territory to another, and the remote and often temporary settlements they built makes for grave difficulties in trying to track down their life-cycle events.

You are unlikely to have ancestors who were all of the same nationality, so you will have to be prepared to hunt for them in a variety of denominational records in different languages. Adherence to a particular sect was not always strict or practical, either. For more information, look in the *Handbook of American Denominations*, by F. Mead, and for current details about churches consult the *Yearbook of American and Canadian Churches*.

One of the major problems of nineteenth-century American genealogy is how to trace migrant families back along the overland trails to their points of departure. Fortunately, there were established routes. Children's baptisms and marriages of people on the move might take place along the way, whilst burial frequently occurred wherever the person died and without any formal record other than a commemorative marker and a mention in a journal, diary or letter. It is often best to begin with someone's death certificate and work back from there.

Local newspapers frequently reported newly arrived individuals and family groups, and the destinations of people leaving town. Look in a contemporary city or town trade and commercial directory for the names and addresses of householders, traders, local churches, clergymen and religious assemblies. State and county histories will tell you about their ethnic and demographic make-up, and the availability of places for religious worship, so are well worth seeking out.

The earliest, Puritan, registers begin in the 1620s. The majority of these early New England church registers have been transcribed and printed. Microfilmed copies and transcriptions of many other registers can be hired in to search in a family history centre. Look in the Family History Library catalogue at **www.familysearch.org**. Extracts of numerous births, baptisms and marriages are embedded in the International Genealogical Index and North American Vital Records Index.

Some of the original church registers of birth, baptism, marriage and burial may now be in state or local historical society libraries, but the majority remain in the hands of the ministers. If you discover that a particular church is defunct, contact the priest of the nearest one of the same denomination.

What the registers contain

The birth, baptism, marriage and burial entries were written in the vernacular.

On the whole, the baptism registrations of children of people with English roots set out the date, the names of the child and his or her parents, and their place of residence. Sometimes the baby's date of birth, and the names of godparents were recorded too. If only the mother's name was given, this did not necessarily indicate that the child was illegitimate, but perhaps that she was the only parent belonging to that congregation. The first Puritan settlers were married by magistrates in civil ceremonies, so the parish clerk was not obliged to commit anything to writing. The registered marriages might note merely the date and names of the groom and bride, or of their publications of intent to marry. However, if your ancestors were Roman Catholic, the couple's ages and birthplaces might be added, as well as where they both then lived, the groom's current occupation or trade, their religious affiliations, and the birthplaces of both named sets of parents. Such entries were normally written in Latin.

Irregular marriages were generally contracted in the safer anonymity of large cities, so search for an elusive wedding in the records of the city nearest to where your ancestors were based.

Most churches and religious assemblies had a graveyard attached to them, and purchased or were donated extra land when this became full or was closed. The burial registers frequently gave the deceased person's date and place of birth, as well as details about his or her date of death and burial. This can be crucial if you are trying to trace someone's origins overseas, or the state or territory from which he or she had trekked. Later, municipal cemeteries and memorial parks were used, away from urban centres.

In rural areas, it was common for families to have personal burial plots on or close to their farm or homestead. Some used durable materials for their gravestones, which were well cared for and remain in good condition, but many have been lost or destroyed or their whereabouts are unknown.

Though commemorative inscriptions survive from the early seventeenth century, most date only from the eighteenth century or later. As the decennial federal censuses did not record everyone's name until 1850, such memorials identify family members who died before this, and whose existence and family relationships might otherwise have stayed undetected.

A number of the early memorial inscriptions have been transcribed and printed, and local enthusiasts have compiled details of the locations of and information on headstones in their counties. You can find out more about these from **www.cyndislist.com**.

13

wills and other probate records in England and Wales

In this chapter you will learn:
- what probate records are and where to find them
- what indexes and digital images are available
- how to use Death Duty registers.

If you already have an ancestor's death certificate, know his or her date and place of burial, or you want to establish approximately when and where someone died, or how any property was disposed of, probate records are for you. As they long pre-date parish registers, wills are your main springboard to the Middle Ages.

Wills, and grants of letters of administration, provide for the distribution of the people's estates after death, so they can help you to sort out family relationships. As binding legal documents, probate records are far more reliable than census returns or other sources where the person him/herself was the informant. A will expresses a person's final instructions, and therefore presents a vivid picture of emotional preferences, prejudices, bonds of loyalty, duty and affection felt towards other family members and towards friends and associates. Not everyone made a will, but after 1815, if someone died without making a will which was taken for probate, he or she was deemed to be intestate, and any estate over a certain value could henceforward only be distributed after letters of administration had been granted. Many estates were too small to be considered worth the cost and inconvenience of the probate process, so were shared out amongst the remaining family.

Where wills were taken to be proved before 1858

Until 9 January 1858, most wills of people leaving property in England and Wales were proved in church courts. In ascending order, the archdeacon's court was utilized when the personal estate (personalty) was confined to a single archdeaconry. If such property was held in more than one archdeaconry, both of which lay in the same diocese, then it was to the bishop's consistory court that the will was taken. The Prerogative Courts of York (PCY) and of Canterbury (PCC) had jurisdiction over property (*bona notabilia*) valued at more than £5 (or £10 in London) which lay in a least two dioceses within their own Province. The Province of York controlled dioceses roughly covering the civil counties of Cheshire, Cumberland, Durham, Lancashire, Northumberland, Nottinghamshire, Westmorland and Yorkshire, and the Isle of Man. The Prerogative Court of Canterbury was the highest church court, and exercised overall authority not only over personal estates in the southern dioceses and in Wales, but also dealt with the estates and assets of military and naval men dying on active Crown service abroad, and overseas residents' personal property in England and Wales. When people possessed property in both provinces, probate grants were applied for in each Prerogative Court.

After the outbreak of the Civil War in 1642, the Prerogative Court of Canterbury was much more widely used, and when the church courts were suspended between 1653 and 1660, it was converted into a Court of Civil Commission, to which all wills were taken to be proved.

There were a number of peculiar and secular courts outside the above framework; these were run under Royal patronage, by bishops whose jurisdictions extended historically to places outside their own dioceses, by deans and cathedral chapters, by certain parishes, by boroughs and city corporations, some manorial lords, and by the chancellors of the Universities of Cambridge and Oxford.

The boundaries of the various probate courts did not coincide with those of civil administrative counties. If you look in *The Phillimore Atlas and Index of Parish Registers,* you will see the various coloured demarcation lines of each probate court set out on the county maps for England and the regional maps for Wales. County probate maps are also gradually being uploaded at **www.familysearch.org**. As executors could take wills to the court which was most locally convenient and qualified to deal with someone's estate, always search every court serving the district where your forebears lived.

Original and/or registered office copies of wills proved in the English and Welsh courts survive only from 1384 for the Prerogative Court of Canterbury, and from 1389 for the Province of York, though some diocesan court probates date from the previous century. The probate records in the Prerogative Court of Canterbury have been transferred to the National Archives, whilst those of the Prerogative Court of York are in the Borthwick Institute for Archives (**www.york.ac.uk/inst/bihr**). Local probates are generally found in diocesan or county record offices, and those relating to the Welsh dioceses are in the National Library of Wales. To discover the actual dates and whereabouts of probate material, and about any indexes and other finding aids, consult *Probate Jurisdictions: Where to Look for Wills,* by J. Gibson and E. Churchill.

You can examine indexed digital images of the PCC registered copies of wills at **www.nationalarchives.gov.uk/documents online**. Access is free in both the National Archives and in the Family Records Centre. The wills are searchable by personal- and/or place-name, by occupation and by date of probate. Printed indexes to PCC wills run up to 1800, and thereafter there are yearly calendars, which are arranged initial-alphabetically by surname, and then chronologically. You can search the indexes between 1750 and 1800 at **www.originsnetwork.com**. Microfilmed copies of the later calendars and of all of the registered wills can be inspected in the National Archives. The calendar volumes and microfilmed copies of the registered wills are held in the Family Records Centre. You can also hire in microfilmed copies to search in a family history centre.

There are printed indexes to the wills proved in the Prerogative Court of York up to 1688, and microfilmed copies of the later indexes can be searched in the Society of Genealogists, or at a family history centre. As with all probate courts apart from PCC, there is a gap between 1653 and 1660. Indexes to the wills proved before 1500, and between 1853 and 1858 are searchable at **www.originsnetwork.com**.

You can search an online index in the National Library of Wales to probate material in all of the Welsh ecclesiastical courts between 1521 and 1858. Indexes to records in some of the local probate courts are being uploaded onto the internet, either by county or by court. Many probate indexes have been printed or are available on microfilm to hire in family history centres.

The indexes reveal at least the year of probate, the deceased's name and last address, and a reference number to help locate the will. The final place of residence might be different from the address when the will was drawn up, especially if this was some years before probate. Sometimes the person's status or occupation, and marital condition were listed too.

Wills proved since 1858

On 12 January 1858, the probate responsibility of the Church and other courts came to an end. Since then, English and Welsh wills have been taken to be proved in civil district probate registries, or in the Principal Probate Registry, in London.

Until 1926, the local jurisdiction of district registries was rigidly applied, but afterwards any office could be used by the executors. Copies of all the wills, regardless of where they were proved, can be viewed in the Principal Registry and local registries for a fee, or posted to you. Registered copies of wills proved in the Welsh district probate registries are also held in the National Library of Wales.

You can inspect printed or microfiche copies of the indexed calendars of wills which were proved more than a year ago in the public search room of the Principal Registry or in any of the district probate registries. Computerized calendars are available for the years since 1992 in the Principal Registry and in the Manchester District Probate Registry. The addresses and contact details of all 12 probate registries and 18 sub-registries can be found at **www.hmcourts-service.gov.uk/HMCSCourtFinder**, and from *The Family and Local History Handbook*. Microfiche or bound copies of the annual calendars, also known as the National Probate Indexes, are widely available, though the end dates vary – consult *Probate Jurisdictions: Where to Look for Wills* for details. The Indexes in the Family Records Centre and in the National Archives run up to 1943, and up to 1972 in the National Library of Wales.

If you prefer, you can make a pre-paid postal application for a four-year search of the indexes and a copy of a specific will by writing to the York Probate Sub-Registry. Quote the person's name, address and date or approximate year of death.

The indexes record each testator's name, last address, status or occupation and his or her date (and up to 1967, the place) of death, plus the date and place of probate. Until 1891, they included the executors' current addresses, occupations and their relationship to the deceased. After 1892, however, merely their names and occupations were copied up. You can also discover the gross value of someone's estate if the will was proved before 3 August 1981, but latterly only the amount it was sworn under.

Tip

If you do not want to buy a certified copy of a death registration, use the probate indexes to find out the person's date of death and then look in the General Register Office indexes after 1866 for his or her age, or after 1 April 1969 for the given date of birth. The probate indexes can also assist you in identifying which of several likely candidates in the registration indexes is correct . If you don't know the year of someone's death, the probate indexes might be quicker to search than the death indexes. However, not everyone left a will.

A will actually only conveys real estate (realty). This consists of freehold land, which was all freely disposable by will after 1660. In 1815, copyholders were permitted to directly will their rented land too, instead of to trustees as before. After 1837, an extract of a will devising customary freehold or copyhold property was copied up in the court records of the relevant lord of the manor. You can find the whereabouts of surviving manorial court records from the Manorial Documents Register, in the National Archives. The catalogues for some counties, and for all the Welsh manors can be trawled at **www.nationalarchives. gov.uk/mdr.**

Any freehold estate entailed or held under a strict settlement was, however, passed on according to the terms of the original deed, which might stipulate its descent over many generations of a family. Entailments and strict settlements were sometimes set up in wills.

A testament makes provision for the disposal of personal estate (personalty). This includes movable goods and chattels, any investments, cash and leasehold interests. For convenience, the will and testament have long been combined together.

Until 1837, personalty could be bequeathed by boys on reaching 14, and girls at 12, since when the minimum age has been 21, as has always been the case with real estate. Today, soldiers and sailors as young as 16, on active service, can legally will their personal effects.

Wills of single people become void on marriage, unless explicitly linked to a specific forthcoming union which actually materializes. This does not apply to soldiers and sailors on active service. A will becomes invalid on the birth of any child after the date it was made if there was no stated provision for this eventuality.

Married women rarely left wills before 1882, unless bequeathing their personal property with their husband's written consent, and from then until 1893 wills of women married after 1 January 1883 leaving personalty and realty had to be re-executed on the husband's death. A husband could revoke his consent at any time, even after his wife had died. However, a family might settle certain goods or an annual income from a piece of land on a bride for her sole use and enjoyment by means of a marriage settlement which was drawn up in anticipation of her marriage (usually on the same day), and to which her future husband was a party. This signed agreement afforded her a measure of independence, though any land was held by trustees for her benefit. The marriage settlement stipulated what should happen to the estate when the wife died or remarried. This was usually for the property to devolve on one or all of her children and their descendants. If the deed allowed her to dispose of the gift without restriction, she might devise it as she wished, but her will had to specifically refer to the settlement, identify the various parties to it, and include its date and clear details about the property or land and the names of the trustees. Her husband's will might also mention the deed to ensure the property remained untouched after his death, since a wife and her goods were treated in law as belonging to her husband. Even if the original settlement deed no longer survives, you should be able to harvest sufficient information about it from the will to discover the bride's maiden surname, her father's name, place of residence and status, and perhaps those of other close relatives who were involved in the agreement, plus its terms and conditions.

What wills tell you

Some of the early wills were written in Latin, but generally they were in English. Sometimes the will and testament were drawn up separately, on the same day, and attached together. They start by giving the name, address, status or occupation of the testator, and the date, although this might be left until the end, before the signatures or marks of the testator and those of at least two witnesses, who all signed in each other's presence.

Look in the preamble for a reference to the testator's current state of health or old age, which might indicate that the will was probably composed not long before death. A request might be expressed for burial in a particular parish or graveyard, hinting at a family connection, though such wishes did not always guarantee they were honoured. Medieval and early Tudor wills often contained instructions for an elaborate funeral. A sum of money might be donated for the saying of masses and obits by a priest in memory of the deceased and named ancestors on special days or anniversaries, or given to construct a chantry chapel.

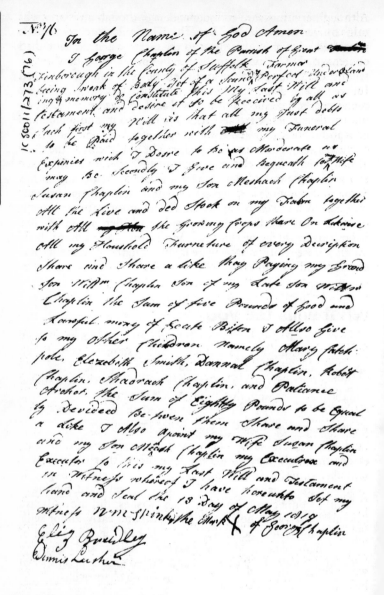

figure 18 George Chaplin's will, 1819
according to his gravestone inscription at Great Finborough, George died the day
before he made his will, which was proved in the Archdeaconry Court of Sudbury.
He was the great-great-great grandfather of Charlie Chaplin
(reproduced by permission of Suffolk Record Office)

Although a wife was usually named in her husband's will, she might have predeceased him. The widow was usually left a parcel of land and/or the marital home or a part of it and its contents for her lifetime or until remarriage. The will directed what should happen thereafter. It was also essential to secure the future of any dependent unmarried and under-age children remaining in the family home, so money was generally set aside under the control of trustees for their maintenance and education. Some children who were known to be living might be excluded altogether from a will. This might be because they had already been financially provided for. For instance, the eldest son would generally be next in line for any freehold property. Some sons and daughters might already have an annual income under a trust, or had been given a portion (lump sum) out of the estate on reaching their majority or when they married, or had been significant beneficiaries in someone else's will. A child might be left only a small legacy as a token of the parent's continuing affection rather than out of any disrespect. Married daughters were occasionally left a specific gift or money for their personal enjoyment to avoid it passing to their husbands.

Unfortunately, kinship descriptions have changed their meaning over time. Be wary of 'nephew' which might indicate a grandson, 'cousin' a nephew or niece, 'natural son' a lawful legitimate child, 'stepson' a son-in-law, 'son-in-law' a stepson or adopted son, 'son' a son-in-law, 'father' a father-in-law (but not necessarily the father of the testator's current wife). 'My now wife' signifies that the testator had been married before, 'my wife's child' that it was a stepchild. 'Cousin' and 'kinsman' were loose terms applied alike to blood relations and people linked by marriage. Occasionally, beneficiaries were identified merely by their forenames, with or without their family connection. You will have to study other family wills to try and sort them out.

A legacy or estate left to a person on condition that he changed his surname to that of the testator, ensured its continuity if the male line would otherwise become extinct. The usual method by which this was done was by Royal Licence. Royal Licences were registered at the College of Arms, as quite frequently the testator was armigerous, and his coat of arms was assigned to the beneficiary and his descendants at the same time. You can find out about name changes by Royal Licence by consulting *An Index to Changes of Name..., 1760–1901,* by W. P. W. Phillimore and E. A. Fry. This is also available on CD-ROM.

Tips

- Legacies to parishes or special groups of people may suggest an enduring personal, family or business link, which is well worth pursuing.
- When friends, neighbours and associates were beneficiaries you might find your ancestor's generosity was reciprocated, or that he was returning a favour, so it is a good idea to study their wills too for references to your family.
- If you draw a blank looking for wills of your own antecedents, examine the wills of other local residents, especially those of the same occupation, and of families into which yours were married.

Holograph wills

A will written by the testator, rather than by someone else, was known as a holograph, and did not require the presence of witnesses to be valid. Three people familiar with his or her handwriting attended the probate court, inspected the script and swore an affidavit acknowledging it to be that of the deceased. Their names, addresses, occupations and length and nature of their acquaintanceship with the dead person were enrolled with the will.

Codicils

If a testator wanted to make minor amendments or additions to the will, this could be done in the form of a codicil. The codicil clearly referred to the date of the original will, and was dated, signed and witnessed in the same way, and physically attached to it. Any number of codicils could be made.

Oral wills

Wills were not always written. Until 1837, in emergencies such as mortal illness, when no scrivener or writing materials were to hand, a dying person could intimate his or her intention of making a last will and testament and dictate it to at least three witnesses. Such oral declarations were called nuncupative wills. The witnesses then repeated what they had been told in the appropriate probate court and the information was duly registered as a dated memorandum. Soldiers, sailors and marines can still make oral wills.

The executors

It was usual for a testator to appoint family members or local friends as executors. In return they might be left a sum of money or the estate residue after the payment of all the debts and legacies.

It is a good idea to note who the executors were, because the attached probate act recorded who actually applied to the court for the grant. An executor might have died before the testator, be under the minimum customary age of 17, be unavailable, or the widow (relict) have remarried. You may discover that only one of the executors was granted probate, and when the absentee returned or the minor came of age another grant had been applied for to enable them to share in the distribution.

If an executor died before he or she was able to complete the disposal of the estate, the deceased executor's own executor took over.

Tip

Wills were generally proved within six months to two years after death, but there might be exceptions, so be prepared to search for up to 20 years. On the whole, the date of probate is a surer guide to when a person died than the date the will was drawn up, unless the two dates were close together, or the testator described him/herself as old, weak or sickly, or the will was contested.

The executors took the testator's latest dated will to the relevant probate court to be validated and approved. They swore an oath to faithfully and honestly carry out its directions and a dated probate grant was appended to the will. When an executor declined to act, was not available, had already died, was under-age, or the will had failed to make a nomination, the probate court intervened and usually appointed the residuary legatee as executor. The will was then listed as an administration with will annexed.

The probate grants were written in Latin until 1733, and then in English, as they were during the Commonwealth period of 1653–60. The grant recorded the name, last place of residence, status or occupation of the testator, the date and place of probate, and the names, addresses, occupations and relationship to the deceased of the executors.

Once the will was approved, an endorsed probate copy was handed back to the executors, and another copy written up in the probate register. The original probated will was filed among the court's records. Sometimes only the registered office-copies of wills survive, because the originals have been lost or destroyed, or they are too fragile for production. The seal and authentic signatures or marks of the testator and witnesses appear only on the original, where clerical errors were less likely. If you are interested in collecting family autographs, or want to compare an ancestor's signature on a variety of documents over time, remember that he or she may have been in extremis when the will was signed, and the writing bear little resemblance to what it was like when the person was in full vigour or much younger.

Contested wills

If a will's validity was challenged, the interested party (the plaintiff) lodged a caveat with the probate court to delay any grant for three months, pending a decision or judgment. The words 'by decree' or 'by sentence', with the names of the litigants and the case outcome were inserted alongside the registered will, and noted in the probate index. An interlocutory decree meant that there was some question that remained to be answered before a final sentence could be passed by the court.

The Court of Chancery dealt with matters concerning realty and trusts, as these lay outside the jurisdiction of the church courts, but by the late seventeenth century, most of the probate cases were presented there.

The church court records were compiled in Latin until 1733, but from their date of commencement in the late fourteenth century, Chancery proceedings were almost always written in English. You can examine the papers relating to cases in the Prerogative Court of Canterbury, and in the Court of Chancery, in the National Archives. Search the *Inheritance Disputes Index, 1574-1714*, by P. W. Coldham, for references to Chancery suits; this is available at **www.originsnetwork.com**, and on the open shelves in the National Archives. The catalogues to some of the Chancery proceedings before 1714 can be searched by personal- and place-name, and by subject, at **www.nationalarchives. gov.uk/catalogue**. The documentation concerning disputes handled by the Chancery Court of the Archbishop of York after 1535 is in the Borthwick Institute for Archives, to which there are printed indexes, whilst the records relating to local church courts have been transferred to diocesan or county record offices, and for the Welsh church courts to the National Library of Wales.

Appeals against decisions made in church courts went first to the Court of Arches of the Prerogative Court of Canterbury, or to the Vicar General of the Prerogative Court of York, and ultimately, up to 1834, to the High Court of Delegates, and later to the Judicial Committee of the Privy Council. Short abstracts of PCC appeals have been published in *Index of Cases in the Records of the Court of Arches at Lambeth Palace Library 1660-1913*, edited by J. Houston. Indexes to the names of many of the High Court of Delegates appellants can be searched at **www.nationalarchives.gov.uk/catalogue**, and to those of the Judicial Committee of the Privy Council appellants up to 1880. The catalogues also provide document references.

Grants of letters of administration

If someone died without making a will and was thus intestate, his or her next of kin or chief creditor could apply to the probate court for a grant of letters of administration, to protect their claims on the personal estate. Until 1925, real estate passed on intestacy to the next legal heir, who was the nearest blood relative, beginning with the eldest son. Since then, any realty has, along with the personal estate, gone on intestacy to the next of kin. For a full explanation of the present-day intestacy rules, visit **www.hmrc.gov.uk/manuals/ihtmanual/ihtm12126.htm** or **www.wisewills.co.uk/intestate.htm**.

The surviving enrolments of administration grants are usually referred to as 'Admons'. They were stored in the same place as wills. Microfilmed copies of grants made by the Prerogative Court of Canterbury between 1559 and 1858 can be searched in the National Archives, the Family Records Centre, and hired in to examine in family history centres. The Prerogative Court of York's administration grants are in the Borthwick Institute for Archives. Copies of the grants made by local courts prior to 1858 have been transferred, like the wills, to diocesan or county record offices, those for the Welsh diocesan courts being in the National Library of Wales. Details of their start dates and whereabouts can be discovered from *Probate Jurisdictions: Where to Look for Wills*.

You can search copies of administration grants made after 12 January 1858 in the Principal Probate Registry, in local district probate registries, or for Wales in the National Library of Wales.

Indexes and transcripts

Until 1858, administration grants were sometimes separately listed. Where there is a joint index or list, wills are usually indicated by 'W' or 'T', and administration grants by 'A'. Consult *Probate Jurisdictions: Where to Look for Wills* for information about published and other copies of indexes. There are printed indexes to the Prerogative Court of Canterbury administration grants between 1559 and 1660. Copies of a typescript index from 1701 to 1749 are available in the National Archives and in the Family Records Centre which also holds a copy of a similar index to grants between 1750 and 1800. The index from 1701 to 1749 is also on microfiche. The original yearly calendars from 1559 to 1858 can be inspected in the Family Records Centre, on microfilm in the National Archives, and hired in to search in family history centres. The published indexes to administration grants in the Prerogative Court of York go up to 1688, though there is a gap between 1653 and 1660 when all the church courts were suspended, and the Prerogative Court of Canterbury became the only probate court. Microfilm copies of the later indexes are available in the Society of Genealogists and for hire in family history centres.

The indexes before 1858 normally record at least the year in which a grant was made, the name, last known whereabouts and occupation of the intestate person, and a document reference. The calendars of PCC administration grants between 1661 and 1700, and from 1750 to 9 January 1858, give the actual month and county of death. You will need this information to locate the correct grant book. After 1714, the grant books were arranged by Seats, depending on the county in which a person died.

The indexed yearly calendars (National Probate Indexes) list administration grants after wills until 1870. The Indexes after 1858 tell you about as much as you could glean from the grant itself. They record the intestate's name, his or her last address, status or occupation, and date of death (including the place up to 1967). You can learn the date and place of issue of the grant, the names and occupations of the administrators and until 1891, their addresses and relationship to the deceased. A gross estate valuation was included for grants before 3 August 1981, and thereafter a 'sworn under' amount.

What grants of letters of administration contain

The actual grants were written in Latin until 1733, except for the years between 1653 and 1660, when they were copied up in English. The registered copies give the date of each grant, the name, place of residence and marital status of the deceased if a bachelor or a woman, and the names and addresses and relationship to him or her of the administrators. From 1792, the gross value of the personal estate was specified as well, with details of the dates by which a probate inventory and probate accounts were to be produced to the court by the administrators.

The next of kin are defined in strict order of precedence. The closest living relative is the spouse, then the children. Any deceased child's children take their parent's place. After this come the intestate's parents, followed by his or her brothers and sisters jointly (their children or grandchildren stepping into their shoes if they have already died), brothers and sisters of the half-blood (or their issue), the deceased's grandparents, uncles and aunts (or their descendants), and finally, the chief creditor. For the want of any of these, the estate passes as *bona vacantia* to the Crown. The shares apportioned to surviving widows and children were determined by the Statute of Distributions in 1670/1 and later enactments.

Up to 30 years after an intestate's death anyone claiming and proving his or her relationship as the rightful next of kin to *bona vacantia* in England and Wales can apply to the Treasury Solicitor, in London, for a decision. The Solicitor for the Duchy of Cornwall and for the Duchy of Lancaster, based in London, deals with property within their jurisdictions. For more details, read **www.bonavacantia.gov.uk**.

Administration grants are therefore especially useful because they identify the nearest living relative at the time someone died. They also provide the names of nearer or equally entitled next of kin who declined, were unavailable or were too young to serve. A guardian acted for a minor until he or she reached 21 and was able to apply for a further grant to administer any remaining estate. Both grants should be cross-referenced.

Should an administrator die without having distributed the whole estate, the court will appoint a replacement, granting an administration *de bonis non*. This is referred to as an 'Admon. d.b.n.'

Probate inventories

Between 1529 and 1732, the submission of a 'true and perfect' probate inventory (valuation of the deceased's personal possessions and assets) was mandatory. After 1733, they were only prepared at the special request of the next of kin or legal representatives.

The inventories were usually filed and listed with the wills or grants, and a number have been published. You can find the dates and whereabouts of surviving inventories and any finding aids in *Probate Jurisdictions: Where to Look for Wills*. Sometimes only the inventory now exists when the will or administration grant has disappeared.

An inventory was compiled within a few days of death to safeguard the interests of the executors and beneficiaries. It was dated, and the names, places of residence and occupations of the deceased and the three or more appraisers were recorded. The inventory covered every stick of furniture and other house contents, each of which was itemized and given an estimated sale price. This was usually conducted room by room, each of which was described in the inventory by its prime function. The contents of barns and outbuildings were valued too, as well as harvested crops, timber, animal carcasses and livestock, leasehold property, cash, and moneys lent out on credit. Certain items, such as wearing apparel (paraphernalia), were traditionally set aside for the widow, so were excluded.

The terms used for certain objects may be unfamiliar, and local dialect or phonetic spellings were commonplace. Consult *A Glossary of Household, Farming and Trade Terms from Probate Inventories*, by R. Milward, or a dictionary of dialect words.

The inventories help you to visualize how your ancestors lived. They tell you about how the various household rooms were furnished. Empty rooms were not included for obvious reasons, but you can still gain a good idea of how big a house was. The work tools may indicate the scale and sophistication of someone's business, or imply a secondary occupation.

Probate accounts

The total assessment generally came to less than the true market value of a person's assets and may have borne little relation to what was left once all the debts and liabilities had been settled, so the final probate accounts presented a more accurate summary, and tell you how much the residuary estate was worth.

From 1540, probate accounts were required by the court, but after 1685, only when requested, especially if the estate looked likely to be in debt or subject to dispute. They were submitted by the executors or administrators six months after the inventory. Probate accounts survive much less often than inventories, but *Probate Accounts of England and Wales*, edited by P. Spufford, contains an index to about 30,000 known extant sets of accounts up to 1857. It excludes those filed in the Prerogative Court of Canterbury. The index is also available on microfiche.

Probate accounts are instructive because they name the deceased's wife and children (who were not always clearly identified in the will itself, or omitted because they had already been provided for), and sometimes their ages, places of residence and occupations are mentioned too. You will certainly learn the names of all the deceased's creditors and debtors. The purchase of clothing, cost of schooling, apprenticeship and maintenance of infant, minor or orphaned children may be detected nowhere else. You can find out about any outlay on medical and funeral expenses and entertainments, mourning rings and other gifts.

Tutors, curators and guardians

When someone died leaving infants under the age of eight, unmarried minors, or a family member who was mentally or physically incapacitated, the tutors and guardians nominated in the will or by the surviving parent first required the probate court's approval. If necessary, the court appointed the next of kin, who had to be over the age of 21. According to civil law, the only woman who could act as tutor was the mother or grandmother, although this did not seem to apply in the Province of York. The court's consent was written up in a special book, which was kept with the rest of the probate records.

The accompanying dated and signed tuition bond set out the tutor's or guardian's name, address and relationship to his or her charge, together with the names and places of residence of sureties willing to be bound as guarantors of the faithful performance of their duties. An inventory of the child's personal possessions was next prepared and lodged with the court, and whilst these could be sold to raise funds with the court's permission, any inherited land remained untouchable.

Boys, on reaching 14, and girls at 12, were able to apply to the court via a proxy to overturn the original arrangement and choose a guardian to replace the tutor. The resulting dated and signed deed of assignment recorded the child's name, age and relationship to their nominees. A curation bond (similar in content to a tuition bond) was then filed with the original documentation, and endorsed to show the court's approval.

Between 1258 and 1724, the probate Court of Husting of the City of London exercised control over the personalty and person of unmarried orphan children of City freemen. Its officers appointed guardians when a freeman's will had failed to do so. The surviving records are currently in London Metropolitan Archives. At least two other city corporations, in Bristol and Exeter, had similar powers.

Death Duty registers

Extracts from wills and administrations can be found in the Death Duty registers, which span the years between 1796 and 1903. The term 'Death Duties' embraced Legacy Duty, which was collected from 1796 until 1949, Succession Duty from 1853 to 1949, and Estate Duty between 1894 and 1975. No files after 1903 are known to have been preserved. The registers only contain those parts of wills and administration grants which were subject to the prevailing Duty collected by the Board of Stamps to 1848, and then by the Board of Inland Revenue.

Individual legacies worth £20 (increased to £100 in 1853), and residuary estates of £100 (reduced to £20 in 1805) were subject to Legacy Duty. The percentage of Duty payable depended on the degree of kinship of the beneficiary to the deceased. Until 1804, any legacies and residual estates bequeathed to spouses, children, parents and grandparents were exempt. From 1805 to 1814, only those gifts to spouses and parents escaped, and in 1815 this was further limited to spousal bequests.

Between 1796 and 1852, real estate was only taken into account if a will directed that it should be sold to fund an annuity, and from 1805 if it was sold to pay legacies or to form the residual estate. After 1853, both personalty and realty were subject to Legacy Duty; any other estate worth over £100 passing on death under a trust or settlement set up outside a will now became liable to Succession Duty. Estate Duty took precedence over Legacy and Succession Duty after 1894, though any part of an estate liable to these was excluded from the calculation of the new Duty. The estates of soldiers, sailors and mariners dying in the service of the Crown were exempt.

Not every estate was caught by Death Duty, perhaps as few as a quarter before 1805, though this increased threefold after 1815, when wills and administration grants were made compulsory. It was not invariably collected if the sum involved was considered insignificant (usually less than one per cent of £1,500) or when an estate was worth more than £1,000,000.

Copies of the registers up to 1857 are available on microfilm in the National Archives and the Family Records Centre, and can be hired in to search in a family history centre. The annual indexes to 1903 are similarly accessible, but the registers from 1858 have to be ordered as original documents in the National Archives. There are no indexes to the extracts from administration grants between 1864 and 1881. Digital copies of all the indexes are searchable at **www.findmypast.com/ HomeServlet**. Indexed digital images of more than 66,000 extracts of wills and administration grants between 1796 and 1811 in all the probate courts (known as the country courts) except the Prerogative Court of Canterbury, can be viewed at **www.nationalarchives.gov.uk/documentsonline**. Access to this website is free in the National Archives and in the Family Records Centre. The index is searchable by name, occupation or status, parish and county, and by date range. It is planned to make digital images of the remaining registers available.

The Death Duty register indexes were arranged initial-alphabetically by the first letter, first letter and first vowel or by the first three letters of each surname and then chronologically. You can find out the deceased's forenames, the names and addresses of his or her executors or administrators, the date and court of the probate or administration grant, though this was heavily abbreviated, and the relevant folio or entry number. Starting in 1889, the indexes also disclose date of death.

Tips

- Where an original will or registered copy no longer exists, as is the case with many of the West Country wills which were destroyed by enemy action in 1940, the Death Duty registers are all that survive to tell you about the distribution of estates over a certain value. The extracts can be used in conjunction with any indexes to local probate court records published before the Second World War. Printed indexes to dutiable Somerset wills and administrations between 1805 and 1857 have been produced by D. T. Hawkings.

- If you already know when and in which court a will was proved, go straight to the annual indexes to see if there is a register entry. Where 'NE' (no entry) was written against someone's name in an index, this signalled that no Duty was payable.

- The Death Duty indexes can be culled to find the relevant probate court if your ancestor's estate was liable.

What the Death Duty registers tell you

Each Death Duty will extract was headed by the name of the deceased, and set out his or her last address, status or occupation and date of death, the dates when the will was made and proved and in which probate court. The names, addresses and occupations of the executors were recorded, together with the gross value the estate was sworn under before deduction of estate debts and expenses. Land was not included in the valuation until 1853. Underneath, in columns, were written details about the liable legacies and residuary estate, their specified purposes, the names of the beneficiaries and their precise relationship to the deceased. If there was any contingency or succession of interest attached to a legacy, the gift was absolute (without any restriction), conditional, or an annuity this was noted too. Finally, the various percentage rates and amounts of Duty were added based on the degree of kinship and when they were received.

A typical contingency arose when a spouse was left copyhold land and/or other possessions for her lifetime or widowhood, after which they were directed to be sold and the proceeds divided according to the testator's instructions. A succession of interest occurred when an estate devolved in a prescribed way down the family, as Duty became payable each time the next entitled person came into the property. Consequently the registers were kept open for many years to allow such events to happen, because although the first estate heir might be exempt under the kinship rules the next in line might not be. The extracts were accordingly annotated with the dates of death, marriage or remarriage of such beneficiaries, noting any absences abroad, and births of any later children and descendants who were in line to inherit. The kinship columns are extremely useful, albeit using acronyms to describe people's degree of relationship to the deceased. Illegitimate issues were treated as strangers of the blood. Any family relationships not made clear in a will should be resolved in the Death Duty register extract. The register extracts also named any relevant posthumous or other children who were unidentified by name in a will, and similarly grandchildren taking a dead parent's share. The age of each annuitant was recorded as at the date of probate, because the calculation of Duty was based on his or her actuarial life expectancy.

The registered extracts of administration grants set out the name, last address, status or occupation and date of death of the intestate, plus the date of the grant and the court where it had been made. The names, addresses, occupations and relationship of the administrators to the deceased were written in, with the names and precise relationship of all the jointly entitled next of kin. The estate's gross value, each person's share and liability were recorded too, and how much Duty was paid.

Table 2 Examples of given abbreviations in the Death Duty registers relating to consanguinity. For a fuller list, visit **www.nationalarchives.gov.uk** and click on the records research guide to interpret Death Duty registers

BF	Brother of a father (uncle)
BM	Brother of a mother (uncle)
DBD	Descendant of a brother (nephew, niece)
DSD	Descendant of a sister (nephew, niece)
DBF	Descendant of a brother of a father (cousin)
DSM	Descendant of a sister of a mother (cousin)
DBGF	Descendant of a brother of a grandfather
G child	Grandchild
G son	Grandson
GG	Great-grandchild
SF	Sister of a father (aunt)
SM	Sister of a mother (aunt)
Str *or* Stra *or* Strag	Stranger of the blood
Stra BL	Brother-in-law
Stra NC	Natural child (illegitimate)
Stra ND	Natural daughter (illegitimate)
Stra NC [of a son or daughter]	Illegitimate child of a son or daughter
Stra (sent)	Servant of the deceased
Stra SL	Son-in-law or sister-in-law
Stra *or* 'daughter'	Natural daughter (illegitimate)

Government stockholders

When people were left stocks and shares, a copy of the approved will or administration grant had to be presented to the bank or company concerned for authorization to transfer the investment. You can search indexes to the Bank of England ledgers of will abstracts, relating to more than 60,500 such assignments of government stock between 1717 and 1845, at **www.originsnetwork.com**. A copy of the index from 1807 to 1845 is available on microfiche and in print, whilst the ledgers are held by the Society of Genealogists.

The indexes record the names and addresses of people who had been left government funds or who were entitled to them as next of kin, together with the date of the probate or administration grant, and the number and stock transfer values. A baptism certificate was generally filed if the beneficiary was a minor, or a burial certificate was produced if appropriate. From about 1810, such probated wills and administration grants were invariably dealt with by the Prerogative Court of Canterbury, probably because this was the only court recognized by the Bank of England.

14

probate records elsewhere in the British Isles, Ireland and the USA

In this chapter you will learn:
- what records survive and how to locate them
- what indexes and digital images are available
- how you can use other records when wills are missing or non-existent.

The Channel Islands

Nominally, the Channel Islands belong to the diocese of Winchester, but local church courts deal with personal estates, and the civil courts with any realty owned by deceased islanders. The records of the Commissary Court of the Bishop of Winchester in the Bailiwick of Guernsey include probates and administration grants for Guernsey, Alderney, Sark, Herm and Jethou after 1660, and are deposited in the Greffe, in St Peter Port. Since 1841 separate wills, devising real estate in the presence of two jurats of the Royal Court, have been taken to the Royal Court of Guernsey, in St Peter Port, for approval and registration. All of the above registered and original wills and administrations are indexed. Similar wills and administration grants regarding land left in Alderney after 1949 are preserved in its Court House, together with a few probates after 1946. All the earlier records were destroyed during the Second World War.

Land in Sark is not disposable by will. It descends instead to the next heir as far as the fifth degree of kinship (the common ancestor being the great-great-great-grandparent), and failing this, it reverts to the Seigneur. A widow has a right of dower to a third of her late husband's land. No land can be disposed of by will in either Herm or Jethou.

Jersey wills were proved in the Ecclesiastical Court of the Dean of Jersey until 25 May 1949. Original wills from about 1660 onwards, enrolled copies between 1714 and 1734, and after 1775, and grants of letters of administration from 1848, are in the custody of the Jersey Archive up to 1948, whilst later records are in the Judicial Greffe, in the Royal Court of Jersey. Before 1851, real estate could not be willed in Jersey, so separate wills, disposing of personalty and of realty, are common. The wills relating to land are filed and recorded in the Public Registry Office, in the Royal Court of Jersey, whilst wills of both personalty and realty, are located in the Judicial Greffe. The Registry is not open to the public, but searches can be undertaken for you for a fee.

The indexes from 1660 to 1847 and calendars from 1848 until 1965, in the Jersey Archive, relate to both the original and registered copies of wills, and include references to the later wills bequeathing both personalty and realty. There are separate indexed volumes for administration grants after 1848. You can trawl the index to Jersey wills at **http://jerseyheritagetrust.jeron.je/archive.html**. Microfilmed copies of both the indexes and wills of personalty and realty up to 1964 can be hired in to inspect in family history centres.

Estates held in England and Wales

Before, 1858, any property left by Channel Islanders in England and Wales was dealt with by the Prerogative Court of Canterbury, and you can search indexed digital images of registered copies of their wills at **www.nationalarchives. gov.uk/documentsonline**. The indexes are searchable by personal- and place-name, by date and by occupation. Unless you are visiting the National Archives or the Family Records Centre, you will have to pay to view the wills. Registered wills and administration grants after 1858 are lodged in the Principal Probate Registry in London. The yearly National Probate Indexes are widely available on microfiche at least until 1943. Look in *Probate Jurisdictions: Where to Look for Wills* for full details. If you know approximately when someone died, you can request a four-year pre-paid search of the Indexes by writing to the York Probate Sub-Registry. The fee includes a copy should a will or administration grant be found.

Isle of Man

Until 1874, two ecclesiastical courts alternately exercised probate jurisdiction over estates in the Isle of Man for a part of each year. These were the Consistory Court of Sodor and Man, the testamentary records of which commence in 1600, and the Archdeaconry Court of Man, with probate material dating from 1631. When the See was suspended between 1644 and 1661, the ecclesiastical officers were replaced by lay 'judices' and a registrar, and the probate process remained otherwise unaffected. From 1875, the Consistory Court acted alone until 1884, and was then replaced by the High Court of Justice, in Douglas.

The probate records up to 1911, and filmed copies up to 1916, are preserved in the Manx National Heritage Library and Archives, from 1912 until 1939 in the Public Record Office of the Isle of Man, and from 1940 onwards in the Deeds and Probate Registry, both in Douglas.

The wills, administration grants and inventories are all indexed, although there are some seventeenth-century gaps. Microfilm copies of the indexed probate records up to 1949 are available for hire in family history centres.

Estates of Manx people held on the mainland or in Ireland

Until 1858, the Prerogative Court of York had authority over estates in the Northern dioceses, which included Sodor and Man, whilst the Prerogative Court of Canterbury dealt with any property in the Southern Province. Look at lists and indexes to wills proved in both of these courts and in local courts for property owned by Manx people on the mainland, particularly in the Consistory Courts of Chester and of Carlisle and in the Archdeaconry Court of Richmond (Western Deaneries). *Probate Jurisdictions: Where to Look for Wills* contains a county by county listing of the dates and whereabouts of wills, administration grants, indexes and any copies for every probate court. You can trace wills and administration grants of English and Welsh estates of Manx people after 1858 in the annual National Probate Indexes, described earlier. Property left in Scotland was dealt with by the Commissary or Sheriff Court of Edinburgh, and in Ireland by the Prerogative Court of Armagh or the Irish Principal Probate Registry, which are described below.

Scotland

From the thirteenth century, rural deans were authorized by their bishops to confirm wills of personal property (movables) up to the value of £40, the bishops themselves dealing with more valuable estates. The testament confirmed the appointment of the executors. After 1560, and until 1823, wills were produced for confirmation (testament testamentar) by the local commissary court. Each commissariot's area of jurisdiction was identical to that of the medieval Catholic diocese, though after the Crown assumed responsibility for probate matters in 1560, the bishops ceased to act. The commissariot boundaries are shown on the Scottish regional maps in *The Phillimore Atlas and Index of Parish Registers*. The chief commissary court, in Edinburgh, handled personal estates valued at £50 or more, and also received the wills of Scots dying overseas and leaving property in Scotland. A list of the various start dates of the commissary courts is included in *Probate Jurisdictions: Where to Look for Wills*. The earliest Scottish probate material, in the Commissariot of Edinburgh, dates from 1514. During the 1650s and until restored in 1662, the commissary courts were abolished, and authority for probate was transferred to local sheriff courts. The commissariots were finally abolished in 1823, and replaced by sheriff courts in 1824, the chief of which is in Edinburgh. The sheriff court districts roughly correspond to those of the civil administrative counties, though some were later enlarged. A list of districts and their constituent parishes can be gleaned from the current *Scottish Law Directory*. You can also find details about the commissariots and sheriff courts at **www.scotlandspeople.gov.uk**, for which there are accompanying county maps. The Commissary Court of Edinburgh lingered on until 1876, when its responsibility for confirming wills of people dying 'furth of Scotland' (abroad) leaving personal property there was transferred to the Court of Session. After 1858, if someone died who was usually resident in England, Wales or Ireland and had movables in Scotland, probate was permitted in the appropriate country, and a 'probate resealed' copy was sent to Edinburgh, and reciprocal arrangements were made for Scots with property in any of these countries.

Special forms were used for soldiers' and sailors' wills, of which about 31,000 survive between 1857 and 1966 for servicemen up to the rank of warrant officer, though there are some for men who were commissioned during the First and Second World Wars, and for officers and men in the Royal Flying Corps and Royal Air Force.

Heritable land was excluded from wills before 1868, although from the early nineteenth century settlements or trusts relating to such estates might be recorded among the commissary and sheriff court registers.

Should a person die intestate, the court drew up a testament dative appointing an administrator, who was usually the person's nominee or a near relative, and the names of any surviving spouse and children were placed in the court records. Most of the commissary and sheriff court registered copies and original confirmed wills, testaments dative, inventories and testamentary deeds are now in the National Archives of Scotland. All the testamentary papers relating to a deceased person were originally kept separate rather than united in one bundle or file.

Contact the Commissary Department of the Edinburgh Sheriff Court for enquiries about confirmed wills and testaments more recent than ten years ago.

Indexes and copies

You can search indexed digital images of all the wills and testaments between 1513 and 1901 at **www.scotlandspeople. gov.uk**. These include the resealed probates of English, Welsh and Irish people who left property in Scotland. The indexes contain the name, title or occupation and place of residence of the deceased, and the date and court of recording. An explanation of abbreviations used in the indexes is available at the website. Copies of the yearly indexed printed calendars of confirmations between 1901 and 1959 are in the National Archives of Scotland, and copies can be searched in many regional archive offices and libraries, including the Mitchell Library, in Glasgow. From 1960 to 1984 the calendars are on microfiche and thereafter, in the National Archives of Scotland, on computer. The calendars disclose the name of the deceased, his or her date and place of death, when and where the testament was recorded. There is an online catalogue to digital copies of the wills of Armed personnel between 1857 and 1966, in the National Archives of Scotland, as the original documents are too fragile for production. Just key in the name of the person concerned.

Consult the National Probate Indexes for references to probates in England and Wales of people leaving property in Scotland. Until 1876, these were indexed at the end of each year. For Ireland, see the section later on in this chapter.

Disputed testaments and *bona vacantia*

Contested testaments were settled in the commissariots, passing on appeal to the Commissary Court of Edinburgh, and finally to the Court of Session. After 1830, the Commissary Court lost its power of appeal. The appeal records are held in the National Archives of Scotland. Full indexes to cases heard in the commissary courts to 1800, and in the Commissary Court of Edinburgh have been published.

If no beneficiary could be located the estate became *bona vacantia* and was sold off by the King's or Queen's and Lord Treasurer's Remembrancer and the proceeds held till any claimant appeared. Nowadays such estates are dealt with by the Crown Office, in Edinburgh.

If there is no known heir of an intestate, his or her property reverts to the Crown as *'ultimus haeres'* (the last heir). The estate is advertised in the press and payment might be made to claimants on moral rather than legal grounds. Otherwise, it is not held indefinitely, and is ultimately taken by the state as 'the Crown's share'. The relevant records are held in the National Archives of Scotland.

Probate inventories

An inventory was normally compiled of the defunct's 'goods, geir, debts and sums of money' by neighbours and friends as soon after death as possible to achieve a valuation of his or her personal effects, and to protect them from being stolen. Almost all the wills and testaments dative had an inventory of some kind, however brief. Some were filed separately. Many of the inventories can be read at www.scotlandspeople.gov.uk with the wills and testaments. Before the civil registration of deaths began in 1855, and where burial registers are defective, inventories may be your sole source about dates of death, and will tell you about people's lifestyles.

Tutors, curators and guardians

When a father died leaving children under 21, and his will had failed to nominate anyone to look after them and their property, Chancery issued a brieve of tutory, appointing a tutor-at-law after a due enquiry directed by the county sheriff. After 1585, similar brieves of idiotry or furiosity were issued for the support of mentally incapacitated relatives of the deceased. The Exchequer could intervene and nominate a tutor-dative should no tutor-nominate or tutor-at-law be appointed.

The nearest kinsman on the paternal (agnate) line, who was aged over 25, became the guardian of the minor's or lunatic's estate, whilst the mother became the person's physical guardian. Starting in 1672, Chancery required an inventory of the individual's personal possessions from the tutor-at-law on taking up his responsibility. Before 1696, on reaching 14, a male minor (a female minor at 12) could apply to Chancery to administer the property him/herself or choose someone else to be curator. After this date curators were appointed in the same way as tutors-at-law, and continued to serve until the minor became 21.

The original records are held in the National Archives of Scotland.

An index to the above services *de tutela* to 1699 has been published in the third volume of *Inquisitionum ad Capellam*

Domini Regis Retornatum ... Abbreviatio, edited by T. Thomson. There is a general index to later tutorships and curations between 1700 and 1897, in the National Archives of Scotland.

The records were compiled in Latin until 1733.

Death duty registers

There are some indexed registers relating to the collection of Legacy Duty from 1804, Succession Duty after 1853 and Estate Duty from 1894 in the National Archives of Scotland. For more information about their likely content, read the relevant section in the previous chapter.

Services (retours) of heirs and sasines

Before 1868, on the owner's death, any heritable land automatically passed to the next rightful heir under the law of primogeniture by a deed of settlement or retour. However, until the twentieth century, most Scots did not own their land.

A landowner might set up a trust for the future management of his or her estate, and details of the trust deed were usually only recorded after the owner's death. The deeds frequently included a settlement of the succession of movables as well. The documentation was called a trust disposition and settlement ('TD and S'). If the person was a major landowner, the register of deeds of the Court of Session, in Edinburgh, was utilized, but for the rest, they were more likely to be enrolled in the register of deeds in the local commissary court up to 1809 and then in the sheriff court, or in the register of deeds of a local royal burgh. However, the deed did not need to be registered to take effect.

The retour (service of the heir) recorded the transfer of the legal title, whereas a sasine recorded when the heir actually took physical possession of the land, after receiving the retour from Chancery. This process might take several years to complete. Only inherited land was dealt with by retours and sasines until 1857, after which leases of 31 years or more became registrable.

After 1868, heritable land could be otherwise disposed of, by will and since 1964, most landed property has been devised, so it is a good idea to search both the retours and confirmed wills.

The county by county registrations of retours are in the National Archives of Scotland.

For a retour to be issued, a brieve of succession was first sent out of Chancery to the county sheriff. His sworn-in local jurors investigated what estates the dead landowner had held there at the time of death, and obtained proof as to the name, age and relationship of the next legal heir. The jury's verdict to the sheriff court was then 'retoured' to Chancery and the heir served with a certified copy of the 'retour' ratifying his or her entitlement. The verdicts were not always recorded.

Personal-name and topographical indexes and short summaries of the county retours between about 1544 and 1699 have been printed in *Inquisitionum ad Capellam Domini Regis Retornatum ... Abbreviatio*. Ten-yearly indexes then cover retours up to 1859, after which they are annual. The indexes invariably specify the relationship of the rightful heir to the deceased. The entries prior to 1860 also frequently contain dated abstracts of the original documentation, and tell you when the landowner died, though the later indexes exclude this.

Until they were abolished in 1747, regality courts, which were exempt from the control of local sheriffdoms, also retoured services of heirs. The courts were gifted by the monarch to Lords of Regality, especially in the Border counties, and in distant or rebellious parts of Scotland, as a reward for their vigilance and loyalty. The courts were presided over by a bailie and his deputy, and they operated in the same way as the sheriff courts. Most of their records are in the National Archives of Scotland too.

The retours were composed in Latin until about 1680, and then increasingly in English, which was also the language used between 1653 and 1660. The retours before 1544 were destroyed, and many of those in the sixteenth century are defective, but they are fairly comprehensive after 1600, except for 1611-14.

The instruments of sasine were written up in a special register of sasines, particularly those after 1540. Like the retours, they were compiled in Latin.

There are three series of registers of sasines after 1599, all of which are in the National Archives of Scotland:

- a secretary's register for every county or district, 1599–1609;
- a particular register for each county or district, 1617-1871; and
- a general register, recording sasines of land held in more than one district or county between 1617 and 1871.

A general register is still kept today, and from 1926 burgh

sasines have been included. Since 6 April 1981, the register has gradually been replaced by a county by county system of registration of title, which is managed by the Registers of Scotland, in Edinburgh.

The first two sets of registers of sasines are only partly indexed, though there is a complete nominal and topographical index to the general register in the National Archives of Scotland. A list of surviving county indexes up to 1780 is at **www.nas.gov.uk/guides/sasines.asp**. You can search printed indexed abridgements for each county of the registered entries from 1781 onwards in the National Archive Scotland, and in many reference libraries and regional archive offices. Sometimes, it may be quicker and easier to purchase a copy of the search sheet for a specific property from the Resgisters of Scotland, as each sheet cites the volume and page numbers of all the sasines and deeds relating to it.

The registers of sasines often refer to earlier transfers of estates within the family, specifying the relationship of each heir to the deceased.

Sasines of land in the 66 Royal burghs were recorded in separate registers. Sasines relating to other burghs were usually copied up into the particular registers described above. Since 1926, they have all been enrolled in the general register. Most of the Royal burgh registers are is now in the National Archives of Scotland, apart from those relating to Aberdeen and Dundee before 1809, and to Glasgow, which are retained in their city archives.

There are almost no published indexes to the burgh sasines before the last century, so you will have to rely on contemporary manuscript or later typescript indexes in the National Archives. There is a complete list of these at **www.nas.gov.uk/guides/sasines.asp**.

Estates in England and Wales

Scots leaving property over the border in England or in Wales had their wills proved in the appropriate local church court before 1858 or in the Prerogative Court of York or of Canterbury. The PCY and PCC indexes after 1707 generally referred to Scots as being of 'North Britain'. You can trace their later wills and administration grants in the annual National Probate Indexes. From 1858 until 1876, the probates and grants of administrations of Scots were listed at the end of each annual index, after which they were integrated with the rest of the entries. Look in the previous chapter for more details about English probate court records.

Ireland

Up to 1858, the wills of Irish people were proved in diocesan consistory courts. The diocesan and civil county boundaries were not identical. When personalty exceeding £5 was held in more than one diocese, the superior Prerogative Court of Armagh was utilized. However, if such property totalled less than this, probate was applied for in the consistory court of the diocese containing the more valuable personal estate. A few peculiar courts operated outside the two-tier hierarchy. To find out which probate courts had jurisdiction over the counties where your ancestors lived, look in *Probate Jurisdictions: Where to Look for Wills*.

In 1858, the church courts were replaced by a civil Principal Probate Registry, in Dublin, and by 11 district probate registries.

The entire collection of original wills and administration grants before 1858, and most of the registered office copies, were destroyed by a fire in Dublin Castle in 1922, along with all the records of the Principal Probate Registry and the original wills and administration grants deposited there by the district probate registries between 1858 and 1903. A list of surviving material is included in *Probate Jurisdictions: Where to Look for Wills*.

Original and registered copies of approved wills and administrations since 1904 are held in the National Archives of Ireland. Wills and administration grants more recent than 20 years ago in the Republic of Ireland are retained by the various probate registries, before being placed in the National Archives of Ireland. Wills and administration grants filed after 1900 in the district probate registries of Belfast, Londonderry and many in Armagh are now in the custody of the Public Record Office of Northern Ireland, whilst probates and grants issued less than ten years ago are kept by the Probate Registry of the Royal Courts of Justice, in Belfast, before being transferred to the Public Record Office.

The Crown Solicitor, in the Treasury Solicitor's Department, in Belfast, deals with *bona vacantia* in Northern Ireland.

Indexes and transcripts

The surviving indexes to the wills and administration bonds in the pre-1858 probate courts testify to what was lost. You can search the indexes from 1484 to 1858 at **www.nationalarchives.ie** and at **www.originsnetwork.com**, and on CD-ROM. There are gaps for most diocesan courts before the mid-eighteenth century, and many recorded probates stem only from the preceding century. There are printed indexes to wills proved in the Prerogative Court of Armagh between 1536 and 1810, and to probate grants in the diocese of Dublin from 1638 to 1857. A manuscript index, in the National Archives of Ireland, covers the remaining period for the Prerogative Court up to 1858, and this is arranged by year and then initial-alphabetically by surname. The indexes usually disclose the testator's or intestate's full name, address, and occupation and the year of probate or administration bond.

Printed copies of the alphabetical annual union calendars of wills and administrations in all the Irish probate registries from 1858 onwards can be inspected in both the National Archives of Ireland and the Public Record Office of Northern Ireland. There is a consolidated index for the period 1858–77. Until 1917, the calendars cover all of Ireland; thenceforward the calendars relating to the 26 southern counties are held in the National Archives of Ireland, and similar calendars for the six northern counties are in the Public Record Office of Northern Ireland. The calendars contain references to will and administration grant book copies, which are complete from 1922. A computerized index between 1983 and 1986 is available in the Dublin Probate Registry and in each of the local district probate registries of southern Ireland. Once 20 years have elapsed, another year is added.

The calendars set out the deceased's name, address, occupation, date and place of death, the date and place of probate or administration grant, and the names, addresses, occupations and relationship to him or her of the executors or administrators. In the case of administration grants, the names of all the entitled next of kin were recorded in the calendars. Gross personal estate valuations were given too.

Fortunately for us, in the early nineteenth century, Sir William Betham compiled sketch pedigrees from his notebooks of genealogical abstracts of almost all the wills proved before 1800 and administration grants up to 1802 in the Prerogative Court of Armagh, and of wills proved in the Consistory Court of Kildare before 1827. His original notebooks can be examined in the National Archives of Ireland. The published index to the Prerogative Court wills is a handy key. The alphabetically listed abstracts of Armagh administration grants, the sketch pedigrees and later amendments and additions, are now in the Genealogical Office, in the National Library of Ireland. Indexed photostat copies of the notebooks and pedigrees are held by the College of Arms, in London, and copies can be studied on microfilm in the library of the Society of Genealogists. Microfilm copies of the unamended sketch pedigrees are available in the Public Record Office of Northern Ireland as well. Consult the Family History Library catalogue at **www.familysearch.org** for references to copies you may hire in look at in a family history centre.

Copies were compiled by the local registries before the original wills and administration grants were sent to Dublin. The resulting will books and administration grant books from 1858 onwards are now in the National Archives of Ireland. Similar will books survive for the Principal Probate Registry only for 1874, 1876, 1891 and 1896, and administration grant books for 1878, 1883, 1891 and 1893, and these too are in the National Archives of Ireland. A complete set of will books for the probate districts of Armagh, Belfast and Londonderry from 1858 to 1900 is available on microfilm in the Public Record Office of Northern Ireland.

A great effort has been made to trace the whereabouts of any other transcripts and researchers' abstracts of destroyed wills and administrations both before and after 1858. A good and growing collection is held by the National Archives of Ireland, to which there is a card index. Indexed transcripts and abstracts of wills before 1858 can also be inspected in the Public Record Office of Northern Ireland. Other concentrations of will abstracts may be found in the Genealogical Office, and in the libraries of the Representative Church Body, Royal Irish Academy, and Trinity College, all of which are in Dublin.

Estates in England, Wales and Scotland

Wills of Irish people leaving property in England or Wales before 1858 were proved in the Prerogative Court of Canterbury, Prerogative Court of York, or in the relevant local diocesan court, especially in London and the North Country.

When personalty was held both in Ireland and England, probate was granted in both countries. Look in *Probate Jurisdictions: Where to Look for Wills* for information about the probate courts serving your county or counties of interest.

You can elicit information about 'resealed' probates of Irish residents leaving property in Englanf or Wales from the National Probate Indexes described earlier. They were listed separately at the end of each year until 1876, and were then absorbed into the main index. As some of these duplicated the documents in the Principal Probate Registry, in Dublin, where the original wills and administrations were destroyed, this source may be a very effective substitute. For more details about the content and whereabouts of the Indexes, see Chapter 13.

The system of 'probate resealing' involved a copy of the proved will being sent by the Principal Probate Registry in Dublin to its London counterpart. A similar arrangement was carried out with the Commissary Court or Court of Session in Edinburgh. A reciprocal scheme was used for British residents with property in Ireland.

Death Duty registers

Irish residuary estates and legacies over a certain value attracted Legacy Duty after 1796, Succession Duty from 1853, and Estate Duty after 1894.

The surviving Legacy Duty registers between 1828 and 1839, containing extracts of liable wills and administrations, are in the National Archives of Ireland. Embedded in them are the name, last address and occupation of the testator or intestate, his or her date of death, the date and place of probate or administration grant, the names, addresses and occupations of the executors or administrators, and details about legacies and/or residuary estate over the minimum dutiable value, with the names of affected beneficiaries or next of kin and their relationship to the deceased, the percentage rate and amount of duty and when it was paid. The entries were amended accordingly if any of the legacies were contingent or to pass in succession, so the marriages and deaths of the relevant future beneficiaries were noted, as were the ages of any nominated annuitants at the date of probate.

The annual indexes to the Death Duty registers, in the National Archives of Ireland run on to 1879, and yield the names and addresses of the deceased, his or her executors or administrators, the date and place of probate or grant of letters of administration. When the original wills and Death Duty registers no longer exist, the indexes convey some idea of when a person died, which is particularly useful before civil registration began in 1864.

Incomplete copies of the registers containing Legacy Duty and Succession Duty abstracts of wills which were proved in the Prerogative Court of Canterbury and in some other local courts between 1821 and 1857 are available in the Public Record Office of Northern Ireland, together with copies of the accompanying annual indexes.

The Registry of Deeds

Another important substitute for lost Irish wills is the collection of enrolments in the Registry of Deeds, in Dublin. The registry was set up in 1708, to protect transfers of land by will or other means against any future litigation, and to prevent Catholics from buying or taking on long leases of land, so the enrolments mostly relate to landowners who belonged to the Church of Ireland. Wills tended to be registered only if someone omitted as a beneficiary was likely to object. Registration was not compulsory in the early years, but became more widespread after 1750, when many Protestant dissenters took advantage of the scheme, especially the Presbyterians in the North of the island. Microfilmed copies of the books of enrolled memorials (containing exact transcripts of the original wills and deeds), can be examined in the Public Record Office of Northern Ireland.

Abstracts of Wills at the Registry of Deeds, edited by P. B. Phair (Eustace) and E. Ellis, includes enrolments from 1708 up to 1832. Copies are available in both the National Library of Ireland and the National Archives of Ireland. From this, you can discover the identities of each testator and beneficiary, and of the witnesses to a will, but not the actual provisions. Use the given enrolment numbers to find the memorial book entries and original witnessed memorials.

There is an alphabetical grantors' index from 1708, but although the surname of the first grantee, and the register volume, page or memorial number are recorded, no property locations or dates were cited before 1832. After this, the county and year of registration were given, which might be as late as two years after probate. The indexes are arranged in blocks of years, and there are no corresponding indexes to the names of grantees. The lands index, running from 1708 to 1947, also in blocks of years, is in two series: one is arranged alphabetically by county and then initial-alphabetically by townland, and the other, commencing in 1828, is organized alphabetically by barony and then by townland, and is thus easier to search. Separate indexes were kept for transfers of land in corporate towns and cities. Microfilmed copies of the indexes can be inspected in the National Library of Ireland, and in the Public Record Office of Northern Ireland. You can hire in copies of the indexes at a family history centre.

If you find the task of searching these indexes too daunting, you may be able to locate the whereabouts and descent of a family's land during the nineteenth century from the Tithe Applotment Books, Primary Valuation and Valuation Office books, described in Chapter 08.

Land Commission records

Indexed copies of some 10,000 nineteenth-century and earlier wills which were deposited with the Irish Land Commission, in Dublin between 1891 and 1923 as a consequence of the Land Purchase Acts might be another fruitful source worth exploring. They were lodged by landowners as proof of title to the smallholdings which they planned to sell to their occupying tenants. The copies are now in the National Archives of Ireland, whilst a card index to the names of the testators is available in the National Library of Ireland.

Britons in India

If your antecedent died in India, his or her will relating to any property there would have been proved in the ecclesiastical court of the appropriate Presidency. Copies were enrolled in the various Court proceedings of the Presidency of Bengal, the Presidency of Bombay and of the Presidency of Madras from about 1704 up to 1780. After this, and until 1948, there is a single indexed register for all the wills, for administration grants after 1774 and for probate inventories from 1780 up to 1938. The records are in the Asia, Pacific and Africa Collections, in the British Library.

When people still owned property in England, Wales, Scotland or Ireland, probate had to take place there as well, so you may find two grants relating to the same person, which were perhaps some years adrift of each other. Read the sections in this book on how to find their whereabouts. It is probable that the chief probate courts of each country were used.

United States of America

The probate procedure adopted by British and post-colonial America largely replicated that of England and Wales, but check the prevailing probate legislation in your state or territory of interest for any variations. Generally, wills of personalty can be made by males on reaching 14, and by girls at 12, but the minimum legal age in Connecticut, Massachusetts and Virginia is 18 for both sexes, 18 for males and 16 for females in the State of New York, and 21 in Vermont. Land can only be devised by will at 21. The rules of intestacy may differ too.

Probate was and still is granted by the county or other district court serving the area where the dead person had his or her property. Sadly, many of the older records have now been lost or badly damaged; surviving documentation is held in the relevant courthouse or probate office. For addresses and contact details of county courthouses, visit **www.genealogy.com/00000174.html** and **www.cyndislist.com/courthouses.htm**. Copies of many of the records can be inspected in family history centres.

The probate process usually has to begin within 30 to 90 days of a person's death, in the county or district court. First, the executor's petition for consent to apply for probate (letters testamentary) is recorded in the probate minute book. As well as the deceased's name, last address, and occupation, his or her date of death, and the names and addresses of the petitioner and of the witnesses to the will, the minutes will tell you the names, addresses and ages of all the deceased's heirs, and the value and whereabouts of his or her real and personal estate. In some jurisdictions the petition is placed in the deceased's probate case packet or file. Next, the will is produced in court, and the witnesses testify to its authenticity, so that a copy can be registered in the will book. In some states, all the identifiable heirs are notified and obliged to attend at this stage, to claim or forfeit any future right to contest the will. The appointment of the executor is then confirmed and minuted by the court.

In cases of intestacy, the petition is presented by the intending administrator. The post of administrator is generally determined by who is the first ranked survivor, starting with the spouse, then the eldest child, the parents, grandparents, siblings, uncles, aunts, nephews, nieces, great-uncles and -aunts, and first cousins of the dead person, and then his or her creditors, and anyone else who is legally competent to deal with the estate, and finally, public administrators step in if there are none of these. There may be variations to the above order of seniority in certain states. The probate minute book may be the only place where you can find the identities and relationships of an intestate's next heirs.

The administrator posts a bond with the court in a sum equal to the total assets, as security. His or her sureties might be relatives, friends or the estate heirs, so these documents can be informative too. The executor is usually specifically spared this formality by the will.

Three independent people are appointed by the court to inventory the deceased's estate for return at its next sitting or within 90 days, to protect the executor or administrator from excessive claims, and the heirs from fraud or theft. The valuation is utilized by the court to fix the probate fees.

As soon as the inventory has been completed, a notice of pending probate is published. In the colonial period, this was done by posting it on the door of the county courthouse, townhall or at the local church, but later it was also advertised for three successive weeks in the chief local newspaper. Copies of the notices were retained by the court or place of posting as proof of publicity.

At this stage, the executor or administrator might pay out interim allowances from the known estate funds to support the deceased's dependants until the final distribution. Often, the widow's right to a third of the estate as her dower might be settled at this point, and the court appoint a guardian to look after any minor or orphaned children. The guardian posts a bond with a friend or relative acting as surety, offering as security a sum equal to the value of the minor's share in the estate, and this remains in force until guardianship ceases on a boy attaining 21 or a girl 18. In order to raise enough money to support the widow and children, or to convert perishable items to cash, the executor or administrator is allowed to sell some off with the court's prior permission. An itemized list of these has first to be furnished with the application, plus an explanation of why the capital is needed, and the expected auction proceeds. A public auctioneer is then appointed, and an account prepared of the various sale takings, together with the purchasers' names and addresses. In some states, the executor, administrator and guardian produce annual accounts to the court, showing all the estate income and expenditure during the year and the purpose of each disbursement. In other states, this might be done only if requested by the estate heirs or creditors. The accounts can be helpful in telling you about any family marriages and deaths during the previous 12 months.

Further notices are published to give possible claimants to the estate a last chance to object before probate or letters of administration are granted, and the executor or administrator then files the final estate accounts, showing how much is left in the estate pot for distribution.

When all the affected parties are agreed, or when all the heirs are of age, the property is divided up. The division documents show how this was done. They name the surviving beneficiaries, their current places of residence, identify the husbands of female heirs, and show if the deceased's widow had remarried. The signed receipts of the beneficiaries reveal how much money or what property each had got, and discharged the executor or administrator or guardian from any further liability to the estate. These papers are usually placed together in the probate case packet or file. In some states, the division documents are deposited in the office of the county land recorder, and copied up into their land entry books.

Indexes and transcripts

The original probate case packets, files and will books are usually indexed. Sometimes, however, you may have to search the county ourthouse records place by place. Visit **www.familysearch.org** for details of copies of indexes you can hire in to search in a family history centre. You can also search uploaded indexes at **www.ancestry.com** or via the links at **www.cyndislist.com**.

Abstracts and transcripts of many colonial wills and administrations have been published, but these are of varying quality and reliability, as are the copies in the will books. However, some of the transcriptions relate to wills which were subsequently lost, and you can use them to locate unindexed probate case packets and files.

Contested wills

Appeals against probate or intestate's estates were handled first by the probate court, and then by the legislative assembly. After the Revolution, each state set up its own Supreme Court (or Court of Last Resort). Deatils of colonial appeals to the governor and council or assembly may be found in the *Calendar of State Papers, Colonial: America and West Indies 1574–1739*, which is also on CD-ROM.

Minors and orphans

Occasionally, guardianship was dealt with by a different court than the one handling probate. An 'orphan' might actually still have one living parent, who was usually appointed as guardian. Boys on reaching 14, and girls at 12 could petition the court for its consent to their nomination of someone else, and a further bond was sworn by the new appointee and a guarantor. The dated applications in such cases contain the names and current ages of the minors, the names both of their nominee and deceased parent. The court clerk recorded its permission in the court order book.

Tips

- Use any indexes and transcriptions as research tools and study the original documentation in case anything was missed out or erroneously copied.
- Since 1811, under federal law, inheritance by primogeniture has been banned on intestacy or by entailment. Each state can otherwise fix its own rules on what should happen to estates that are otherwise unprovided for on death. Look for the most recent probate statute in a published State Law Code for a reference to the next most recent enactment, and work back in time until you find the acts which were in force during your ancestors' lifetimes. Copies are available in most reference and law libraries.
- In some jurisdictions, testators could have their wills probated whilst they were still alive, thereby ensuring that their wishes were carried out.
- When the original probate records have been destroyed, look for any trust deeds, deeds of settlement and maps concerning the partition of real estate, and for copies which were enrolled in the county courthouse land entry books.

- Legatees might be referred to in certain probate documents without surnames or without their relationship to the testator, so work your way through the entire packet or file for further clarification. The definition of some family relationships has changed over time too, so always write them down as they appear in the record and interpret them later. For example, '-in-law' might indicate a step-child, or adopted kin, as well as a connection by marriage.

American estates in the United Kingdom and Ireland

Sometimes colonial wills were proved not only in the colonial county court, but in the Prerogative Court of Canterbury too for reasons of security or in expectation of future litigation. If the county records have been lost, this avenue is worth exploring. The English grant might, however, come some years after the colonist's death, and his or her last place of abode be listed in the indexes as 'Parts'.

You can view indexed digital images of PCC wills from 1384 up to 1858 at **www.nationalarchives.gov.uk/documentsonline**, which is searchable by personal- and place-name as well as by date and occupation. Uutilize this to find the wills of contemporary family members who stayed behind, who may have mentioned relatives abroad.

Consult *American Wills and Administrations in the Prerogative Court of Canterbury, 1610–1857*, by P. W. Coldham, for brief abstracts of the probate act books. The entries are arranged alphabetically by each testator's or intestate's name and forename, and disclose his or her last place of residence and death, the name of the executor(s) or administrator(s), the date of the will and of probate or of the administration grant, and cite the whereabouts of any known printed abstract or transcript. There are indexes to ships'- and to place-names, which is helpful if you want to trace the wills of fellow travellers or of other settlers leaving property in the same place, for references to your family.

You may be able to discover the precise dates and places of death of people dying abroad from the eighteenth century and later PCC warrants issued to executors authorizing probate and to administrators so that they could obtain grants of letters of administration. You can inspect the chronological bundles of warrants in the National Archives, at Kew.

Probate inventories exist only in any quantity in the Prerogative Court of Canterbury after 1660, though some date from as early as the fifteenth century. Search the personal-name indexes at **www.nationalarchives.gov.uk/catalogue** for document references. The inventories demonstrate the widespread practice of borrowing and lending among overseas merchants and traders and their continued links with and visits home, as well as the estimated values of the contents of their houses and warehouses, trade stock and merchandise.

American Wills proved in London, 1611–1775, also compiled by P. W. Coldham, concentrates on probates in the Bishop of London's Consistory Court. For probated estates of Americans in England and Wales after 1858, search the National Probate Indexes, described in Chapter 13.

Indexes to Scottish wills and testaments and Irish probates of wills should also be searched for references to property left there by emigrants or travellers overseas. You can examine indexed digital images of the Scottish documents from 1513 until 1901 at **www.scotlandspeople.gov.uk** and the index to Irish wills between 1484 and 1858 at **www.originsnetwork.com** and on CD-ROM, though few Irish wills now survive.

Look in *Scottish-American Heirs, 1683–1883*, by D. Dobson, for information about their retours and sasines.

When wills of overseas residents were contested in the Prerogative Court of Canterbury and/or in the Court of Chancery, the litigation often gave rise to a wealth of background and biographical information. Some of the Chancery proceedings, in the National Archives, at Kew, have been indexed online by personal- and place-name, and by subject, at **www.nationalarchives.gov.uk/catalogue**. Try this to see if your ancestor was a litigant or the deceased, whose estate was the subject of a dispute. Such Chancery suits are listed in the *Inheritance Disputes Index, 1574–1714*, which is searchable at **www.originsnetwork.com**.

Death Duties

Americans leaving property in the United Kingdom were subject to Legacy Duty, Succession Duty and Estate Duty in the same way as British residents. You can search digital images of the yearly indexes to the Death Duty registers between 1796 and 1903 at **www.findmyfamily.com/HomeServlet**. Microfilm copies of all the indexes and of the registers up to 1857 can be hired in to study in a family history centre. The original registers from 1858 to 1903 can be inspected in the National Archives, in Kew, and microfilm copies of the indexes up to 1903, and of the registers as far as 1857 are available there and in the Family Records Centre. It is planned to upload digital images of all the registers.

The register entries tell you where the overseas resient was last living and his or her date of death, as well probate or administration grant details about liable parts of the estate.

15

across the divide: pursuing your migrant ancestors

In this chapter you will learn:
- how to find when and where your immigrant ancestor arrived in North America
- how to follow your emigrant ancestor's trail
- how to locate naturalization papers.

The prime sources I have already described in this book may have told you that your ancestors or other relatives were emigrants from the United Kingdom to North America. If this happened more than a generation ago, all former ties are likely to have been severed. As genealogy is a global pursuit, the break may not be permanent, as you can make use of the many online message boards, family-name associations and people finders to try and trace their present-day descendants.

Don't forget that one country's emigrant is another country's immigrant, so you will have to examine records of both. Sometimes, emigration took place in stages, which might mean several countries were involved, for instance, a family or individual might first move from Scotland to Ireland, or from Ireland to England, before the Atlantic voyage. An emigrant might originally have gone to the West Indies, eventually settling in America, or have disembarked at an American port before crossing the border into Canada, or vice versa. Read *Tracing Your West Indian Ancestors*, by G. Grannum (PRO Publications, 2002) for information about sources.

You will find some knowledge of the history and pattern of settlement of the colony, plantation, state or territory will be helpful, as well as of the political, economic and religious climate in which your ancestors lived, and the prevailing local industrial, agricultural and cultural conditions they left behind. Use a search engine or your library catalogue for books that will give you a general overview and study their bibliographies for specific topics. Read *The Peopling of British North America: An Introduction*, by B. Bailyn (Vintage Books USA, 1988), *Scottish Emigration to Colonial America, 1607–1785* by D. Dobson (University of Georgia Press, 2004), and *History of the Irish in America*, by A. K. Bradley (Chartwell Publishing, 1986). Some other titles are listed in the select bibliography at the end of this book.

In the seventeenth century, it was mainly the North American Eastern seaboard which was colonized, but gradually the vast hinterland began to be opened up. By the second half of the nineteenth century, people were able to move faster by rail than by wagon or handcart so ventured further West, particularly to seek work in the burgeoning manufacturing cities and towns, to mine coal, build railroads, prospect for gold, or to farm.

Where the colonies were run by governors, councils and assemblies under the close supervision of the Crown, their reports and correspondence, settlers' petitions and land grants will be located in British records. Where the Crown transferred control over colonial government to trustees, proprietors or individuals, any surviving documentation will be in state archives. Read *Emigration and Expats, A Guide to Sources on UK Emigration and Residents Overseas*, by R. Kershaw (PRO Publications, 2002), for an introduction to a wide range of available government and other records on both sides of the Atlantic.

After independence, each American state or territory became virtually autonomous, except in matters of defence and federal taxation, so their records were kept locally, as were those of the town and county courts responsible for local justice and administration. Consult *Courthouse Research for Family Historians: Your Guide to Genealogical Treasures*, by C. Rose (Rose Family Assn, 2004), and *The Genealogist's Address Book*, by E.P. Bentley (Genealogical Publishing Company, 1998), for more information.

Ships' passenger lists and border crossings

If your relatives went to North America in the last two centuries, you could start by trawling the indexed digital images of the ships' passenger lists of arrivals in the Port of New York between 1820 and 1957, and at other American ports, which you can view at **www.ancestry.com**. This huge immigration database includes alien passengers passing through Castle Garden Immigration Center between 1855 and 1890, the Barge Office 1890–91 and arrivals at Ellis Island from 1892 to 1924, which are also searchable at **www.castlegarden.org/index.html** and **www.ellisislandrecords.org** respectively. Control over immigration began in the United States of America in 1820. The digitized images are of the ships' manifests which were filed from that year up to 1905 in the port customs houses in Boston, New York, Baltimore, Philadelphia, Mobile, New Bedford and New Orleans; and of the immigration passenger lists, compiled for the State Department, for Philadelphia from 1883, and most other American ports after 1891. Look at the listed end-dates for each port. You can view images of the entire passenger lists and pictures of the vessels at these websites.

Microfilm copies of the above are held in the National Archives Building in Washington, DC, in some of its regional facilities, state and city archives, and for hire in family history centres. The customs house lists were variously written up, according to family group, strictly alphabetically, by ticket number or in order of boarding, whilst the immigration passenger lists were compiled initial-alphabetically by surname. The customs house lists set out the ship's name, port of embarkation, ports of call and destination, and the name, country of origin, gender, age, occupation and the passenger's country, city or town of residence at the time the ticket was bought. The given city or town was not necessarily where the emigrant originally came from. The immigration passenger lists added each passenger's marital status and nationality, when and where he or she had been in the USA before and, if they were going to join a relative, that person's name, address and family relationship. After 1907, the name and address of a relative in the country of provenance was given too. You can thus quickly find out exactly when your relatives set foot in America, where they were going, and the whereabouts of a family member left behind. You may even come across certain passengers' names several times, as they went to and fro across the Atlantic, and pick up the names of other relatives who went to join them. There are some earlier cargo ships' manifests of passenger arrivals in American ports before 1820, but these are rarely indexed or complete. Look in *Maritime Folklife Resources: a Directory and Index*, by P. Bartis and M. Hufford (Washington DC: American Folklife Centre, 1980), for details of known collections, any finding aids and published lists.

Where your ancestor lived is likely to have determined at which port he or she embarked, for instance, for Scots emigrants the voyage was shorter to the Canadian ports. Personal-name indexes to ships' passengers arriving there between 1925 and 1935 are searchable at **www.collectionscanada.ca/ archivianet/02011802_e.html**. From these you can learn each passenger's age and nationality, the name of the ship and shipping line, the year and port of arrival and the relevant volume, page and microfilm numbers, so that you can order a copy to study in provincial or territorial archives (**www.archivescanada.ca/**), or to borrow using the inter-library loan service (**www.collectionscanada.ca/gateway/s22-200-e.html**). The database excludes returning Canadians, tourists, visitors and people in transit to the United States.

You can examine copies of the incoming ships' passenger lists from 1865 onwards in Library and Archives Canada, which include copies of ships' manifests lodged in Canadian ports of call by masters of vessels on their way to America. The lists are arranged by port and date of landing up to 31 May 1921, and from 1 January 1925 onwards, whilst individual forms were compiled for every passenger intending to proceed directly to Canada between 1 June 1921 and the end of 1924. You can inspect digital images of the lists from 1865 up to 1922 at **www.collectionscanada.ca/archivianet/passenger/001045-100.01-e.php**, although you will need to know the name of the ship, shipping line, year or port of arrival or of departure to view them. The lists up to 1921 reveal only the age, country of origin, occupation and intended destination of each immigrant, but the later forms and lists are more informative and similar to the American lists described above. However, wives and accompanied young children often went unrecorded.

There are no comprehensive ships' passenger lists of Canadian port arrivals before 1865, although you can search a miscellaneous immigration index to 15,000 names of incoming passengers from the British Isles between 1801 and 1849, relating mostly to Quebec and Ontario, at **www.ingeneas.com**. Later passenger lists, from 1 January 1936, are held by Citizenship and Immigration Canada, in Ottawa. You can write requesting a search on your behalf, but you will need to supply the full name, date of birth and year of entry of the passenger, and there are certain terms and conditions for disclosure of information.

Links to other online indexes and digital images or transcriptions of names of passengers on incoming vessels to American ports are accessible at **www.archives.gov/genealogy/immigration**, and to both American and Canadian ports at **www.cyndislist.com/ships**. It is worth trying all the website links in case of indexing errors and variations, and don't forget to look out for those that are free. People's names were often spelled in unfamiliar ways, so try every likely permutation and phonetic spellings.

In 1803, the British government began to regulate ships carrying emigrants to North America, and ships' masters were required to leave a list of passengers at the port of departure. Copies were also lodged at every port of call and at the final destination, and the shipping line itself kept a copy. To find the dates and whereabouts of UK shipping company records, visit **www.nationalarchives.gov.uk/nra**, **www.liverpoolmuseums.org.uk/maritime** and **www.proni.gov.uk/records/emigrate.htm**.

Another excellent source of this information is *Shipping: A Survey of Historical Records*, by P. Mathias and W. H. Pearsall (David & Charles PLC, 1971), which contains indexes to ships' names, shipowners, shipping lines and places.

Indexed digital images and transcriptions of centrally preserved passenger lists of outgoing ships leaving UK ports after 1890 are gradually being uploaded at **www.findmypast.com/HomeServlet**. You can search these by personal- or ship's name, by port and by date. The lists themselves, running up to 1960, relate only to vessels bound for destinations outside Europe and the Mediterranean, and are in the National Archives, at Kew. The lists are arranged by port and chronologically by departure date. Liverpool was the most popular English port of embarkation for North America, and was easily reached from Ireland, as well as Irish ports being used en route. After the 1860s, Southampton overtook Liverpool as the port of choice for steamships, and was more convenient for European emigrants. The lists of outgoing passengers complement the incoming passenger lists in North America and may make up for any gaps. As well as each person's age, occupation, nationality and port and country of destination, the lists from 1922 onwards give his or her last UK address and from 1956, exact date of birth. If you know on which ship your ancestor sailed, search the yearly registers of ships' passenger lists between 1906 and 1951. However, up to October 1908 they relate only to the ports of Bristol, Southampton and Weymouth. The monthly entries (daily from 1921) record the names of ships leaving each port, so that you can identify the correct box of passenger lists.

An exceptional collection of ships' passenger lists, in the National Archives, at Kew, consists of the weekly returns of vessels leaving English and Welsh ports between 1773 and 1776, and of emigrants departing from Scottish ports in 1774 and 1775. The lists relating to passengers bound for America have been published in *Emigrants to the American Colonies, 1773-1776*, by P. W. Coldham (Clearfield Co, 1988), which is searchable at **www.ancestry.com**, and in the *Directory of Scottish Settlers in North America, 1625-1825*, by D. Dobson (Genealogical Publishing Company, 1985). From these, you can discover each person's name, age, last address and occupation, the purpose of his or her journey, the date and place of embarkation, on which ship, the intended port of disembarkation and ultimate destination.

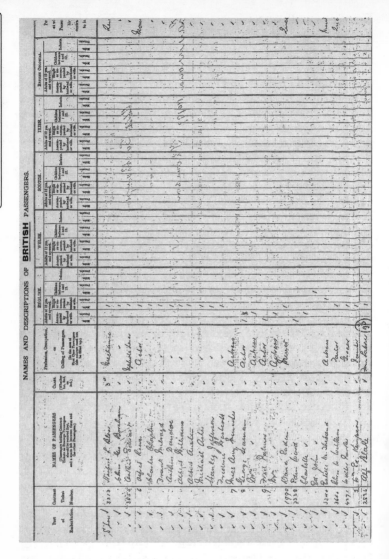

Figure 19 part of the ship's passenger list of SS Cairnrona, which left Southampton for Quebec and Montreal on 20 September 1910. Among the third class passengers bound for Montreal were Charles Chaplin, Stanley Jefferson (later known as Stan Laurel) and Frederick Westcott (Fred Karno), all of whom were described as actors
(reproduced by permission of The National Archives)

Border crossings

Before April 1908, people were able to move freely over the American/Canadian border, so there will be no formal record of their movements, except what births, baptisms and marriages you might circumstantially turn up in the International Genealogical Index or North American Vital Records Index. Border crossing entry lists exist for the years between 1908 and 1935, and are deposited in Library and Archives Canada. Until 1918, the entry lists are arranged by border land point or seaport, and date of entry. If you don't have this information, you will have to search the entries for each port, month by month. The lists record the name, age, country of birth, last address, occupation, and the destination in Canada of each entrant. Individual forms were used between 1919 and 1924, but the border entry lists were restored in 1925. From 1925, the country, state and place of birth were included, plus the name of the relative, friend or employer in Canada to whom the person was going, and the name and address of a relative in the country of origin. Border crossing entries between 1925 and 1935, of people whose surnames began with 'C', are indexed with the ships' passenger lists at **www.collectionscanada.ca/ archivianet/02011802_e.html**, but the indexes between 1925 and 1935 are otherwise closed to the public, although searches can be made for you, if you can provide the year of entry. Visit **www.collectionscanada.ca/genealogy/022-908.005-e.html** for more information. The lists after 1935 are held by Citizenship and Immigration Canada.

You can examine microfilmed copies of the so-called 'St Albans Lists', in the National Archives Building, for details about passengers crossing the border in the other direction, from Canada into the United States. Copies can be hired in to search in family history centres too. The lists were compiled between 1895 and 1954, after the American government had set up border ports to issue certificates of admission to alien ships' and railroad passengers who had first undergone quarantine in Canada. After October 1906, Canadian-born immigrants to the United States were included. The earlier lists are filed by year and month and then alphabetically by port, but from 1925 the port records are all filed together by month. There are two filmed Soundex personal-name indexes to the lists between 1895 and 1927, which are incomplete after 1917, and from 1924 to 1952.

Some printed and electronic resources

Consult *Passenger and Immigration Lists Index*, edited by P. W. Filby and M. K. Meyer (Gale, 1997), and the yearly supplements for any published references to your migrant ancestors between 1538 and about 1905, which include some seventeenth-century ships' passenger lists and oaths of allegiance to the English Crown. You can access the index and its supplements at **www.ancestry.com** and on CD-ROM. The alphabetical entries are cross-referenced to cited publications, which you should then study for more information, and look for the original context of each reference. The indexes often contain multiple references to the same individual.

There are lots of databases about UK emigrants and North American immigrants, many of which are searchable at **www.ancestry.com** and on CD-ROM. A particularly useful index, to five million names of Irish famine emigrants who arrived at the Port of New York between 1846 and 1851, is available at the same website, at **http://aad.archives.gov/aad**, at **www.familyrelatives.com**, and in *The Famine Immigrants*, edited by I. A. Glazer and M. Tepper (7 vols. Genealogical Publishing, 1983–87). The index includes ships leaving both Irish and non-Irish ports, and you can find out the name of each passenger, his or her age, gender, occupation, native country or port of embarkation, the ultimate place or country of destination, date of arrival and manifest identification number.

An Irish Emigration Database is under preparation for passengers to America and Canada between 1845 and 1870, so visit **www.qub.ac.uk/cms** for progress reports. The database is held in the Centre for Migration Studies, at the Ulster-American Folk Park, in Castletown, where it is accessible to researchers, as well as in the Public Record Office of Northern Ireland, and in Northern Irish local studies departments.

Special groups of emigrants

The New England Historic Genealogical Society has been very active in publishing English and American records about its colonial communities and their inhabitants. It is currently engaged in the Great Migration Project, 1620-43 (**www.greatmigration.org**), to create a massive database containing every known fact about early New England settlers and their families. You can read their biographies in *The Great*

Migration Begins: Immigrants to New England, 1620-1633 (New England Historic Genealogical Society, 1995), and in *The Great Migration: Immigrants to New England, 1634-1635* (New England Historic Genealogical Society, 1999), both edited by R. C. Anderson, the first of which is also available at **www.ancestry.com** and on CD-ROM. A list of names included in these books is being uploaded at this website. The same author has compiled *The Pilgrim Migration: Immigrants to Plymouth Colony, 1620-1633* (New England Historic Genealogical Society, 2004), which focuses on the first wave of Puritan settlers.

During and after the American Revolution, many of the colonists who had stayed loyal to the British Crown fled North into Canada, or returned to Britain. You can discover their stories from the compensation and pension claims which were filed with the British government after the American Loyalists Act of 1783. The original indexed claim papers and reports between 1776 and 1831 are in the National Archives, at Kew, and abstracts have been published in *American Migrations, 1765-1799, The Lives, Times and Families of Colonial Americans, Who Remained Loyal to the British Crown*, by P. W. Coldham (Genealogical Publishing Company, 2000). The memorials, depositions and other supporting documents will tell you where the person was then living, about his or her former estates and legal title to them, the family's lifestyle before, during and after the Revolutionary War, who were their dependants and the circumstances and exact nature of their alleged losses. Consult *United Empire Loyalists, a Guide to Tracing Loyalist Ancestors in Upper Canada (Ontario)*, by B. D. Merriman (Global Heritage Press Inc., 2006), for more information. Once in Canada, each head of family was allotted 100 acres of land, with a further 50 acres for each child, the same as was given to single men. Records about these can be found in the National Archives and in Canadian provincial archives.

Details about British soldiers who defected during the American Revolutionary War may sometimes be traced in the surviving three-monthly regimental musters, in the National Archives, at Kew. The list of non-effectives at the end of each muster recorded the soldier's birthplace and date of joining, and his date and reason for leaving the regiment, whilst a similar list of new recruits covering the date of enlistment would have recorded his age and former occupation or trade. It might also be worth trawling the American military service and pension records, in the National Archives Building, for men who changed sides,

figure 20 part of Lieutenant-Colonel Ralph Gore's petition to the Lieutenant Governor of the Province of Lower Canada for a land grant in the townships of Ireland and Halifax, 1825. The memorial records that he fought at the Battle of Waterloo in 1815, and was now on half-pay. He requested an extra 6000 acres so that he could establish Irish settlers

(reproduced by permission of The National Archives)

although their true identities might have been concealed. Retired military personnel were encouraged to settle in the colony where they were last stationed. Land was offered as a sweetener, the amount being determined by rank and other factors. Copies of their applications and details of the grants can be found in the National Archives, at Kew.

You can find out about many former soldiers who stayed on in Canada from *British Army Pensioners Abroad, 1772-1899*, by N. K. Crowder (Clearfield Co., 1995). The author drew on the quarterly pay district pension records in the National Archives, at Kew. The receipted entries are arranged by date of going to pension, and list each soldier's name, last rank, regiment and regimental number, how much and when he was paid, when and where he moved to another pay district, or died. The regimental attestation, service and discharge papers of British Army pensioners, in the National Archives, at Kew, start in 1760. You can search the personal-name index to the records up to 1854 at **www.nationalarchives.gov.uk/catalogue**. For more information about these and later service records, see Chapter 6.

figure 21 the quarterly return from 1 April to 30 June 1856 of British Army out-pensioners in the Toronto pay district, showing former regiment, pension rate, date of going to pension, rank, name and movements of each former soldier, and when transferred from the district
(reproduced by permission of The National Archives)

Between 1797 and 1835, letters of protection from impressment into the Royal Navy were issued to naturalized American seamen by British consuls in American ports. You can find some examples among the Foreign Office records in the National Archives, at Kew. The documents explain how the protection had been acquired, and set out any aliases used by the seaman, a physical description, his age, birthplace and place of baptism, the names and address of living parents, the father's occupation, and the names and addresses of the spouse and any siblings.

Assisted emigration

In Virginia, a headright system was applied, whereby a reward of 50 acres was given to the person paying for the voyage of an indentured servant or other immigrant. Any number of tickets could be purchased, which was an attractive proposition for someone wishing to build up a large landholding. The land was often sold on to raise cash or exchanged to consolidate an existing holding. Indentured servants might also have contracted themselves for four or more years in return for a free passage, or sold their labour to the highest bidder on arrival, to redeem the cost of the voyage. You can find out about the places of origin of many of the headright passengers, indentured servants and redemptioners in *The Complete Book of Emigrants, 1607-1776*, by P. W. Coldham (Genealogical Publishing Company, 1992), which is also available on CD-ROM.

Under a series of statutes regulating the legal settlement of the poor in England and Wales after 1662, destitute families could be sent to the American colonies under the authority of the county quarter sessions. You can find published details about many of them in *The Complete Book of Emigrants, 1607-1776*. In 1850, the local Boards of Guardians running the New Poor Law Unions were empowered to dispatch paupers and orphans to the British Dominions and colonies. You can trace some of the emigrants' names, ages, personal circumstances and their dates and destinations abroad from the minutes of the regular Union Board meetings, which are deposited in county record offices. The Board's correspondence with the Poor Law authorities in London up to 1909, and with the government's Land and Emigration Commission between 1836 and 1876, are also worth investigation. These records are in the National Archives, at Kew. You can find catalogue references to some quarter sessions and Poor Law records at **www.a2a.org.uk**, and good county-by-county guides to their dates and whereabouts are

Quarter Sessions Records for Family Historians: A Select List, by J. Gibson (Genealogical Publishing Company, 1992), and *Poor Law Union Records*, by J. Gibson, C. Rogers and C. Webb (Federation of Family History Societies, 1993).

In 1833, a special government Land and Emigration Commission was formed to sponsor and assist adult emigration and to make colonial land grants. The applications for a free or assisted passage were processed by local government agents, who were instructed to find the most suitable people, ideally, workers and craftsmen between the ages of 14 and 35, who were married, but childless. The related correspondence and petitions run chronologically from 1817 to 1851, and are in the National Archives, at Kew. They record the applicants' ages, addresses, occupations, marital status and the number and ages of any children, and tell you whether they were successful. Other Land and Emigration Commission papers between 1840 and 1876 can also be examined there.

The Highlands and Islands Emigration Society was founded in Scotland in 1852, and its records are held in the National Archives of Scotland. You can search an index to the names of sponsored emigrants between 1852 and 1857 at **www.scan.org.uk/ researchrtools/emigration.htm**, and discover their ages, last place of residence, who in the family accompanied them, the name of the ship and the date and port of embarkation.

A discrete group of assisted emigrants were the early Mormons, the first of whom sailed from Liverpool in 1840 to help build up the newly founded community in Nauvoo, in Illinois. The converts mostly came from Lancashire and the Northwest of England, where the first British Mission had been active. Many such emigrants were poor, so their chartered voyages were partly or wholly paid for by local branches of the Church, or out of a central Perpetual Emigration Fund. The arrival at New Orleans was followed by an onward journey by river, or after 1848, by wagon or handcart to Utah. Between 1840 and 1870, more than 45,000 such English emigrants had arrived. Read *Expectations Westward: The Mormons and the Emigration of their Converts in the Nineteenth Century*, by P.A.M. Taylor (Oliver & Boyd, 1965), for an account of their experiences. Indexed transcriptions of the ships' manifests from 1840 to 1890 are searchable on CD-ROM, as part of the Mormon Immigration Index. You can discover personal information not only about individual passengers, but about everyone else on board, view a picture of their ship and read some of their journals, letters and diaries.

Starting in 1617, the Common Council of the City of London began to send young orphans and children of impoverished City freemen to Jamestown in Virginia, and then to other American and West Indian colonial settlements, effectively as cheap labour. You can find details about them in *Child Apprentices in America from Christ's Hospital London, 1617-1778*, by P. W. Coldham (Clearfield Co., 1988), which is also accessible at **www.ancestry.com**. The school registers are in the Guildhall Library. Other cities, boroughs and parishes followed suit after 1620, and any surviving material is likely to be found in corporation and borough archives.

In the nineteenth and twentieth centuries, various religious and charitable bodies helped to fund child emigration to some mid-West American agricultural states, to Canada and to other British Dominions and colonies as domestic servants and farm workers. From 1869 until the late 1930s, more than 100,000 youngsters were sent to Canada from Great Britain, many of them under the auspices of the Farm School Movement. You can search a database containing the names of the so-called 'Home Children' at **www.collectionscanada.ca/archivianet/02011_e.html**, which runs up to 1930 and is based on material in Library and Archives Canada. Before 1925, however, you will learn little about them beyond their ages, destinations and sending agencies.

Government reports on the housing and welfare of pauper children in Canada between 1887 and 1892 can be examined in the National Archives, at Kew. The reports record their names and ages, the Union or parish where they came from, the names and addresses of their hosts, and the children's opinions of them, as well as the observations of the Secretary of the Department of Agriculture sent to conduct the interviews. Microfilmed copies of the Juvenile Inspection Report cards, compiled between about 1914 and the 1930s, are available in Library and Archives Canada. The Reports are arranged alphabetically, and record each child's date of birth, year and ship of arrival, the title of the sending organization, and the name(s) and address(es) of the farmer(s) with whom he or she was placed. You can find a list of sending organizations at **www.collectionscanada.ca/genealogy/022-908.009-e.html**.

Many of the child emigrants later served in the Canadian or British Expeditionary Forces during the First and Second World Wars. Indexed digital images of parts of the personnel files of 600,000 servicemen in the Canadian Expeditionary Force between 1914 and 1918 can be viewed at **www.collectionscanada.ca/ archivianet/020106_e.html**. The complete files are in Library and Archives Canada, as is information about people enlisting after 1918 and dying in the Second World War. For information about British military service records, see Chapter 06.

Some material relating to young emigrants to Canada who were charitably sponsored is held in the National Archives, at Kew, but most charity archives are preserved elsewhere. Visit **www.dcs.uwaterloo.ca/%7EMarj/genealogy/homeadd.html** for details about the various charitable emigration schemes and the dates and location of their records between 1833 and 1935, and read *Labouring Children: British Immigrant Apprentices to Canada, 1869-1924*, by J. Parr (University of Toranto Press, 1994), and *The Little Immigrants: The Orphans Who Came to Canada*, by K. Bagnall (Dundurn Group Ltd., 2001), for background information.

If you want to try to trace your own origins as a child emigrant, or those of another family member who was sent overseas as a child, or to locate their present whereabouts, contact the National Council of Voluntary Child Care Organizations, in London (**www.ncvcco.org**).

During the Second World War, until September 1940, the Children's Overseas Reception Board evacuated 17,000 children from cities and larger towns to safety in the British Dominions and to the USA to escape the threat of German air raids or invasion. Look for their names among outgoing and incoming ships' passenger lists. These also include details about children of wealthier families who were sent at their parents' expense to join relatives abroad.

An act of 1718 provided for the reduction of the death sentence to transportation for 14 years or for life, or for seven years for non-capital offences. Until 1776, convicted felons were transported to the West Indian and American Plantations, particularly in Maryland and Virginia. Once freed, the convicts were rarely able to afford a return passage. Consult *The Complete Book of Emigrants in Bondage, 1614-1775* (Clearfield Co., 1988), and *More Emigrants in Bondage*, by P. W. Coldham (Genealogical Publishing Company, 2002), and *Directory of Scots Banished to the American Plantations, 1650-1775*, by D. Dobson (Clearfield Co., 2001), for useful biographical information about them. The first three publications are also searchable at **www.ancestry.com** and on

CD-ROM, whilst *British Emigrants in Bondage 1614-1788*, by P. W. Coldham (Genealogical Publishing Company, 2005), including details about Irish felons, is on CD-ROM too. The entries record the name and place of origin of each convict, as well as his or her offence, court, month and year when sentenced, the months of embarkation and landing, and the ultimate destination. You should then be able to track down the relevant bundle of English and Welsh Assize court indictments or Crown minute book, in the National Archives, at Kew, for more details of the trial. The records are listed at **www.nationalarchives.gov.uk/catalogue**. You can search indexed transcriptions of the printed proceedings between April 1674 and October 1834 at the Old Bailey Sessions, in London, at **www.oldbaileyonline.org**. It is also worth trawling the Australian convict transportation database from 1788 to 1868, at **www.nationalarchives.ie/** and on CD-ROM, for references to convicts going to New South Wales, Tasmania and Western Australia, who later made their way to the United States. This will tell you the convict's age or birth year and birthplace, occupation and marital status, when and where he or she was tried, and details about the voyage and year of arrival.

Read *Emigrants in Chains*, by P. W. Coldham (Genealogical Publishing Company, 1992), for an overview of all types of forced emigration to the West Indies and North America.

Following an emigrant's paper trail

If all of this fails, you will need to establish the date and place of your ancestor's first appearance in North American records, and/or last mention in those of the former country, and hopefully marry them up. You may already have been able to do a certain amount of this from your researches in the sources described so far. For instance, the indexed online ten-yearly census returns may have told you where your ancestor was last found in the United Kingdom and picked him or her up later in North America. The US census was taken a year earlier than in the UK, so this will reduce your research focus to nine years. However, only the country of birth rather than the exact birthplace was given for first-generation settlers, so the census evidence for concluding that the entries both relate to the same person will be circumstantial or may eventually turn out to be coincidental. You will have to rely on other factors, such as consistency of age, and the given details about other family members or associates who were present with him or her on both occasions. As the American census returns after 1890 tell you about immigrants' years of arrival, they give you a headstart. Foreign parentage is also indicated from 1870 onwards, too, so that you will know straightaway if your ancestor was a first- or second-generation settler. Year of immigration and date of birth were also given in the 1901 and 1911 Canadian census returns, digital images of which you can search by personal-name at **www.ancestry.ca** or by place-name at **www.collectionscanada.ca/genealogy/022-911-e.html**.

American birth and marriage certificates usually note the countries of birth of parents who were immigrants, and marriage certificates detail the foreign origins of couples. Death certificates since 1910 have usually recorded the deceased's actual date of birth, so that the three pieced together can provide good clues to which UK civil registration and other life-cycle records you should be pursuing next.

You can retrace an immigrant's movements back to his or her point of embarkation and place of origin, or take the reverse route, by following the emigrant's journey from the beginning. Think about the various steps involved in planning emigration.

- A landowner or tenant would have to dispose of his or her property, so there should be a dated deed of conveyance of a freehold or leasehold estate, or a manorial court surrender of copyhold property to the lord of the manor. Other personal goods and furniture might be sold by auction.
- Having raised sufficient cash, a ticket would be bought for the voyage, or alternatively, an application might be made for an assisted or fully funded passage. He or she might lodge close to a port and work until enough had been saved for the ticket or until a vacant berth was available. In the meantime, he or she might marry and have children. Search the International Genealogical Index, British Isles Vital Records Index and National Burial Index for references to people who were on the move, trawl the indexes to civil registrations, and examine parish and chapel records. Visit **www.movinghere.org. uk/galleries/roots/irish/irish.htm** for guidance on sources about the Irish on the mainland.
- An application might be made for a UK passport, although this was not essential before 1915. Printed references to Crown licences issued to pass beyond the seas between 1573 and 1677 can be found in the *Passenger and Immigration*

Lists Index. Indexed digital images of many of the passport applications between 1851 and 1903 are accessible at **www.findmypast.com/HomeServlet**. However, only the date of issue and the name of the person are included, and before 1874, the passport number. Nevertheless, this information will help you to pin down an approximate departure date.

- The Atlantic voyage could last over a month, until the advent of steamships in the 1860s reduced the length of the trip to between a week and a fortnight. Search for any family births, marriages and deaths at sea between 1854 and 1890, at **www.findmypast.com/HomeServlet**, and in the Registrar General's indexed Marine Returns from 1 July 1837 at the same website, and at **www.familyrelatives.com**. See Chapter 06 for more information about registered life-cycle events at sea. Many emigrants kept diaries or logs of the voyage, so it is worth asking your family or enquiring about any that have been donated to a Pioneers' Museum, local history society or local studies library.

- After 1718, on disembarkation, incoming aliens to North America were examined by medical officers of the port authority as to their state of their health. Some surviving hospital certificates of good health may be tracked down in state archives or historical society libraries.

- Accommodation had to be found quickly, but this might only be temporary until the immigrant met up with relatives already living in America, or had obtained employment. The newcomer might try to trace such relatives, by advertising in local newspapers. Conversely, the press often announced recent passenger arrivals. Some newspapers have been indexed and uploaded, so try the A-Z list of titles at **www.cyndislist.com/newspaper.htm** for website links, and **www.genealogybank.com/gbnk/keyword.html** for indexed digital images of historical American newspapers published between 1690 and 1977. A person might change addresses many times before finally settling down. Local newspapers frequently printed personal details about people who were new to the district and about the destinations of departing residents. The accounts of fellow travellers, especially those written along the overland trails to the West, and across Canada, may contain incidental references to your migrant family, so are worth investigating. A number have been published, and many have been deposited in state, provincial, historical society libraries and other institutions.

- If your ancestor belonged to a close religious group, a letter of recommendation or a testimonial might be sent ahead of the emigrant by the local minister or church elders to the receiving congregation by way of introduction. From these you can learn not only where the person came from, but something about his or her character. Any surviving documents will be located among the relevant church, chapel or religious assembly records, wherever they are now preserved, and some have been published. The minutes of the Quaker preparative meetings are particularly informative in this respect.
- Ask around your family and try local and maritime archive collections about the existence of any emigrants' letters reporting safe arrival, and giving a postal address. The Public Record Office of Northern Ireland has a particularly good cache of such correspondence.
- Registration as an alien was compulsory in the United States between 1802 and 1828, and under the Alien Registration Acts of 1929 and 1940. Many of the first, local court, records of registration have been published, and are included in *Passenger and Immigration Lists Index*. The original registration documents from 1929 are held in the National Archives Building. The details were annually updated, to keep track of each alien's current address and place of employment. Once registered, he or she was issued with a personal identification card, incorporating the dates of lawful entry into America and of registration, and secondly, with a certificate of arrival, giving his or her name, date and port of entry. Under the 1940 statute, every alien over 14 was obliged to register at the local post office within 30 days of arrival in the country, and received an alien card in return. If you are a direct descendant, you can request a search of the 1929 and 1940 registrations, under the Freedom of Information Act.
- Try the International Genealogical Index, North American Vital Records Index and state vital registration indexes for registered births, baptisms, marriages and deaths of immigrants and their families.

Naturalization

Once firmly settled in the United States, the immigrant might apply for citizenship, although this was not obligatory. During the colonial era, British settlers did not need to be naturalized, but after 1776, British immigrants were treated as aliens until they became naturalized as American citizens. The 1870 American census returns tell you if someone was already naturalized, and the census returns after 1890 tell of his or her current citizenship status.

Up to 1906, American citizenship could be granted by any state court of record, although some federal grants were made too. Unfortunately, the state where the person applied to be naturalized might not be where he or she first resided in America. Each state set its own residency rules for naturalization, but in 1795 it became fixed at a total of five years in the United States, of which one year had to have been spent in the state where the application was made. The total residency regulation was relaxed to three years in 1922. A declaration of intention to apply to become an American citizen (called 'first papers') could be presented after two years, and the petition itself after a further three. The declaration and petition might be filed in different courts. Until 1870, naturalization was only open to free white males over the age of 21.

The documents relating to naturalization are mostly preserved among state, regional and county court archives. Some personal-name indexes, state naturalization papers, or microfilm copies, are available for examination in the National Archives Building, and they are listed state by state at **www.archives.gov/genealogy/ naturalization/naturalization. html.** You can find the addresses of state archives at **www.archives.gov/research/alic/ reference/state-archives.html** and of county courthouses at **www.cyndislit.com/courthouses.htm.**

After 1906, the local courts forwarded copies of naturalization certificates to the Immigration and Naturalization Service, in Washington, DC.

Indexed copies of the earlier federal grants and those since September 1906 have been transferred to the appropriate regional facilities of the National Archives, those for Washington, DC, being held in the National Archives Building. Their contact details can be found at **www.archives.gov/ locations.** You can request to see naturalization papers after 1 July 1924, under the Freedom of Information Act, by contacting the Department of Homeland Security, in the Bureau of US Citizenship and Immigration Services, in Washington, DC.

The naturalization papers consist of the declaration of intention, the petition, a swearing-in document, and a naturalization certificate. The dated declaration recorded the person's name, address, occupation, current marital condition, country of birth and nationality, his or her country of origin, birth date or age, and was accompanied by a personal description, last foreign address, port and date of entry and the name of the ship on which he or she had arrived. The dated, signed and witnessed petition contained similar information, but gave the applicant's length of stay in America, and the names and ages of any spouse and children, and the spouse's address. Between 1790 and 1922, the wives of naturalized Americans were granted derivative citizenship, as were, between 1790 and 1940, any of their children under 21. The swearing-in document, renouncing the previous nationality and taking the American oath of allegiance, recorded the person's age, present and former addresses. The naturalization certificate gave the new American citizen's name and address, exact birthplace or former nationality, his or her country of origin, birth date or age, a personal description, and his or her marital status, with the name, age or date of birth of the spouse and the names, ages and addresses of any children. When the given age or birth date came after the start of civil registration in the country of origin, search the appropriate indexes and obtain a copy of the full details. If it was before, try the International Genealogical Index and British Isles Vital Records Index. If the applicant had married and had children before leaving for America, look for these registrations too. For more information, read *Guide to Naturalization Records of the United States*, by C. K. Schaefer (Genealogical Publishing Company, 1997).

Naturalization qualified a person to petition for a plot of land. Look in the records of state-land states and federal government sources relating to public-land states for the petitions, warrants, surveys (plats) and grants or patents. Indexed digital images of some federal government documents between 1789 and 1980 are searchable at **www.genealogybank.com/gbnk/ keyword.html**. These include grants of homesteads too.

During the colonial era, the Crown, acting through its appointed governors, granted land by patent to private individuals or groups. You can find indexed summaries of the petitions, related correspondence and copies of many of these land grants in the printed *Calendar of State Papers Colonial: America and West Indies, 1574-1739*, a more comprehensively indexed version of which is on CD-ROM. The documents themselves are in the National Archives, at Kew. Certain proprietors were granted vast tracts of land by the Crown, which they divided up into smaller parcels for sale or lease, as was the case in Virginia and North Carolina. When the Crown delegated total control over a colony's government to a private citizen or named trustees, which was what happened in Pennsylvania and in Georgia, they were empowered to make their own land grants. Such registered land grants and deeds are preserved in land offices, some of which are attached to the state archives. Most of the deed books before 1915 have been microfilmed and can be hired in to family history centres. They are useful because they may tell you where the buyer or grantee came from.

Many of the disputes concerning colonists' estates were handled by the equity Court of Chancery, in London. From the early seventeenth century until 1714, documentation relating to a specific case was often spread over six different clerks' filing systems, where it was listed by its current title. This might change if a plaintiff dropped out, died or was replaced by someone else, or when joint defendants sent in separate answers, making them difficult to reunite, especially as litigation could drag on for many years, and perhaps not even reach a court hearing. You can search personal- and place-name and subject indexes to a number of the seventeenth-century cases in the National Archives, at Kew, at **www.nationalarchives.gov.uk/ catalogue,** and there are published or manuscript indexes to the names of the chief plaintiffs and defendants up to 1714 and beyond. Because the bills of complaint, answers and sworn depositions of the supporting witnesses frequently refer to people and events retrospectively over a long period, they can reveal much about the date and circumstance of an original grant and the descent of the estate through several generations or branches of a family, and make up for the want of any other surviving evidence. They have the added advantage of being written in English. Any court orders and decrees were recorded in special books and rolls. Read *The National Archives, A Practical Guide for Family Historians*, by S. Colwell (The National Archives, 2006), for an introduction to the records, and *Tracing Your Ancestors in the National Archives: The Website and Beyond*, by A. Bevan (PRO Publications), for a thorough description.

If your ancestor officially changed his or her name in the colonies before 1782, study *An Index to Change of Name Under*

Authority of Act of Parliament or by Royal Licence, and Including Irregular Changes, from 1 George lll to 64 Victoria, 1760-1901, by W. P. W. Phillimore and E. A. Fry, also on CD-Rom, for details. Later name changes were formalized by application to a state court. Many people did not bother with a legal process and their new names became accepted by common repute.

Sometimes, colonists sent their children back to England to be educated or apprenticed to other relatives or business partners. Some of the more well-known schools have published their admission registers of pupils, which are kept among school archives. The enrolments of apprenticeships to burgesses are included among borough archives, whilst those concerning apprentices to freemen of city livery companies, are found in company records. Most of the apprenticeship bindings books and freedom registers of the City of London livery companies are now in the Guildhall Library. A number have been indexed and published, but always check these against the originals for verification and further details. The bindings tell you each apprentice's name and that of his or her father or guardian, his status or occupation and current place of residence, and the name, trade and address of the master taking the child on, for how long (usually seven or eight years), from what date, and at what premium. The freedom registers disclose when the young adult (customarily over the age of 24) was admitted as a freeman of the company, and became qualified to employ his or her own apprentices. The given place of parental residence is a powerful clue to an apprentice's birthplace, as they were usually bound out between the ages of 12 and 14.

Settlers and their families might occasionally return to visit relatives or friends, to attend to family or commercial business, to claim an inheritance or to check up on the running of an estate. The wills and administration grants of emigrants, which were registered in both UK and North American probate courts, testify to their continuing Trans-Atlantic family links and interests. Conversely, the wills of family members who stayed behind, often mentioned relatives abroad. For details about taxable estates in England and Wales of overseas residents between 1796 and 1903, inspect the indexes at **www.findmypast. com/HomeServlet**.

Tips

- Don't ignore printed and manuscript pedigrees and family histories for references to emigrants and where they went.
- If you cannot locate the place of origin of your own ancestor, but know with whom he or she travelled, try researching that family's history in case they came from the same parish or district.
- Take care when searching electronic and printed indexes and transcriptions as they may be inaccurate, misleading or incomplete.
- Use microfilmed copies or inter-library loan services whenever you can, to avoid having to travel all over the place in pursuit of your ancestors. A lot of the British emigration records have been copied and may be hired to search in family history centres throughout the world, so search the Family History Library catalogue at **www.familysearch.org**, to find out what is available.

It may take a long time, but just think of the satisfaction when you do clinch your ancestral link between the old country and the new!

16

writing it all up

In this chapter you will learn:
- how to relate your family's story
- what questions to ask yourself about presentation
- how to publish.

When I was ten years old I wrote my autobiography. Reading through it now I can vividly relive how it felt growing up in a Lakeland village of the 1950s, and revive half-forgotten memories of the various local characters and their goings-on.

When and where do you begin?

One of the most pleasurable and personal ways of bringing the past alive is to write up your family's history. When should you start? It is never too soon, for the longer you delay the more material you will have to negotiate, and the less inclined you will be to tackle and unravel it all. Writing up your story concentrates the mind wonderfully, pulls your researches together, and draws your attention to any queries which can be settled before you climb any further up your family tree. Older relatives may be able to help you to sort out some of the riddles, to pepper your story with family anecdotes and photographs, and to lend encouragement.

Who is it for?

Decide first for whom your story is intended. Is it for your own delectation, for your descendants, all your known kinsfolk, or a wider audience? Is it for private circulation only, or publication? You will have to be careful about the amount of detail and disclosure you indulge in if you want a broad readership. You should try to avoid your narrative becoming bogged down in minutiae, and offending the very people who have given you support.

Have a look at others' writings, to see which ones grip you the most and analyse why this is. Two evocative books are *The Simple Annals*, by P. Sanders, an account of how he traced a family's migration over two centuries from Stansted Mountfitchet, in Essex, into London; and *Hannah, The Complete Story*, by H. Hauxwell with B. Cockroft, which reminisces about a farmer's life in the Yorkshire Dales, and describes, house by house, the histories of their occupiers and their convoluted family networks. You will have your own favourites and by adopting a similar approach as well as constructing an unvarnished and flowing narrative, you will soon warm to your task, and your script will move at a cracking pace, which you can prune and edit later.

From present to past or fast forward?

You could begin by explaining the possible origins and distribution of your surname and its variants over time, with a map plotting out its incidence. This may involve a one-name study, a look at current phone books, and a tour round the internet to find out how your surname has evolved and spread over time. Visit **www.last-names.net** for suggestions about surname meanings and origins. This could be followed by a potted history of your own family down to the present day. If you want to cite the earliest reference to the places where your ancestors lived, look at **www.nationalarchives.gov.uk/ domesday** to see if they appeared in any of the Domesday Surveys around 1086, and in the relevant county volumes of the English Place-Name Society.

Conversely, you may prefer to act as the family's storyteller, working back in time. This has the advantage of carrying your readers with you on your quest, sharing in your discoveries and disappointments, and you can continue to add to the narrative as you progress further, without detriment to the earlier sections. Try not to let your text get out of hand, by running on forever, so fix a structure and stick to it.

The essentials

Decide if you want the work to contain profiles of individual family members, confine it to your direct ancestors, or to widen the story to say something about their social life and times in the wider community, perhaps relying on other people's published research.

Bear in mind the following points too:

- Always date your text and identify yourself as the author. Do not overlook your own story, and do draw on the reminiscences of living relatives, taking care that they consent to their inclusion first. If you doubt the truth of a statement, you can always preface it by saying 'it is alleged', 'according to', 'supposedly', or 'it is said', because you do not want to alienate family goodwill or risk being sued for libel.
- Describe how and why certain events happened if you can, rather than what and when they were.
- Stick to the facts and don't make false assumptions that cannot be backed up.

- Resist the temptation to express a personal opinion or judgement about people's actions. You live in a different cultural environment or era to that of your ancestors.
- If you pad out your narrative with short quotes from the writings or sound recordings of other people, always acknowledge your sources and be careful not to use huge chunks of someone else's work so that you contravene their copyright. If in doubt, check with the publisher. Always cite the full title, author's name, publisher or place of publication, and the date, or the date and whereabouts of the recording, and give full acknowledgements. The reader can then follow up the quotations by studying or listening to the original in full.
- Numbered footnotes at the bottom of a page, or end-notes at the conclusion of each chapter of your story, can be used to expand on certain statements or words, and for source references. The references let the reader check them up for him/herself, and might suggest new avenues of research. Be sparing with footnotes and end-notes, though, as it can be a maddening experience ploughing through pages dotted with countless numbered references inviting you to follow them up.

Adding pictures

Break up your narrative with accurate, clear and simple family trees, pictures and diagrams. Always ensure they are appropriate to their place in the text, sufficiently sharp or legible, and that they enhance rather than conflict with or detract from their context. Acknowledge where they came from, date and identify any people in photographs. If your illustrations come from a record office, or publication, make sure you have the appropriate permissions to use them. Most repositories will have a standard form of words for you to use in reproducing copies of their documents. Include these in the caption, as well as the full document reference. The caption should explain what the picture is all about.

A map of the area covered in the story is another must, especially for readers who might be unfamiliar with it. Shade in the places mentioned in your text. Do not neglect to give compass bearings and the map's scale.

Never pass original drawings or photographs to anyone else before they go to a printer, in case of loss or damage; use photocopies of them if necessary.

Editing your script

Think about the length, final layout and presentation of your family's history. If you plan to create a website or put it on disk rather than publish your story on paper, these considerations will be crucial. It is helpful to have an independent and sympathetic outsider read a copy of your script, which should be double-spaced until finalized. Any constructive suggestions about its strengths and weaknesses will be invaluable at this stage, before it is exposed to a wider audience. You may need to prune or rewrite parts to make your account clearer or punchier. This is particularly the case with the introduction, which is what most people will read first, before deciding whether they like your style of writing and are enticed into reading more.

When you are happy with your text, save a master version, print a copy and then leave it a week or two. When you next read it, you will be amazed how some of your sentences that once made sense, no longer do, or fail to make a point strongly enough. You may even discover you have overlooked important bits of the story.

How are you going to publish?

Decide on the medium. If you want to upload your narrative, you will need to keep it short and lively to sustain the viewer's interest. Appearances count, so make sure your website is easy to navigate and the home page is not cluttered with unnecessary or confusing signposts. Don't swamp the home page with glaring colours that absorb or overwhelm the text. Look at other people's websites to see what works best, enrol on a course or arm yourself with a simple practical manual. When you illustrate your story with pictures remember that these take up a lot of space, and may be very slow to come up on-screen. A thumbnail of each picture, which you can click on to enlarge the image is probably best. Do you want to include film footage and any sound features? Not everyone will have a computer system compatible with yours, so be careful if these are to be integral to your story.

Always insert a dated copyright notice to protect your text and the date when your text was last updated.

You may want to make your website by subscription only. You should certainly include a feedback section to make it interactive, and to log the number of website visits. You will have to read your feedback regularly, update and tweak your narrative. You might want to add acknowledged and authenticated contributions from your website visitors too. An online newsletter is another possibility, but don't be too ambitious, give yourself too much work, and stand the risk of it all getting out of control. A good many websites are short-lived, so make sure yours isn't one of these. It would be a shame to let your efforts go for nothing at the final hurdle.

Another option is to save your material on CD-ROM or DVD. The same principles about text length and layout apply. The illustrations can be loaded in full, and you can burn as many copies as you like. You might want to import film footage, oral testimonies and a commentary too, so this medium is very versatile. Make sure you include your dated copyright notice. If you use a good quality re-writable disk (CD-RW) as the master, you can make any later dated alterations and additions to this and then burn and circulate the new version. You can cost out how much you will charge for each copy disk.

If you want to restrict circulation to a few bound copies, have adequate computer software, and a high-quality printer, consider going on a desktop publishing course, where you can learn, share and discuss design skills. If you elect for photocopying, this is likely to prove expensive, and the quality of reproduced illustrations will not be very sharp.

If you would prefer to use a professional printer, you can generally submit camera-ready text, using crop-marks to indicate page size, which will keep down the cost. You will have to design the page layouts and placements of any pictures and diagrams. If you have no inclination or aptitude for this, ask a local printer to undertake the design and layout for you. You can produce your text on floppy disk or CD-ROM with a printout, or as a paginated paper copy from which he or she will prepare artwork for you to inspect and approve before printing. The overall final layout, and page lengths should be closely scrutinized for consistency, and all the illustrations studied to make sure they appear in the right places, the proper way up and right way round, are consecutively and correctly numbered and captioned. Check that your dated copyright notice is clearly displayed at the front of your narrative.

If you are submitting your story on disk, ensure that your own software is compatible with the printer's, as otherwise there may be a fee to convert the disk. A printout will show the printer any encoding such as italics, in case this is lost during the conversion.

Always keep an updated back-up copy on disk.

Discuss with several printers the different paper qualities and weights on offer. What about the cover design and colours? What type of binding would be strongest and best for the approximate number of pages of your text? Study other published family histories to see what makes them look attractive, sturdy or flimsy.

The charge for publishing will also be governed by word length, the total number and type of your illustrations, paper quality, number of jacket colours and the print-run. By casting around for pre-paid subscriptions, you can estimate how many extra copies you may need to sell to recoup your initial outlay. Try to recover at least part of the cost, if not all of it, before you have to settle up with the printer. Are you going to charge each person a calculated proportion of the price of printing plus postage and packing? If so, you will need to know the actual weight, type of wrapping and the final postal charge. Your relatives might be persuaded by a special pre-publication discount, but you will have to convince them that their investment will be worthwhile, in other words, that there is something in it for them. It is no good selling your story to members of the family who are not mentioned in it, or who will learn nothing new. You will also need to make sure you acknowledge everyone who has helped you, in however small a way, at the front of the book.

Obtain several quotations from different printers for the cost of a print-run of 100, 250, 500 and 1,000 copies. These will vary, as some specialize in print-runs lower than 2,000 and will offer a better price than printers used to producing bulk printings. You then need to calculate the unit cost per copy, dividing the total amount by the number of copies to be printed, multiplying this figure by three, four or five to achieve a competitive selling price. Take into account any permission fees you have had to pay, free presentation copies on which you will make nothing, the cost of advertising and other hidden unforeseen extras, to ensure you at least break even.

Decide how you wish to market your story, as harbouring spare copies indefinitely will not only turn out to be inconvenient, and take up precious space, but they will gradually deteriorate. Extra unbound copies can easily have dust jackets added later. Before committing yourself financially, approach likely outlets in the district with which your family was associated or where its members were prominent to see if they will sell some stock, but be sure you agree on written trade terms in advance. Bookshops are in business to make money, and not all authors are good at self-promotion. You could draft a flyer for distribution and display, compose a short item for the local press, publicize your book via the local family history society at its events or in its magazine, and of course advertise it online on a message board at sites like **www.rootsweb.com** or **www.ancestry.com**. In this way you will reach a global audience, but remember that your overseas postal costs will increase each time someone makes a purchase, so fix a price for the publication itself and say that postage and packing are extra. Always advise your customer of the final cost, and receive the moneys before dispatching any order, confirming by e-mail when this has been done.

Once customers have paid their dues they will expect the book to be delivered promptly. Printers usually hold their quotations firm for a month or so, and when you know your print-run (trying to avoid the need for a small reprint, which can be expensive), submit your text in the agreed format. Printing may be turned round in as little as ten days, but may take up to a month. Always agree a timescale with the printer to avoid any misunderstandings, and add an extra fortnight for any unforeseen eventualities. Planning publication to coincide with a special family event or with Christmas is more likely to kindle demand, provided you give sufficient notice, and can meet the deadline.

Ensuring permanent preservation and publicity

Lodge a copy of your work with the relevant county record office, local studies collection, and any family history society that you think appropriate, and put your name and dated address inside if you would welcome feedback. You can request reviews by sending copies to relevant magazines with a large readership, but remember that a free copy is lost money. However, that free copy may generate sales of a few more thus reducing any surplus stock. The local newspaper is another good sales outlet, if the editor is prepared to run a small feature article about your story, particularly if it contains something sensational (which is true and does not reflect badly on living or recent family members).

And finally ...

The more sound and and accurately researched family histories there are the more others interested in the past can safely and happily draw on them to compare the stories of other families and to add to our knowledge about how local and regional communities have developed over time.

Tracing your ancestry is a constant adventure. A family's history is never finished, and it is much more fun reconstructing it for yourself. Having read this book, you should now be able to assemble the basic structure of your personal pedigree. Use the given clues in the four given prime genealogical sources as a springboard, to flesh out your existing knowledge about your ancestors, and then extend your researches into other archives. You never know who you might find lurking in your family tree!

Author's note

As one door closes...
The Family Records Centre, in London, is due to close by the end of 2008 and the various services offered by the National Archives will be relocated to Kew. Early in the same year, digital images of newly created indexes to the birth, marriage and death registers held by the Office for National Statistics, in Southport, will start to be made available online. The existing paper and microfiche indexes now in the FRC will be transferred to Kew as well, where you will be able to continue to search them until the digitization project is completed. For progress reports, visit **www.nationalarchives.gov.uk** and **www.gro.gov.uk/gro/content**.

...another one opens
The General Register Office for Scotland is working with the National Archives of Scotland and the Court of the Lord Lyon to create a new family history centre, to be known as the 'Scotlands' People Centre'. This is designed to be a one-stop shop for family historians in the heart of Edinburgh, based on Princes Street, close to the GRO and New Register House Buildings. It will contain electronic facilities offering a streamlined service for researchers, and is expected to open late in 2007. For more information, visit **www.scotlandspeoplehub.gov.uk**.

taking it further

Addresses and websites

Before going to any of the repositories, first visit their website, e-mail or telephone to check on their current whereabouts, opening times, fees and search regulations. You may need to add the international dialling code.

United Kingdom and Ireland

Adoption Board, Shelbourne House, Shelbourne Road, Dublin 4 Tel: 1800 309 300 (freephone), (0)1 230 9300 e-mail: **adoptioninfo@health.irlgov.ie** website: **www.adoptionboard.ie**

Association of Family History Societies of Wales, c/o Phil Bufton, 3 Cagebrook Avenue, Hunderton, Hereford HR2 7AS e-mail: **secretary@fhswales.info** website: **www.fhswales.info**

Association of Genealogists and Researchers in Archives, Joint Secretaries, 29 Badgers Close, Horsham, West Sussex RH12 5RU e-mail: **agra@agra.org.uk** website: **www.agra.org.uk**

Association of Professional Genealogists in Ireland, Hon. Secretary, 30 Harlech Crescent, Clonskeagh, Dublin 14 e-mail: **info@apgi.ie** website: **www.apgi.ie**

Association of Scottish Genealogists and Researchers in Archives, 93 Colinton Road, Edinburgh EH10 5DF Tel: (0)131 313 1104 website: **www.asgra.co.uk**

Birthlink, 21 Castle Street, Edinburgh EH2 3DN
Tel: (0)131 225 6441
e-mail: **winnie@birthlink.org.uk**
website: **www.birthlink.org.uk**

Bodleian Library, Department of Special Collections and
Western Manuscripts, University of Oxford,
road Street, Oxford OX1 3BG
Tel: (0)1865 277158
e-mail: **western.manuscripts@bodley.ox. ac.uk**
website: **www.bodley.ox.ac.uk/dept/scwmss/wmss/
online/online.htm**

Borthwick Institute for Archives, University of York,
Heslington, York YO10 5DD Tel: (0)1904 321 166
website: **www.york.ac.uk/inst/bihr**

British Association for Cemeteries in South Asia
website: **www.bacsa.org.uk**

British Library, St Pancras, 96 Euston Road, London
NW1 2DB Tel: (0)20 7412 7676 (reader information)
website: **www.bl.uk**
Department of Manuscripts Tel: (0)20 7412 7513
e-mail: **mss@bl.uk**
website: **www.bl.uk/catalogues/manuscripts**
Asia, Pacific and Africa Collections
Tel: (0)20 7412 7873
e-mail: **apac-enquiries@bl.uk**
website: **www.bl.uk/collections/asiapacificafrica.html**
British Library Newspapers, Colindale Avenue, London
NW9 5HE Tel: (0)20 7412 7353
website: **www.bl.uk/catalogues/ newspapers**

BT Group Archives, Third Floor, Holborn Telephone
Exchange, 268-270 High Holborn, London WC1V 7EE
Tel: (0)20 7440 4220
e-mail: **archives@bt.com**
website: **www.btplc.com/Thegroup/BTsHistory/
BTgrouparchives/index.htm**

Centre for Migration Studies at the Ulster-American Folk Park,
2 Mellon Road, Castletown, Omagh, Co. Tyrone BT78 5QY
Tel: (0)28 8225 6315
e-mail: **CentreMigStudies@ni-libraries.net**
website: **www.qub.ac.uk/cms**

Channel Islands Family History Society, PO Box 507,
St Helier, Jersey JE4 5TN
e-mail: **picus@euseymail.co.uk**
website: **www.channelislands history.com**

Children's Service, Social Services, Maison Le Pape,
  The Parade, St Helier, Jersey JE2 3PU Tel: (0)1534 623500

Civil Registry Office, Registries Building, Deemster's Walk,
  Bucks Road, Douglas, Isle of Man IM1 3AR
  Tel: (0)1624 687039
  e-mail: civil@registry.gov.im
  website: www.gov.im/registries/general/civilregistry/

Clans of Ireland Ltd., 93 Beech Park, Lucan, Co. Dublin
  e-mail: Clansofireland@eircom.net
  website: www.theclansofireland.ie

College of Arms, Queen Victoria Street, London EC4V 4BT
  Tel: (0)20 7248 2762
  website: www.college-of-arms.gov.uk

Commissary Department, Sheriff Court, 27 Chambers Street,
  Edinburgh EH1 1LB

Commonwealth War Graves Commission, 2 Marlow Road,
  Maidenhead, Berkshire SL6 7DX
  Tel: (0)1628 634221, (0)1628 507200 (casualty information
  and enquiries)
  website: www.cwgc.org

Court House, Alderney GY9 3AA
  Tel: (0)1481 822 817

Court of the Lord Lyon, HM New Register House,
  Edinburgh EH1 3YT
  website: www.lyon-court.com/lordlyon

Crown Office, Queen's and Lord Treasurer's Remembrancer,
  25 Chambers Court, Edinburgh EH1 1LA
  Tel: (0)131 226 2626
  website: www.crownoffice.gov.uk

Deeds and Probate Registry, Registries Building,
  Deemster's Walk, Bucks Road, Douglas IM1 3AR
  website: www.gov.im/registries/general/deedsandpro.xml

Duchy of Cornwall, Solicitor, Farrer and Co.,
  66 Lincoln's Inn Fields, London WC2A 3LH

Duchy of Lancaster, Solicitor, Farrer and Co.,
  66 Lincoln's Inn Fields, London WC2A 3LH

Edinburgh Sheriff Court, Commissary Department,
  27 Chambers Street, Edinburgh EH1 1LB

Families in British India Society
  website: www.fibis.org

Family Records Centre, 1 Myddelton Street, London EC1R 1UW
  Tel: (0)20 8392 5300
  e-mail: frc@nationalarchives.gov.uk
  website: www.familyrecords.gov.uk/frc

Federation of Family History Societies, The Administrator,
PO Box 2425, Coventry, West Midlands CV5 6YX
e-mail: **info@ffhs.org.uk**
website: **www.ffhs.org.uk**

Friends Historical Library, Quaker House, Stocking Lane,
Rathfarnham, Dublin 16 Tel: (0)1 495 6890
website: **www.quakers-in-ireland.org**

Genealogical Office (see National Library of Ireland)

Genealogical Society of Ireland, Hon. Secretary,
11 Desmond Avenue, Dún Laoghaire, Co. Dublin
e-mail: **eolas@familyhistory.ie**
website: **www.familyhistory.ie**

General Register Office for England and Wales, Certificate
Services Section, PO Box 2, Southport, Merseyside PR8 2JD
Tel: (0)845 603 7788 (includes still births),
fax: 01704 550013
e-mail: **certificate.services@ons.gsi.gov.uk** (certificate
enquiries), **col.admin@ons.gsi.gov.uk** (enquiries)
website: **www.gro.gov.uk/gro/content**
Abandoned Children's Register
Tel: (0)151 471 4806
e-mail: **corrections.and.re.reg.section@ons.gsi.gov.uk**
Adoptions Section, Room 201, General Register Office,
Trafalgar Road, Southport, Merseyside PR8 2HH
Tel: (0)151 471 4830 fax: (0)151 471 4755
website: **www.gro.gov.uk/gro/content/adoptions**
Overseas Section, General Register Office, Trafalgar Road,
Birkdale, Southport, Merseyside PR8 2HH
Tel: (0)151 471 4801, fax: (0)1633 652988
e-mail: **overseas.gro@ons.gsi.gov.uk**
Traceline Tel: (0)151 471 4811
website: **www.gro.gov.uk/gro/content/research/
traceline/index.asp**

General Register Office for Scotland, New Register House,
3 West Register Street, Edinburgh EH1 3YT
Tel: (0)131 334 0380
e-mail: **www.gro-scotland.gov.uk/ contacts/contact-form.html**
website: **www.gro-scotland. gov.uk**

General Register Office (Northern Ireland),
Oxford House, 49–55 Chichester Street, Belfast BT1 4HL
Tel: (0)28 90 252 000
e-mail: **gro.nisra@dfpni.gov.uk** (birth, marriage and death
enquiries) **groreg.nisra@dfpni.gov.uk** (marriages, re-
registrations and adoptions)
website: **www.groni.gov.uk**

General Register Office of Ireland, Joyce House, 8–11 Lombard Street East, Dublin 2 (postal address: General Register Office, Government Offices, Convent Road, Roscommon)
Tel: (0)90 663 2900, fax: (0)90 663 2999
website: **www.groireland.ie**

Glamorgan Record Office, The Glamorgan Building, King Edward VII Avenue, Cathays Park, Cardiff CF10 3NE
Tel: (0)29 2078 0282
e-mail: **GlamRO@cardiff.ac.uk**
website: **www.glamro.gov.uk**

The Greffe, La Chasse Marette, Sark GY9 0SF
Tel: (0)1481 832012
website: **www.sark.gov.gg/**

The Greffe, Royal Court House, St Peter Port, Guernsey GY1 2PB
Tel: (0)1481 725277
e-mail: **hm_greffier@court1. guernsey.gov.uk**

Guernsey Island Archives Service, St Barnabas, Cornet Street, St Peter Port, Guernsey GY1 1LF
Tel: (0)1481 724512
e-mail: **archives@gov.gg**

Guildhall Library, Aldermanbury, London EC2P 2EJ
Tel: (0)20 7332 1868 or 1870 (printed books)
e-mail: **printedbooks.guildhall@cityoflondon.gov.uk**
website: **www.cityoflondon.gov.uk/Corporation/leisure _heritage/libraries_archives_museums_galleries**
Tel: (0)20 7332 1863 (manuscripts)
e-mail: **manuscripts.guildhall@cityoflondon.gov.uk**
website: **www.history.ac.uk/gh**
Tel: (0)20 7332 1839 (prints and maps)
e-mail: **prints&maps@cityoflondon.gov.uk**

Guild of One-Name Studies, The Secretary, Box G, 14 Charterhouse Buildings, Goswell Road, London EC1M 7BA
Tel: (0)800 011 2182
e-mail: **guild@one-name.org, registrar@one-name.org** (to register your surname)
website: **www.one-name.org**

Harleian Society, Hon. Secretary and Treasurer, College of Arms, Queen Victoria Street, London EC4 4BT
website: **http://harleian.co.uk**

Irish Family History Foundation, The Secretary, Co. Wexford Heritage and Genealogy Society, Yola Farmstead, Folk Park, Tagoat, Rosslare, Co. Wexford

Tel: (0)53 32611 e-mail: **wexgen@eircom.net**
website: **www.irish-roots.net**

Irish Manuscripts Commission, 45 Merrion Square, Dublin 2
Tel: (0)1 676 1610
e-mail: **support@irishmanuscripts.ie**
website: **www.irmss.ie**

Isle of Man Family History Society Library, 13 Michael Street,
Peel, Isle of Man IM5 1HB
Tel: (0)1624 843105
e-mail **iomfhs@manx.net**
website: **www.isle-of-man.com/interests/genealogy/fhs**

Jersey Archive, Clarence Road, St Helier, Jersey JE2 4JY
Tel: (0)1534 833333
e-mail: **archives@jerseyheritagetrust.org**
website: **www.jerseyheritagetrust.org**

Jersey Library, Halkett Place, St Helier, Jersey JE2 4WH
Tel: (0)1534 759992

Judicial Greffe, Royal Court House, Royal Square, St Helier,
Jersey JE1 1JG
Tel: (0)1534 441300
e-mail: **jgreffe@gov.je**
website: **www.judicialgreffe.gov.je**

Lambeth Palace Library, London SE1 7JU
Tel: (0)20 7898 1400
e-mail: **lpl.staff@c-of-e.org.uk**
website: **www.lambethpalacelibrary.org**

Linen Hall Library, 17 Donegall Square North, Belfast BT1 5GB
Tel: (0)28 9032 1707
e-mail: **info@linenhall.com**
website: **www.linenhall.com**

Lord Coutanche Library, The Société Jersiaise, 7 Pier Road,
St Helier, Jersey JE2 4XW
Tel: (0)1534 730538
e-mail: **genealogyinfo@societe-jersiaise.org**
website: **www.societe-jersiaise.org**

London Metropolitan Archives, 40 Northampton Road,
London EC1R 0HB
Tel: (0)20 7332 3820
email: **ask.lma@cityoflondon.gov.uk** website:
www.corpoflondon.gov.uk/Corporation/leisure_
heritage/libraries_archives_museums_galleries

Manx National Heritage Library and Archives, Kingswood
Grove, Douglas, Isle of Man IM1 3LY
Tel: (0)1624 648000
e-mail: **library@mnh.gov.im**
website: **www.gov.im/mnh**

Maritime Archives and Library, Merseyside Maritime Museum,
Albert Dock, Liverpool L3 4AQ
Website: **www.liverpoolmuseums.org.uk/maritime/archive**

Mitchell Library, North Street, Glasgow G3 7DN
Tel: (0)141 287 2999
e-mail: **lil@cls.glasgow.gov.uk**
website: **www.mitchelllibrary.org**

Mrs M. Mignot, 88 St Martins, Alderney, Guernsey GY9 3UB

National Archives, Ruskin Avenue, Kew, Richmond, Surrey
TW9 4DU Tel: (0)20 8876 3444
e-mail: **www.nationalarchives.gov.uk/contact/form**
website: **www.nationalarchives.gov.uk**

National Archives of Ireland, Bishop Street, Dublin 8
Tel: (0)1 407 2300
e-mail: **mail@nationalarchives.ie**
website: **www.nationalarchives.ie**

National Archives of Scotland, HM General Register House,
2 Princes Street, Edinburgh EH1 3YY
Tel: (0)131 535 1314
e-mail: **enquiries@nas.gov.uk**
website: **www.nas.gov.uk**

National Council of Voluntary Child Care Organizations,
Unit 4 Pride Court, 80-82 White Lion Street, London N1 9PF
Tel: (0)20 7833 3319
e-mail: **office@ncvcco.org**
website: **www.ncvcco.org**

National Library of Ireland, Kildare Street, Dublin 2
Tel: (0)1 603 0200
e-mail: **info@nli.ie**
website: **www.nli.ie**

National Library of Scotland, Map Collections, Causewayside
Buildings, 33 Salisbury Place, Edinburgh EH9 1SL
Tel: (0)131 623 3970
e-mail: **maps@nls.uk**
website: **www.nls.uk/collections/maps/subjectinfo/ord_survey.html**

National Library of Wales, Department of Manuscripts and
Records, Aberystwyth SY23 3BU
Tel: (0)1970 632 800 (general) or (0)1970 632 933

(enquiries) e-mail: **www.llgc.org.uk/ymholiadau.htm**
website: **www.llgc.org.uk**

National Organization for the Counselling of Adoptees and
Parents (NORCAP), 112 Church Road, Wheatley,
Oxfordshire OX33 1LU
Tel: (0)1865 875000
website: **www.norcap.org.uk**

Office for National Statistics (see General Register Office for
England and Wales)

Presbyterian Historical Society, Presbyterian Church in Ireland,
Church House, Fisherwick Place, Belfast BT1 6DW
Tel: (0)28 9032 2284 x268
email: **info@presbyterianireland.org**
website: **www.presbyterianireland.orgphsi/index.html**

Presbyterian Historical Society, United Reformed Church
House, 86 Tavistock Place, London WC1H 9RT
Tel: (0)20 7916 2020

Priaulx Library, Candie House, Candie Road, St Peter Port,
Guernsey GY1 1UG
Tel: (0)1481 721998
website: **www.priaulx.gov.gg**

Principal Registry of the Family Division, Probate Department,
First Avenue House, 42–49 High Holborn, London
WC1V 6NP
Tel: (0)20 7947 6983 (Probate Search Room)
website: **www.theprobateservice.gov.uk**
Tel: (0)20 7947 7017 (Decree Absolute Search Section)

Probate Sub-Registry, Postal Searches and Copies Department,
1st Floor, Castle Chambers, Clifford Street, York YO1 9RG
Tel: (0)1904 666 777

Public Record Office of the Isle of Man, Unit 40a, Spring
Valley Industrial Estate, Douglas IM2 2QR
Tel: (0)1624 693569
e-mail: **public.records@registry.gov.im**
website: **www.gov.im/registries/publicrecords/**

Public Record Office of Northern Ireland, 66 Balmoral Avenue,
Belfast BT9 6NY
Tel: (0)28 9025 5905
e-mail: **proni@dcalni.gov.uk**
website: **www.proni.gov.uk**

Registry for Births, Deaths, Companies, Land and Marriages, St Anne, Alderney GY9 3AA

Registers of Scotland, Erskine House, 68 Queen Street, Edinburgh EH2 4NF

Registry of Deeds, Kings Inns, Henrietta Street, Dublin 7
Tel: (0)1 670 7500
website: **www.landregistry.ie**

Religious Society of Friends Library, Friends House, 173-177 Euston Road, London NW1 2BJ
Tel: (0)20 7663 1135
website: **www.quaker.org.uk**

Representative Church Body Library, Braemor Park, Churchtown, Dublin 14
Tel: (0)1 492 3979
e-mail: **library@ireland.anglican.org**
website: **www.ireland.anglican.org/library/index.html**

Royal Court of Guernsey, Royal Court House, St Peter Port, Guernsey GY1 2PB

Royal Court of Jersey, Public Registry Office, Royal Square, St Helier, Jersey JE1 1JG

Royal Courts of Justice, Probate Registry, Chichester Street, Belfast BT1 3JY Tel: (0)28 9023 5111

Royal Irish Academy, 19 Dawson Street, Dublin 2
Tel: (0)1 6762 570
website: **www.ria.ie**

Scottish Association of Family History Societies
website: **www.safhs.org.uk/**

Society of Friends Library, Meeting House, Railway Street, Lisburn, Co. Antrim

Scottish Genealogy Society, The Hon. Secretary, 15 Victoria Terrace, Edinburgh EH1 2JL
Tel: (0)131 220 3677
e-mail: **info@scotsgenealogy.com**
website: **www.scotsgenealogy.com**

La Société Guernesiaise (Family History Section), PO Box 314, Candie, St Peter Port, Guernsey GY1 3TG
website: **www.societe.org.gg/sections/familyhistorysec.htm**

The Société Jersiaise (see Lord Coutanche Library)

Society of Genealogists, 14 Charterhouse Buildings, Goswell Road, London EC1M 7BA
Tel: (0)20 7251 8799
e-mail: **genealogy@sog.org.uk**
website: **www.sog.org.uk**

Superintendent Registrar, 10 Royal Square, St Helier,
Jersey JE2 4WA Tel: (0)1534 441335

Traceline (see General Register Office for England and Wales)

Treasury Solicitor, Treasury Solicitor's Department,
One Kemble Street, London WC2B 4TS Tel: (0)20 7210 3000
e-mail: **Thetreasurysolicitor@tsol.gsi. gov.uk**
website: **www.treasury-solicitor.gov.uk/**

Trinity College Dublin, College Green, Dublin 2
Tel: (0)1 896 1000
website: **www.tcd.ie**

Ulster Historical Foundation, Unit 7, Cotton Court,
Waring Street, Belfast BT1 2ED
Tel: (0)28 90 332288
e-mail: **enquiry@uhf.org.uk**
website: **www.ancestryireland.com**

Valuation Office, Irish Life Centre, Abbey Street Lower, Dublin 1
Tel: (0)1 817 1045 or 1041
e-mail: **info@valoff.ie**
website: **www.valoff.ie**

United States of America and Canada

American Antiquarian Society, 185 Salisbury Street, Worcester,
MA 01609-1634 Tel: 508 755 5221
website: **www.americanantiquarian.org**

American Battle Monuments Commission, Courthouse Plaza II,
Suite 500, 2300 Clarendon Boulevard, Arlington,
VA 22201-3367 Tel: 703 696 6900
e-mail: **info@abmc.gov**
website: **www.abmc.gov**

Army Casualty and Memorial Affairs Operation Center,
US Army Total Personnel Command, TAPC-PED,
2461 Eisenhower Avenue, Alexandria, VA 22331-0482

British Isles Family History Society, 2531 Sawtelle Boulevard
PMB 134, Los Angeles, CA 90064-3124
website: **www.rootsweb.com/~bifhsusa**

Bureau of Land Management, Department of the Interior
(BLM-ES0), 7450 Boston Boulevard, Springfield,
VA 22153-3121 Tel: 703 440 1600
e-mail: **records@blm.gov**
website: **www.glorecords.blm.gov**

Citizenship and Immigration Canada, Public Rights
Administration, 360 Laurier Avenue West, 10th Floor,
Ottawa, Ontario K1A 1LI

Department of Homeland Security, Bureau of US Citizenship and Immigration Services, Historical Reference Library, Ullico Building, 111 Massachusetts Avenue NW, Washington, DC 20529
e-mail: **CISHistory.Library@dhs.gov**
website: **www.uscis. gov/graphics/index.htm**

Family History Library of the Church of Jesus Christ of Latter-day Saints, 35 North West Temple Street, Salt Lake City, UT 84150-3400
Tel: 801 240 2584 or 866 406 1830
e-mail: **fhl@familysearch.org**
website: **www.familysearch.org**

Federation of Genealogical Societies, PO Box 200940, Austin, TX 78720-0940
Tel: 888 FGS 1500
e-mail: **fgs-office@fgs.org**
website: **www.fgs.org/**

Godfrey Memorial Library, 134 Newfield Street, Middletown, CT 06457–2534
e-mail: **Library@Godfrey.org**
website: **wwwgodfrey.org**

International Society for British Genealogy and Family History, PO Box 350459, Westminster, CO 80035-0459
e-mail: **isbgfh@yahoo.com**
website: **www.isbgfh.org**

International Soundex Reunion Registry, PO Box 2312, Carson City, NV 8902
Tel: 775 882 7755
website: **www.isrr.net/**

Library and Archives Canada, 395 Wellington Street, Ottawa, Ontario K1A 0N4
Tel: 613 996 5115
website: **www.collectionscanada.ca**

Library of Congress, 101 Independence Avenue, SE, Washington, DC 20540
Tel: 202 707 8000
website: **www.loc.gov**

National Archives and Records Administration, 700 Pennsylvania Avenue, NW, Washington, DC 20408-0001

National Archives at College Park (Archives ll), 8601 Adelphi Road, College Park, MD 20740-6001
Tel: 866 272 6272
e-mail: www.archives.gov/contact/inquire-form.html#part-b
website: www.archives.gov
Civilian Records (Room 2600, National Archives at College Park) Fax: 301 837 1919
e-mail: www.archives.gov/contact/inquire-form.html
National Personnel Records Center, Military Personnel Records, 9700 Page Avenue, St Louis, MO 63132-5100
Tel: 314 801 0850
e-mail: center@nara.gov
National Society of Daughters of the American Revolution Library, 1776 D Street, NW, Washington, DC 20006-5303
Tel: 202 879 3229
website: www.dar.org
Newberry Library, Local and Family History Section, 60 West Walton Street, Chicago, ILL 60610-3305
Tel: 312 255 3512
e-mail: geneaalogy@newberry.org
website: www.newberry.org/
New England Historic Genealogical Society, 101 Newbury Street, Boston, MA 02116-3007
Tel: 617 536 5740
e-mail: info@nehgs.org
website: www.newenglandancestors.org/
New York Genealogical and Biographical Society, 122 East 58th Street, New York, NY 10022-1939
Tel: 212 755 8532
e-mail: library@nygbs.org
website: www.newyorkfamilyhistory.org/
Passport Services, US Department of State, Vital Records Sections, 1111 19th Street, NW, Suite 510, Washington, DC 20522-1705 Tel: 202 955 0307
website: www.travel.state.gov/passport/get/first_825.hmtl

Bibliography

The following list includes all the books mentioned in the text.

Acts of the Privy Council, Colonial Series, 1613–1783, 6 vols (London, 1908–12)

Adams, J. T., rev. by K. T. Jackson, *Atlas of American History* (New York, 1978)

Anderson, R. C., *The Great Migration Begins: Immigrants to New England, 1620–33*, 3 vols (Boston, 1996)

Anderson, R. C., *The Great Migration: Immigrants to New England, 1634–1635*, 4 vols (A–I) (Boston, 1999–2005) Vols 1 and 2 with G. H. Sanburn, Jr., and M. L. Sanburn

Anderson, R. C., *The Pilgrim Migration: Immigrants to Plymouth Colony, 1620–1633* (Boston, 2004)

Atkins, P. J., *The Directories of London, 1677–1977* (London, 1990)

Atterbury, T. E. (ed.), *Trade Associations and Professional Bodies of the United Kingdom and Eire* (London, 17th edn, 2003)

Bagnall, K., *The Little Immigrants; The Orphans who came to Canada* (Toronto, *c.* 2001)

Bailyn, B., *The Peopling of British North America: An Introduction* (London, 1986)

Bailyn, B. and DeWolfe, B., *Voyagers to the West: Emigration from Britain to America on the Eve of the Revolution* (London, 1987)

Bardsley, C. W., *A Dictionary of English and Welsh Surnames, with Special American Instances* (London, 1901, rev. repr. 1981)

Barrow, G. B., *The Genealogist's Guide: An Index to Printed British Pedigrees and Family Histories, 1950–1975* (London, 1977)

Bartis, P. and Hufford, M., *Maritime Folklife Resources: a Directory and Index* (Washington, DC, 1980)

Beech, G. and Mitchell, R., *Maps for Family and Local History, The Records of the Tithe, Valuation Office and National Farm Surveys of England and Wales, 1836–1943* (The National Archives, 2nd edn 2004)

Bentley, E. P., *The Genealogist's Address Book* (5th edition, Baltimore, 2005)

Bevan, A., *Tracing Your Ancestors in the National Archives: The Website and Beyond* (The National Archives, 7th edn, 2006)

Bigwood, R., *Tracing Scottish Ancestors: A Practical Guide to Scottish Genealogy* (Glasgow, updated edn, 2001)

Billington, R. A., and Ridge, M., *Westward Expansion* (New York, 1982)

Black, G. F., *The Surnames of Scotland* (New York, 1946)

Blatchford, R. (ed. and comp.), *The Family and Local History Handbook* (Nether Poppleton, 10th edn, 2006)

Bradley, A. K., *History of the Irish in America* (Chartwell, 1986)

Brigham, C.B., *History and Bibliography of American Newspapers, 1690–1820*, 2 vols (Worcester, Mass, 1947)

Calendar of State Papers, Colonial: America and West Indies, 1574–1739 (London, 1860–1994)

Campbell, L., Steer, F. W. and Yorke, R., *A Catalogue of Manuscripts in the College of Arms, Vol 1* (London, 1988)

CBD Research Ltd, *Directory of British Associations and Associations in Ireland* (Beckenham, 18th edn, 2006)

Chapman, J., *A Guide to Parliamentary Enclosures in Wales* (Cardiff, 1992)

Cheffins, R. H. A., *Parliamentary Constituencies and their Registers since 1832* (British Library, 1998)

Cheney, C. R., rev. by M. Jones, *A Handbook of Dates for Students of English History* (Cambridge, 1945, 2000)

Christian, P., *The Genealogist's Internet* (The National Archives, 3rd expanded edn, 2005)

Clarke, R. S. J., *Gravestone Inscriptions*, 19 vols (Ulster Historical Foundation, 1966–83)

Coldham, P. W., *American Migrations 1765–1799, The Lives, Times, and Families of Colonial Americans, Who Remained Loyal to the British Crown* (Baltimore, 2000)

Coldham, P. W., *American Wills and Administrations in the Prerogative Court of Canterbury, 1610–1857* (Baltimore, 1989)

Coldham, P. W., *American Wills proved in London, 1611–1775* (Baltimore, 1992)

Coldham, P. W., *The Bristol Registers of Servants Sent to Foreign Plantations, 1654–1686* (Baltimore, 1988)

Coldham, P. W., *British Emigrants in Bondage 1614–1788*, (Baltimore, 2005)

Coldham, P. W., *Child Apprentices in America from Christ's Hospital London, 1617–1778* (Baltimore, 1988)

Coldham, P. W., *The Complete Book of Emigrants, 1607–1776*, 4 vols (Baltimore, 1992–2003)

Coldham, P. W., *The Complete Book of Emigrants in Bondage 1614–1775* (Baltimore, 1988) and *Supplement* (1992), and *More Emigants in Bondage* (2002)

Coldham, P. W., *Emigrants from England to the American Colonies, 1773–1776,* (Baltimore, 1989)

Coldham, P. W., *Emigrants in Chains* (Baltimore, 1992, repr. 1994)

Coldham, P. W., *The King's Passengers: Transportation Coming into Maryland, Virginia,* 2 vols (Westminster, 1998–99)

Coldham, P. W., *The King's Passengers: Transportation to Maryland and Virginia* (Westminster, 1997)

Cole, J. and Church, R., *In and Around Record Repositories in Great Britain and Ireland* (Ramsey, 4th edn, 1998)

Colwell, S., *The Family Records Centre, A User's Guide* (PRO Publications, 2nd edn, 2002)

Colwell, S., *The National Archives, A Practical Guide for Family Historians* (The National Archives, 2006)

Craig, F. W. S., *Boundaries of Parliamentary Constituencies, 1885–1972* (Chichester, 1972)

Crosson, B., and M., *A Census of Pensioners for Revolutionary or Military Services (1841),* (Apollo, 1978)

Crowder, N. K., *British Army Pensioners Abroad, 1772–1899* (Baltimore, 1995)

De Breffny, B., *Bibliography of Irish Family History and Genealogy* (Cork, 1974)

Dickson, R. J., *Ulster Emigrants to Colonial America 1718–1775* (Belfast, 1988)

Dobson, D., *Directory of Scots Banished to the American Plantations, 1650–1775* (Baltimore, 1983)

Dobson, D., *Directory of Scottish Settlers in North America, 1625–1825,* 7 vols (Baltimore, 19854–93)

Dobson, D., *Irish Emigration in North America* (Baltimore, 2004)

Dobson, D., *Scottish-American Heirs, 1683–1883* (Baltimore, 1990)

Dobson, D., *Scottish-American Wills, 1650–1900* (Baltimore, 1991)

Dobson, D., *Scottish Emigration to Colonial America, 1607–1785* (University of Georgia Press, 2004)

Dollarhide, W., *Getting Started in Genealogy Online* (Baltimore, 2006)

Dollarhide, W., *Map Guide to American Migration Routes 1735–1815* (Bountiful, 1997)

Dubester, H.J., *An Annotated Bibliography of Censuses Taken After the Year 1790 by States and Territories of the United States* (New York, 1969)

Eales, E. B. and Kvasnicka, R. M. (eds) *Guide to Genealogical Research in the National Archives of the United States* (Washington DC, 3rd edn, 2000)

Eichholz, A. (ed.), *Ancestry's Red Book, American State, County and Town Sources* (Provo, 3rd edn, 2004)

Ellis, M., *Using Manorial Records* (PRO Publications, 1997)

Ethridge, J. M., and Marlow, C. A. (eds), *The Directory of Directories* (Detroit, 5th edn, 1988)

Estcourt, E. E. and Payne, J. O. (eds), *The English Catholic Non-Jurors of 1715...* ([London, 1885], facsimile edn, 1969)

Falley, M. D., *Irish and Scotch–Irish Ancestral Research* (Baltimore, repr. 1998)

Ferguson, J. P. S., *Scottish Family Histories* (Edinburgh, 2nd edn, 1986)

Filby, P. W. and Meyer, M. K. (eds), *Passenger and Immigration Lists Index*, 3 vols (Michigan, 1981, with annual supplements by P. W. Filby and various co-editors)

Gandy, M. (ed.), *Catholic Missions and Registers, 1700–1880,* 6 vols, (London, 1993, 1998)

Gandy, M. (ed.), *Catholic Parishes in England, Wales and Scotland, an Atlas* (London, 1993)

Gibson, J., *Bishops' Transcripts and Marriage Licences, Bonds and Allegations: A Guide to Their Location and Indexes* (Birmingham, 5th edn, 2001)

Gibson, J., *The Hearth Tax, Other Later Stuart Tax Lists and the Association Oath Rolls* (Birmingham, 2nd edn, 1996)

Gibson, J., *Quarter Sessions Records for Family Historians: A Select List* (Birmingham, 4th edn, 1995)

Gibson, J. and Churchill, E., *Probate Jurisdictions: Where to Look for Wills* (Birmingham, 5th edn, 2002)

Gibson, J. and Hampson, E., *Marriage and Census Indexes for Family Historians* (Birmingham, 8th edn, 2000)

Gibson, J. and Medlycott, M., *Local Census Listings, 1522–1930: Holdings in the British Isles* (Birmingham, 2nd edn, 1994)

Gibson, J., Medlycott, M. and Mills, D., *Land and Window Tax Assessments* (Birmingham, 2nd edn, 1998)

Gibson, J. and Peskett, P., *Record Offices: How to Find Them* (Bury, 9th edn, 2002)

Gibson, J. and Rogers, C., *Electoral Registers since 1832; and Burgess Rolls* (Birmingham, 2nd edn, 1990)

Gibson, J. and Rogers, C., *Poll Books and Lists, c.1696–1872: A Directory of Holdings in Great Britain* (Birmingham, 3rd edn, 1994)

Gibson, J., Rogers, C. and Webb, C., *Poor Law Union Records*, 3 parts (Birmingham, 2nd edns, 1997)

Gibson, J. and Youngs, F. A., Jr., *Poor Law Union Records: Pt 4: Gazetteer of England and Wales* (Birmingham, 1993)

Glazer, I. A., and Tepper, M. (eds), *The Famine Immigrants*, 7 vols (Baltimore, 1988)

Good, J. A., *A Register of Royal Marine Deaths, 1914–1919* (Royal Marine Historical Society, 1991)

Good, J. A., *A Register of Royal Marine Deaths, 1939–1945* (Royal Marine Historical Society, 1991)

Gooder, E. A., *Introduction to Latin for Local History* (London, 1961)

Grannum, G., *Tracing Your West Indian Ancestors* (PRO Publications, 2nd rev. edn, 2002)

Grannum, G. and Taylor, N., *Wills and Other Probate Records, a Practical Guide to Researching your Ancestors' Last Documents* (The National Archives, 2004)

Greenwood, V. D., *The Researcher's Guide to American Genealogy* (Baltimore, 3rd edn, 2000)

Gregory, W., *American Newspapers [1821–1936]: A Union List of Files Available in the United States and Canada* (New York, 1937)

Grenham, J., *Tracing Your Irish Ancestors: the Complete Guide* (Dublin, 3rd edn, 2006)

Grieve, H. E. P., *Examples of English Handwriting 1150–1750* (Essex Record Office, 1954, 5th impression 1981)

Groome, F., *Gazetteer of Scotland*, 6 vols (Edinburgh, 1882–85)

Guildhall Library Research Guide 2: *The British Overseas: A Guide to Records of Births, Baptisms, Marriages, Deaths and Burials available in the UK* (London, 1995)

Harper, M., *Adventurers and Exiles: The Great Scottish Exodus* (London, 2003)

Hatcher, P. L., *Locating Your Roots: Discover Your Ancestors Using Land Records* (Cincinnati, 2003)

Hauxwell, H., with Cockroft, B., *Hannah, The Complete Story* (London, 1991)

Hawkings, D. T., *Index to Somerset Estate Duty Office Wills and Letters of Administration, 1805–1811*, 2 vols (Weston-super-Mare, 1995)

Hawkings, D. T., *Index to Somerset Estate Duty Office Wills 1812–57, and Letters of Administration, 1812–1857*, 2 vols (Weston-super-Mare, 1995)

Heads of Families at the First Census of the United States Taken in the year 1790, 12 vols (Washington, DC, 1907–08, repr. Baltimore, 1965–75)

Herber, M., *Clandestine Marriages in the Chapel and Rules of the Fleet Prison 1680–1754*, 3 vols (London, 1998–2001)

Hinkley, K. W., *Your Guide to the Federal Census* (Cincinnati, 2002)

Houston, J., *Index of Cases in the Records of the Court of Arches at Lambeth Palace Library 1660–1913* (London, 1972)

Humphery-Smith, C. R. (ed.), *The Phillimore Atlas and Index of Parish Registers* (Chichester, 3rd edn, 2003)

Ifans, D. (ed.), *Nonconformist Registers of Wales* (National Library of Wales and Welsh County Archivists Group, 1994)

Johnson, K. A. and Sainty, M. R. (eds), *Genealogical Research Directory, National and International* (Sydney, annual 1981–)

Kain, R. J. P. and Oliver, R. R., *The Tithe Maps of England and Wales, Cartographic Analysis and County by County Catalogue* (Cambridge, 1995)

Kaminkow, M.J. (comp. and ed.), *A Complement to Genealogies in the Library of Congress: a Bibliography* (Maryland, 1981)

Kaminkow, M. J., *Genealogies in the Library of Congress: A Bibliography* (Baltimore, 1972), with *Supplements 1972–76* (1977), *1976–86* (1987), and *1992–2000* (2001)

Kemp, T. J., *International Vital Records Handbook* (Baltimore, 4th edn, 2000, 3rd repr. 2002)

Kershaw, R., *Emigrants and Expats, a Guide to Sources on UK Emigration and Residents Overseas* (PRO Publications, 2002)

Kershaw, R. and Pearsall, M., *Immigrants and Aliens, Guide to Sources on UK Immigration and Citizenship* (The National Archives, 2nd edn, 2004)

Lainhart, A. S. (ed.) *State Census Records* (Baltimore, 1992, repr. 2000)

Lewis, S., *Topographical Dictionary of Ireland* (London, 1837)

MacLysaght, E., *Bibliography of Irish Family History* (Dublin, 1982)

Marshall, G. W., *The Genealogist's Guide* (London, 1903, repr. 1980)

Marshall, H., *Palaeography for Family and Local Historians* (Chichester, 2004)

Martin, C. T., *The Record Interpreter, a Collection of Abbreviations, Latin Words and Names used in English Historical Manuscripts and Records* (London, 1910, repr. 1994)

Mathias, P., and Pearsall, A. W. H., *Shipping: A Survey of Historical Records* (Newton Abbot, 1980)

Maxwell, I. and McGrath, G., *Tracing your Ancestors in Northern Ireland* (Edinburgh, 1997)

Mead, F., *Handbook of American Denominations* (5th edn, Nashville, 1970)

Meller, H., *London Cemeteries, an Illustrated Guide and Gazetteer* (Brookfield, Vermont, 3rd edn, 1994)

Merriman, B. D., *United Empire Loyalists, A Guide to Tracing Loyalist Ancestors in Upper Canada (Ontario)*, (Campbellville, Ontario, 2006)

Meyerink, K. (ed.), *Ancestry's Printed Sources: A Guide to Published Genealogical Sources* (Salt Lake City, 1998)

Milward, R., *A Glossary of Household, Farming and Trade Terms from Probate Inventories* (Derbyshire Record Society, 3rd edn, 1986, repr. 1993)

Mitchell, B., *Guide to Irish Parish Records* (Baltimore, 1987)

Mitchell, B., *A New Genealogical Atlas of Ireland* (Baltimore, 1986)

Morgan, T. J., and Morgan, P., *Welsh Surnames* (Cardiff, 1985)

Munby, L. M., *How Much is That Worth?* (Chichester, 2nd edn, 1996)

Narasimham, J., *The Manx Family Tree: A Beginner's Guide to Records in the Isle of Man* (Isle of Man, 3rd edn, 2000)

National Archives of Scotland, *Tracing Your Scottish Ancestors: A Guide to Ancestry Research in the National Archives of Scotland* (Edinburgh, 3rd edn, 2003)

Norton, J. E., *Guide to National and Provincial Directories of England and Wales, Excluding London, Published Before 1856* (London, 1950)

Oswald, D.T., *Fire Insurance Maps: Their History and Applications* (College Station, 1997)

Pappalardo, B., *Royal Naval Lieutenants: Passing Certificates 1691–1902* (List and Index Society, Vols 289 and 290, 2002)

Parr, J., *Labouring Children: British Immigrants and Apprentices to Canada, 1869–1924* (London, 1980)

Phair (Eustace), P. B. and Ellis, E., *Abstracts of Wills at the Registry of Deeds*, 3 vols (Irish Manuscripts Commission, 1954–88)

Phillimore, W. P. W. and Fry, E. A., *An Index to Changes of Name under Authority of Act of Parliament or by Royal Licence, and Including Irregular Changes, from 1 George lll to 64 Victoria, 1760–1901* (London, 1905, repr. 1986)

Public Record Office of Northern Ireland, *Guide to Church Records: Public Record Office of Northern Ireland* (PRONI, 1994)

Raymond, S. A., *Monumental Inscriptions on the Web* (Bury, 2002)

Raymond, S. A., *Occupational Sources for Genealogists: A Bibliography* (Birmingham, 2nd edn, 1996)

Return of Owners of Land of One Acre and Upwards in England (excluding the Metropolis), and Wales 1873, 2 vols, (London, 1875)

Return of Owners of Land of One Acre and Upwards in Ireland (London, 1876)

Return of Owners of Land of One Acre and Upwards in Scotland, 1872–3 (London, 1874)

Reynard, K. W. (ed.), *The ASLIB Directory of Information Sources in the United Kingdom* (London, 13th edn, 2004)

Richards, E., *Britannia's Children: Emigration from England, Scotland, Ireland and Wales since 1600* (London, 2004)

Richards, M., *Welsh Administrative and Territorial Units* (Cardiff, 1969)

Rose, C., *Courthouse Research for Family Historians: Your Guide to Genealogical Treasures* (San José, 2004)

Rosie, A., *Scottish Handwriting 1500–1700: A Self-help Pack* (Scottish Records Association and National Archives of Scotland, 1994)

Ryan, J. G., *Irish Records: Sources for Family and Local History* (Salt Lake City, rev. edn, 1997)

Sanders, P., *The Simple Annals, the History of an Essex and East End Family* (Gloucester, 1989)

Schaefer, C. K., *Guide to Naturalization Records of the United States* (Baltimore, 1997)

Shaw, G. and Tipper, A., *British Directories: A Bibliography and Guide to Directories Published in England and Wales (1850–1950) and Scotland (1773–1950)* (London, 2nd edn, 1997)

Shorney, D., *Protestant Nonconformity and Roman Catholicism, Guide to Sources in the Public Record Office* (PRO Publications, 1996)

Society of Genealogists, *Index to the Bank of Englanf Will Extracts 1807–1845* (London, 1991)

Society of Genealogists, *A List of Parishes in Boyd's Marriage Index* (London, 6th edn, corrected repr. 1994)

Society of Genealogists, *Marriage Licences: Abstracts and Indexes in the Library of the Society of Genealogists* (London, 4th edn, 1991)

Society of Genealogists, *Monumental Inscriptions in the Library of the Society of Genealogists*, 2 parts (London, 1984, 1987)

Society of Genealogists, *Parish Register Copies in the Library of the Society of Genealogists* (London, 11th edn, 1995)

Society of Genealogists, *The Trinity House Petitions: 1787–1854* (London, 1987)

Spufford, P. (ed.), *Index to the Probate Accounts of England and Wales*, 2 vols (British Record Society, 1999)

Squibb, G. D., *Visitation Pedigrees and the Genealogist* (London, 2nd edn, 1978)

Steel, D.J., *National Index of Parish Registers, Vols 1–111* (Chichester, 1974, London 1968, 1973)

Steel, D. J., with Steel, A.E. F., *National Index of Parish Registers, Vol. X11: Sources for Scottish Genealogy and Family History* (Chichester, 1970)

Stevenson, D. and W. B. (eds), *Scottish Texts and Calendars: An Analytical Guide to Serial Publications* (Edinburgh, 1987)

Stryker-Rodda, H., *Understanding Colonial Handwriting* (Baltimore, 1986, repr. 2002)

Stuart, D., *Latin for Local and Family Historians* (Chichester, 1995)

Stuart, M., *Scottish Family History, Guide to Works of Reference on the History and Genealogy of Scottish Families... To which is prefixed an essay on 'How to write the history of a family, by Sir James Balfour Paul'* (Edinburgh, 1930)

Szucs, L. D. and Luebking, S. H. (eds), *The Source: A Guidebook of American Genealogy* (Provo, 3rd edn, 2006)

Tate, W. E., *A Domesday of English Enclosure Acts and Awards* (Reading, 1978)

Taylor, P. A. M., *Expectations Westward: The Mormons and the Emigration of their Converts in the Nineteenth Century* (Edinburgh, 1965)

Thomas, J. A., Helm, M. L and A. L., and Barratt, N., *Genealogy Online for Dummies* (Chichester, 2006)

Thompson, R., *Mobility and Migration: East Anglian Founders of New England, 1629–1640* (Amherst, 1994)

Thomson, T. (ed.), *Inquistionum ad Capellam Domini Regis Retornatum, quae in publicis archivis Scotiae adhuc servantur, Abbreviatio,* 3 vols (London, 1811–16, 1900)

Thomson, T. R., *Catalogue of British Family Histories* (London, 3rd edn, 1980 with Addenda)

Thorndale, W. and Dollarhide, W., *Map Guide to the United States Federal Censuses 1790–1920* (Baltimore, 1987, repr. 2005)

The Times Tercentenary Handlist … of English and Welsh Newspapers, Magazines and Reviews 1620–1920 (*The Times,* 1920)

Thiry, C. J. J. (ed.) *The Guide to US Map Resources* (Landham, 2005)

Turner, G. Lyon, *Original Records of Nonconformity under Persecution and Indulgence,* 3 vols (London, 1911–14)

Wagner, A. R., *The Records and Collections of the College of Arms* (London, 1952)

Wagner, A. R. *English Genealogy* (Chichester, 3rd edn, 1983)

Walsh, B. B., *Telephone and City Directories in the Library of Congress, A Finding Guide* (Washington, DC, 1994)

Waters, C., *A Dictionary of Old Trades, Titles and Occupations* (Newbury, expanded edn, 2002)

Watt, H., *Welsh Manors and their Records* (Aberystwyth, 2000)

Whitmore, J. B., *A Genealogical Guide: An Index to British Pedigrees in Continuation of Marshall's Genealogist's Guide* (London, 1953)

Williams, C. J. and Watts-Williams, S. J. (comps), *National Index of Parish Registers, Vol. 13: Parish Registers of Wales* (National Library of Wales and Welsh County Archivists Group, 1986)

Willing's Press Guide, 3 parts (Chesham, 2003)

Wolfston, P. S., rev. by C. Webb, *Greater London Cemeteries and Crematoria* (London, 6th edn, 1999)

Whyte, D., *A Dictionary of Scottish Emigrants to Canada before Confederation,* 2 vols (Ontario Genealogical Society, 1986, 1995)

Whyte, D., *A Dictionary of Scottish Emigrants to the United States of America,* 2 vols (Baltimore, 1972, 1986)

index

abandoned children **49**
accessing records **152–67**
  dating of documents **164–5**
  drawing up a checklist **154–5**
  facsimiles and transcriptions
    of documents **162**
  filing and storage systems **2,
    21, 165–7**
  handling old documents
    158–9
  interpreting your findings **165**
  online **153**
  reading old handwriting
    159–62
  understanding Latin
    documents **163**
  working with numbers **163–4**
  see also archives
administration grants **222, 233–5**
  Channel Islands **244–5**
  and Death Duty registers
    238–41
  emigrants **289**
  and government stockholders
    242
  Ireland **253–5**
  Isle of Man **245–6**
  National Probate Indexes of
    58, 234
  next of kin defined in **235**
  and probate inventories **236**

Scotland **247**
Adoption Contact Register **48–9**
adoptions
  American **95–6**
  birth registrations **47–9**
  Channel Islands **66–7**
  on family trees **23**
  indexes to **46–7**
  Ireland **76**
  Isle of Man **67**
  Scotland **69**
African Americans, census
    returns **127**
ages
  in census returns **108, 109,
    111, 130**
  of death **59**
  of marriage **51, 93, 179**
Alderney **65, 103, 204, 244**
annulments **55**
apprenticeship records **289**
archival boxes **166–7**
archives **155–67**
  preparatory work online **156–7**
  understanding dialect **162–3**
  visiting an archive office
    155–6, 157–8
  see also accessing records
Armed Forces *see* servicemen
Asia, British in **90–1**

baptisms **60, 169, 170, 172, 174, 175–8, 184, 186**
American **219**
Channel Islands **204**
Ireland **212–13, 214**
Isle of Man **204–5**
nonconformist **192, 193–4**
Roman Catholic **177, 201, 202, 212**
Scotland **205–6, 210, 212**
Baptists **191, 193**
Irish **216**
Bibles, family **10**
bigamists **56**
birth-briefs **26, 29**
births
alternative sources of information on **60–3**
at sea and abroad **79–81, 83–4**
baptism registers **60, 169, 170**
and censuses **102, 169**
certificates **44–6, 50, 75**
buying copies of **40, 42**
Channel Islands **65–6, 204**
Ireland **73–4, 75**
Isle of Man **67, 204–5**
nonconformist registers **194, 196–7**
Quakers **197–8, 211**
registrations **2, 37, 38, 43–9, 65–77, 91–3**
reasons for inability to find **43–4**
Scotland **68–9, 205–6**
service families **81–2**
stillbirths **49, 69, 76**
in the USA **91–3, 218, 219**
border crossings **273**
British Colonies, Commonwealth, Dominions or Territories **81**
burials **169, 170, 174, 175, 186–9, 200**
Channel Islands **204**

gravestone inscriptions **59, 189, 195–6**
indexes **188**
Ireland **213, 214–15**
nonconformists **192, 194–6**
Quakers **198, 200**
Roman Catholic **202, 212**
Scotland **205–6, 209, 212**
in the USA **220**

Canada
border crossings **273**
Canadian archives **157**
child emigrants to **280–81**
ships' passenger lists **269–70**
canals, census returns and people on **114**
cemetery registers **17, 59, 170, 187–8**
Ireland **75**
Scotland **209**
censuses **2, 101–31, 169**
1841 returns **108–9, 112**
1851 returns **109, 112**
American **119–20, 218**
earlier in the UK (before **1841**) **117–18**
and emigrants **283–4**
enumerators **102**
first census **102**
general advice on tackling **129–31**
household information in **108–12**
indexes, digital images and transcriptions **104–8, 129, 131**
India **119**
Ireland **116–17, 213**
organization **102–4**
overseas surveys **118–19**
people at sea or on inland waterways **114**
people in institutions **114**

Scotland **115**
seasonal workers **112**
unlisted townships,
    communities or
    settlements **108**
in the USA **220**
Wales **103, 108, 129–30**
Channel Islands **65–7, 103**
parish registers **204**
probate records **244–5**
chapel registers *see*
    nonconformists
children
in census returns **112**
child emigration **280–1**
recording on family trees **21, 22**
tutors, curators and guardians
    nominated in wills **237–8**
in wills **226, 229, 237–8**
American **262–3**
Scottish **249–50**
see also illegitimate children
church courts
annulments/divorces **55–6**
wills proved in **222–3, 232–3**
Ireland **253**
Scotland **246**
church registers *see* parish
    registers
churchyard burials **17, 170, 187**
civil registrations *see* births;
    deaths; marriages
collateral branches of families
    26–7
College of Arms **30–1**
commercial directories **135, 137**
American **139–40**
computers
digital copies of family
    souvenirs **10**
genealogical software
    packages **21–2**
records on **12, 166**
see also internet searches

coroners' inquests **60**
cremation registers **59, 170,
    187–8**

Data Protection Act (2008) **16**
Death Duty registers **238–41**
and Americans leaving property
    in the UK **265**
Ireland **256–7**
Scotland **250**
deaths **56–60**
alternative sources of
    information on **60–3**
at sea and abroad **79–81, 83–5**
certificates **57, 58–9, 72, 75**
buying copies of **40, 42**
Channel Islands **65–6**
coroners' inquests **60**
Ireland **73–4, 75**
Isle of Man **67**
mortality schedules in
    American census returns
    128, 218
parish registers **169, 170**
Quakers **198, 200**
registrations **2, 37–8, 56,
    65–77, 94–5**
Scotland **71, 72**
servicemen **86–90**
families of **81–2**
in the USA **94–5, 98–9, 218,
    219**
war casualties **82–3, 86, 98–9**
see also burials
dialect, understanding **162–3**
diaries **10**
directories of names **135–8**
additional name lists **151**
American **138–40**
London directories **137–8**
provincial **135, 136–7**
district registrars **37, 38**
divorces **53–6**
Ireland **77**

Scotland 70–1
  in the USA 96–7
DNA sample matching xiii
documents *see* accessing records

e-mailing relatives 15
electoral registers 133–4
  American 138
emigrants *see* migrants

family group sheets 21, 166
family souvenirs 10
family trees
  earliest dates on 37
  known relatives 5–8
  published 33–4
  transferring information to 21–7
filing systems 2, 21, 165–6
forenames
  in baptism registers 176, 178
  in census returns 108, 109, 111
  in indexes and transcriptions of
    parish registers 173–4
  in Scotland 207

General Register Office indexes
    38–40, 41
  adoptions 46–7
  deaths 56, 58–9
  Ireland 73–4, 85
  marriages 50
  overseas entries 79
  and probate indexes 225
  Scotland 67–8
  war casualties 82–3
government stockholders, and
    wills/administration grants
    242
grants of letters of administration
    see administration grants
gravestone inscriptions 59, 189
  American 220
  Irish 214–15
  nonconformists 195–6

Roman Catholics 202
  Scottish 209
Gregorian calendar 164
Guernsey 65, 66, 204, 244

handwriting, reading old 159–62
holograph wills 230
hospital records 63

illegitimate children 23, 56
  baptism registers 175, 177
  birth registrations 43
  and Death Duty registers 241
  in Scotland 207
immigrants *see* migrants
India, Britons in 90–1
  census returns 119
  wills 258–9
institutions, census returns for 114
internet publication 295–6
internet searches xiii–xvi, 153
  archives 156–7, 158
  census records 104–8
  collections of pedigrees 29–30,
    34–5
  family surnames 17–19
  migrants 273
  portal or gateway sites xv
  Registrar General's indexes
    38–9
  Scottish civil registration records
    68
interviews with relatives 10–13
  dealing with different types of
    10–11
  and personal descriptions 9
  questions to ask 8–9
  tape-recorded 12–14
Ireland 73–7
  adoptions 76
  census returns 116–17, 213
  collections of pedigrees 31
  directories of names 135–6
  divorces 77

Irish Catholics in Scotland
211–12
marriage registers 73
migrants 84–5
nonconformists 215–16
Ordnance Survey maps 141,
149
parish registers 212–17
Primary Valuation of 147–8
probate records 253–8
Land Commission records
258
Registry of Deeds 257–8
Quakers 216
Roman Catholic parish registers
216–17
school registers 215
stillbirths 76
surnames 28, 74
tithe maps 144–5
Isle of Man 67, 204–5
probate records 245–6

Jersey 65–6, 66–7, 103, 204
probate records 244–5
Jews, marriage registers 37, 38,
170
Julian calendar 164

land records, American 149–50
laptop computers 12
Latin documents 163
letters 10
living relatives
contacting and visiting 8
interviews with 10–13
memories of 9, 11
none known 16–17
recording information about 21
tracing missing 15–16
writing to 14–16
local indexes 41–2
London directories 137–8

magazines
advertising in 17
family history press 18
manorial court records 226
manuscript collections of
pedigrees 30–3
maps 140–4
American 149
Ordnance Survey 140–1, 149
tithe maps and apportionments
141–5
town plans 140–1
marital status, in census returns
109, 111, 117
marriages
at sea and abroad 79–81, 83–4
banns 179, 182, 183, 207, 208
certificates 51–3, 75
buying copies of 40
Channel Islands 65–6, 204
clandestine and irregular 183–4,
208, 220
divorces 53–6
indexes of 185–6
Ireland 73–4, 75, 213
Isle of Man 67, 205
licenses 179–83
nonconformist registers 194
parish registers 169–70, 172,
174, 179–86
press announcements of 63
Quakers 37, 38, 170, 198, 200,
211
recording on family trees 21–2
registrations 2, 37–8, 41, 50–3,
65–77, 93–4
service families 81–2
Roman Catholic 202, 212
Scotland 70, 183, 184, 205–6,
207–8, 212
in the USA 93–4, 218, 219–20
married women and wills 226–7
maternal line 5
medieval documents 163

memories of relatives **9, 11**
merchant seamen **89–90, 114**
Methodists **192, 193, 196–7, 210**
  Irish **216**
migrants **266–90**
  and alien registration **285**
  American colonies **267–8,
    287–8**
  assisted emigration **278–82**
  border crossings **273**
  child emigration **280–1**
  databases on **274**
  Irish Catholics in Scotland
    211–12
  Mormons **270–80**
  naturalization **285–9**
  New England settlers **274–5**
  records of **31, 282–5**
  ships' passenger lists **268–71,
    274**
  soldiers from the American
    Revolutionary War **275–8**
  transported convicts **281–2**

names *see* directories of names;
    forenames; surnames
naturalization, as American
    citizens **285–9**
New England
  church registers **219**
  divorces **96–7**
  marriage bonds **93**
  settlers **274–5**
newspapers
  advertising in **17**
  American
    and emigrants **284**
    obituaries in **95**
nonconformists **190–202**
  chapels **191**
  foreign Protestants **193**
  in Ireland **215–16**
  in the Isle of Man **205**
  London birth registries **196–7**

registers **2, 37, 192–5**
  marriages **41, 50**
  in Scotland **210–12**
  see also Quakers (Religious
    Society of Friends)
Northern Ireland **74–5, 76, 77, 85**
numbers, working with **163–4**

occupations, in census returns
    108, 109, 111–12
Old Poor Law settlement papers
    150–1
oral wills **230**
Ordnance Survey maps **140–1,
    149**
overseas census surveys **118–19**
overseas registrations **79–81**
  Americans abroad **98**
  British in India and Asia **90–1**
  Scottish travellers **83–4**
  servicemen **86–90**
    families of **81–2**
    war casualties **82–3, 86**

parish registers
  American **218–20**
  Channel Islands **204**
  England and Wales **2, 168–89**
    baptisms **60, 169, 170, 172,
      174, 175–8, 184, 186**
    burials **169, 170, 174, 175,
      186–9**
    indexes and transcriptions
      172–5
    loss or disruption of **169–70**
    marriages **169–70, 172, 174,
      179–86**
    where to find **171**
  Ireland **212–17**
  Isle of Man **204–5**
  Scotland **205–12**
  see also nonconformists
passports **10, 283–4**
paternal line **5**

pedigrees, collections of **29–33,
    34–5, 233**
photographs **10**
Post Office London Directory
    137–8
Prerogative Courts
    Canterbury (PCC) **222–4, 233,
        237, 242, 246, 255, 264**
    York (PCY) **222, 224, 233, 246,
        255**
Presbyterians **191, 192, 208**
    in Ireland **215–16**
press advertising **17**
probate accounts **236–7**
probate courts **222–4**
probate inventories **236**
    Scotland **249**
probate records
    American **259–65**
        emigrants **289**
    Channel Islands **244–5**
    England and Wales **222–42**
    Ireland **253–8**
    Isle of Man **245–6**
    Scotland **246–53**
    see also administration grants;
        wills
provincial directories **136–7**
publication **295–8**
published family histories **33–4**

Quakers (Religious Society of
        Friends) **37, 38, 164, 170,
        191, 197–200**
    in Ireland **216**
    in Scotland **211**

registration cards **10**
Religious Creed and General
        Register **61**
religious denominations
    and census returns in Ireland
        117, 118
    tracing emigrants **285**

Religious Society of Friends *see*
        Quakers (Religious Society
        of Friends)
Roman Catholics **177, 201–2**
    parish registers in Ireland
        216–17
    in Scotland **211–12**
Roman numerals **163–4**

Sark **65, 103, 204, 244**
school registers **60–1, 151**
    children from the American
        colonies **289**
    Ireland **215**
Scotland **67–72, 205–12**
    birth registers **68–9**
    census returns **115**
    clandestine marriages **183, 184**
    Court of the Lord Lyon **31**
    dating of documents **164**
    death certificates **72**
    death registers **71**
    dissenters in **210–11**
    emigrants to Canada/USA **279**
    General Register Office records
        67–8
    local records **68**
    marriage registers **70**
    parish kirk session registers **210**
    parish registers **205–12**
    probate records **246–53**
        estates in England and Wales
            252–3
        services (retours) of hiers and
            sasines **250–2**
    Roman Catholics **211–12**
    surnames **28, 68, 206, 207, 209**
    tithe maps **144**
    Valuation Office records **147**
Scottish travellers, overseas
        records **83–4**
servicemen
    American **98–9**
    in census returns **114**

discharges and deaths in
service **86–90**
and electoral registers **134**
families of **81–2**
men at war **82–3**
wills **226, 247**
see also war casualties
ships
births, marriages and deaths of
Britons at sea **79–80, 83–4**
census returns from **114, 115**
and movements of emigrants
283–4
passenger lists **268–71, 274**
slaves in the United States,
census returns **127**
smallpox vaccination registers
62–3
stillbirths **49**
Ireland **76**
Scotland **69**
superintendent registrar's indexes
41
surnames **5**
in baptism registers **175–6, 177,
178**
on birth certificates **44**
in census returns **108, 109, 111,
129–30**
changes of **59**
American colonists **288–9**
death certificates **59**
in indexes and transcriptions of
parish registers **173–4**
Irish **28, 74**
marriage certificates **50, 53**
in medieval documents **163**
misspelling of **42**
name changes by Royal Licence
229
in nonconformist registers **194**
Scottish **28, 68, 206, 207, 209**
searching of family surnames
17–19

tracing origins and distribution
of **27–9**
Welsh **42, 129–30, 173**
writing about **293**

tape-recorded interviews **12–14**
tithe maps and apportionments
141–5
town plans **140–1**
Traceline **15–16**
trade directories **135**
American **139–40**

United States of America **91–100**
adoption records **95–6**
Americans abroad **98**
archives **157**
birth registrations **91–3**
census returns **119–29, 218,
220**
colonial, state and local **129**
indexes, digital images and
transcriptions **120–1**
information contained in
121–2
mortality schedules **128, 218**
slaves **127**
special uses of **122–6**
war veterans **127**
colonists **267–8, 287–9**
death registrations **94–5**
directories **138–40**
divorces **96–7**
electoral registers **138**
land records **149–50**
maps **149**
marriage registrations **93–4**
parish registers **218–20**
probate records **259–65**
contested wills **262**
estates in the UK and Ireland
263–5
indexes and transcripts of **261**
minors and orphans **262–3**

service records **99–100**
war casualties **98–9**
see also migrants

vaccination registers **62–3**
Valuation Office records **145–9**
voters, registers of **133–4**

Wagner, Sir Anthony **153**
Wales
  census returns **103, 108,
    129–30**
  chapel registers **193**
  grants of letters of
    administration **222, 233–5**
  parish registers **173–4**
  probate courts **224**
  surnames **42, 129–30, 173**
  Welsh pedigrees **32**
war casualties **82–3, 86**
  American **98–9**
war veterans, in American census
    returns **127**
wills **2, 221–42**
  American **259–65**
  Channel Islands **244–5**
    estates held in England and
      Wales **245**
  and children **226, 229, 237–8,
    249–50, 262–3**
  codicils to **230**
  contested **232–3**
    American **262**
    Scottish **248–9**
  date of probate **231**
  and Death Duty registers
    238–41

of emigrants **289**
entailments in **226**
executors **231–2**
and freehold land **226**
and government stockholders
    242
guardianship in **237–8**
  Scotland **249–50**
holograph **230**
intestacy **222, 233**
Ireland **253–8**
Isle of Man **245–6**
kinship descriptions in **229**
and married women **226–7**
name changes by Royal
    Licence **229**
National Probate Indexes of **58**
oral wills **230**
and personalty **226**
probate courts **222–4, 231**
probate indexes of **224–6**
and probate inventories **236**
Scotland **246–50**
and widows **229**
see also administration grants;
    probate records
writing it up **291–9**
  adding pictures **294**
  beginnings **292–3**
  editing your script **295**
  essentials of **293–4**
  publication **295–8**
  sales outlets **298**
writing to relatives **14–16**
written accounts **12**

teach® yourself

From Advanced Sudoku to Zulu, you'll find everything you need in the **teach yourself** range, in books, on CD and on DVD.

Visit **www.teachyourself.co.uk** for more details.

Advanced Sudoku and Kakuro
Afrikaans
Alexander Technique
Algebra
Ancient Greek
Applied Psychology
Arabic
Aromatherapy
Art History
Astrology
Astronomy
AutoCAD 2004
AutoCAD 2007
Ayurveda
Baby Massage and Yoga
Baby Signing
Baby Sleep
Bach Flower Remedies
Backgammon
Ballroom Dancing
Basic Accounting
Basic Computer Skills
Basic Mathematics
Beauty
Beekeeping
Beginner's Arabic Script
Beginner's Chinese Script
Beginner's Dutch

Beginner's French
Beginner's German
Beginner's Greek
Beginner's Greek Script
Beginner's Hindi
Beginner's Italian
Beginner's Japanese
Beginner's Japanese Script
Beginner's Latin
Beginner's Mandarin Chinese
Beginner's Portuguese
Beginner's Russian
Beginner's Russian Script
Beginner's Spanish
Beginner's Turkish
Beginner's Urdu Script
Bengali
Better Bridge
Better Chess
Better Driving
Better Handwriting
Biblical Hebrew
Biology
Birdwatching
Blogging
Body Language
Book Keeping
Brazilian Portuguese

Bridge
British Empire, The
British Monarchy from Henry VIII, The
Buddhism
Bulgarian
Business Chinese
Business French
Business Japanese
Business Plans
Business Spanish
Business Studies
Buying a Home in France
Buying a Home in Italy
Buying a Home in Portugal
Buying a Home in Spain
C++
Calculus
Calligraphy
Cantonese
Car Buying and Maintenance
Card Games
Catalan
Chess
Chi Kung
Chinese Medicine
Christianity
Classical Music
Coaching
Cold War, The
Collecting
Computing for the Over 50s
Consulting
Copywriting
Correct English
Counselling
Creative Writing
Cricket
Croatian
Crystal Healing
CVs
Czech
Danish
Decluttering
Desktop Publishing
Detox

Digital Home Movie Making
Digital Photography
Dog Training
Drawing
Dream Interpretation
Dutch
Dutch Conversation
Dutch Dictionary
Dutch Grammar
Eastern Philosophy
Electronics
English as a Foreign Language
English for International Business
English Grammar
English Grammar as a Foreign Language
English Vocabulary
Entrepreneurship
Estonian
Ethics
Excel 2003
Feng Shui
Film Making
Film Studies
Finance for Non-Financial Managers
Finnish
First World War, The
Fitness
Flash 8
Flash MX
Flexible Working
Flirting
Flower Arranging
Franchising
French
French Conversation
French Dictionary
French Grammar
French Phrasebook
French Starter Kit
French Verbs
French Vocabulary
Freud
Gaelic

Gardening
Genetics
Geology
German
German Conversation
German Grammar
German Phrasebook
German Verbs
German Vocabulary
Globalization
Go
Golf
Good Study Skills
Great Sex
Greek
Greek Conversation
Greek Phrasebook
Growing Your Business
Guitar
Gulf Arabic
Hand Reflexology
Hausa
Herbal Medicine
Hieroglyphics
Hindi
Hindi Conversation
Hinduism
History of Ireland, The
Home PC Maintenance and
  Networking
How to DJ
How to Run a Marathon
How to Win at Casino Games
How to Win at Horse Racing
How to Win at Online Gambling
How to Win at Poker
How to Write a Blockbuster
Human Anatomy & Physiology
Hungarian
Icelandic
Improve Your French
Improve Your German
Improve Your Italian
Improve Your Spanish
Improving Your Employability

Indian Head Massage
Indonesian
Instant French
Instant German
Instant Greek
Instant Italian
Instant Japanese
Instant Portuguese
Instant Russian
Instant Spanish
Internet, The
Irish
Irish Conversation
Irish Grammar
Islam
Italian
Italian Conversation
Italian Grammar
Italian Phrasebook
Italian Starter Kit
Italian Verbs
Italian Vocabulary
Japanese
Japanese Conversation
Java
JavaScript
Jazz
Jewellery Making
Judaism
Jung
Kama Sutra, The
Keeping Aquarium Fish
Keeping Pigs
Keeping Poultry
Keeping a Rabbit
Knitting
Korean
Latin
Latin American Spanish
Latin Dictionary
Latin Grammar
Latvian
Letter Writing Skills
Life at 50: For Men
Life at 50: For Women

Life Coaching
Linguistics
LINUX
Lithuanian
Magic
Mahjong
Malay
Managing Stress
Managing Your Own Career
Mandarin Chinese
Mandarin Chinese Conversation
Marketing
Marx
Massage
Mathematics
Meditation
Middle East Since 1945, The
Modern China
Modern Hebrew
Modern Persian
Mosaics
Music Theory
Mussolini's Italy
Nazi Germany
Negotiating
Nepali
New Testament Greek
NLP
Norwegian
Norwegian Conversation
Old English
One-Day French
One-Day French – the DVD
One-Day German
One-Day Greek
One-Day Italian
One-Day Portuguese
One-Day Spanish
One-Day Spanish – the DVD
Origami
Owning a Cat
Owning a Horse
Panjabi
PC Networking for Small
   Businesses

Personal Safety and Self
   Defence
Philosophy
Philosophy of Mind
Philosophy of Religion
Photography
Photoshop
PHP with MySQL
Physics
Piano
Pilates
Planning Your Wedding
Polish
Polish Conversation
Politics
Portuguese
Portuguese Conversation
Portuguese Grammar
Portuguese Phrasebook
Postmodernism
Pottery
PowerPoint 2003
PR
Project Management
Psychology
Quick Fix French Grammar
Quick Fix German Grammar
Quick Fix Italian Grammar
Quick Fix Spanish Grammar
Quick Fix: Access 2002
Quick Fix: Excel 2000
Quick Fix: Excel 2002
Quick Fix: HTML
Quick Fix: Windows XP
Quick Fix: Word
Quilting
Recruitment
Reflexology
Reiki
Relaxation
Retaining Staff
Romanian
Running Your Own Business
Russian
Russian Conversation

Russian Grammar
Sage Line 50
Sanskrit
Screenwriting
Second World War, The
Serbian
Setting Up a Small Business
Shorthand Pitman 2000
Sikhism
Singing
Slovene
Small Business Accounting
Small Business Health Check
Songwriting
Spanish
Spanish Conversation
Spanish Dictionary
Spanish Grammar
Spanish Phrasebook
Spanish Starter Kit
Spanish Verbs
Spanish Vocabulary
Speaking On Special Occasions
Speed Reading
Stalin's Russia
Stand Up Comedy
Statistics
Stop Smoking
Sudoku
Swahili
Swahili Dictionary
Swedish
Swedish Conversation
Tagalog
Tai Chi
Tantric Sex
Tap Dancing
Teaching English as a Foreign
    Language
Teams & Team Working
Thai
Theatre
Time Management
Tracing Your Family History
Training

Travel Writing
Trigonometry
Turkish
Turkish Conversation
Twentieth Century USA
Typing
Ukrainian
Understanding Tax for Small
    Businesses
Understanding Terrorism
Urdu
Vietnamese
Visual Basic
Volcanoes
Watercolour Painting
Weight Control through Diet &
    Exercise
Welsh
Welsh Dictionary
Welsh Grammar
Wills & Probate
Windows XP
Wine Tasting
Winning at Job Interviews
Word 2003
World Cultures: China
World Cultures: England
World Cultures: Germany
World Cultures: Italy
World Cultures: Japan
World Cultures: Portugal
World Cultures: Russia
World Cultures: Spain
World Cultures: Wales
World Faiths
Writing Crime Fiction
Writing for Children
Writing for Magazines
Writing a Novel
Writing Poetry
Xhosa
Yiddish
Yoga
Zen
Zulu